Algebra 2

LARSON
BOSWELL
KANOLD
STIFF

Applications • Equations • Graphs

Practice Workbook with Examples

The Practice Workbook provides additional
practice with worked-out examples for every lesson.
The workbook covers essential skills and vocabulary.
Space is provided for students to show their work.

McDougal Littell
A HOUGHTON MIFFLIN COMPANY
Evanston, Illinois • Boston • Dallas

ISBN-13: 978-0-618-02034-8   ISBN-10: 0-618-02034-9

18 19 20 VEI 10 09 08 07

Contents

Contents

Practice with Examples

For use with pages 3–10

GOAL **Use a number line to graph and order real numbers and identify properties of and use operations with real numbers**

VOCABULARY

The **graph** of a real number is the point on a real number line that corresponds to the number. On a number line, the numbers increase from left to right, and the point labeled 0 is the origin.

The number that corresponds to a point on a number line is the **coordinate** of the point.

The **opposite,** or *additive inverse,* of any number a is $-a$.

The **reciprocal,** or *multiplicative inverse,* of any nonzero number a is $\dfrac{1}{a}$.

EXAMPLE 1 ## *Graphing and Ordering Real Numbers*

Graph and write the numbers in increasing order: $-\sqrt{7}, 0, \frac{3}{2}, 2, \frac{3}{8}$.

SOLUTION

$-\sqrt{7} \approx -2.6, \frac{3}{2} = 1.5, \frac{3}{8} \approx 0.4$ Rewrite each number in decimal form.

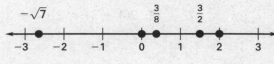

Plot the points on the real number line.

$-\sqrt{7}, 0, \frac{3}{8}, \frac{3}{2}, 2$ Write the numbers from least to greatest.

Exercises for Example 1

Write the numbers in increasing order.

1. $1, \frac{1}{3}, \sqrt{2}$

2. $\frac{3}{5}, -1, 1$

3. $\sqrt{5}, \frac{2}{3}, 3.25$

4. $-4, 1, -1$

5. $0, -2, \frac{1}{3}$

6. $-\sqrt{2}, -15, 5.7$

7. $\frac{5}{2}, -5, -10$

8. $3, -5, 0$

NAME _____ DATE _____

Practice with Examples

For use with pages 3–10

EXAMPLE 2 *Identifying Properties of Real Numbers*

Identify the property shown.

a. $5(10 + 2) = 5 \cdot 10 + 5 \cdot 2$

b. $(6 \cdot 4)5 = 6(4 \cdot 5)$

SOLUTION

a. Distributive property

b. Associative property of multiplication

Exercises for Example 2

Identify the property shown.

9. $5 + 3 = 3 + 5$

10. $7 + (-7) = 0$

11. $-2 + 0 = -2$

12. $2(4 + 1) = 2 \cdot 4 + 2 \cdot 1$

13. $8 \cdot \frac{1}{8} = 1$

14. $(5 + 7) + 3 = 5 + (7 + 3)$

Practice with Examples

For use with pages 3–10

EXAMPLE 3 ## *Operations with Real Numbers*

At rest, the average person's heart beats 65 times per minute. During aerobic exercise, this rate increases by 40%.

a. How many times does the average person's heart beat per hour?

b. How many times will the average person's heart beat per minute during aerobic exercise?

SOLUTION

a. $\left(\dfrac{65 \text{ beats}}{1 \text{ minute}}\right)\left(\dfrac{60 \text{ minutes}}{1 \text{ hour}}\right) = 3900$ beats per hour

b. To find 40% of 65, multiply.

$$40\% \times 65 = 0.4 \times 65 \qquad \text{Rewrite 40\% as 0.4.}$$
$$= 26 \qquad\qquad \text{Simplify.}$$

During aerobic exercise, the average person's heart would beat $65 + 26 = 91$ times per minute.

Exercises for Example 3

In Exercises 15 and 16, use the following information.

At Indianapolis Motor Speedway, one lap is 2.5 miles in length. The average speed of an Indy racing car is 190 miles per hour.

15. Find the length of one lap in yards.

16. How many seconds would it take to complete one lap?

NAME _____ DATE _____

Practice with Examples

For use with pages 11–17

GOAL **Evaluate algebraic expressions and simplify algebraic expressions by combining like terms**

VOCABULARY

A **variable** is a letter that is used to represent one or more numbers.

An **algebraic expression** is an expression involving variables.

Like terms are expressions that have the same variable part. **Constant terms** such as -4 and 2 are also like terms.

The **base** of an exponent is the number or variable that is used as a factor in repeated multiplication. For example, in the expression 4^b, 4 is the base.

An **exponent** is the number or variable that represents the number of times the base is used as a factor. For example, in the expression 4^b, b is the exponent.

A **power** is the result of repeated multiplication. For example, in the expression $4^2 = 16$, 16 is the second power of 4.

Any number used to replace a variable is a **value of the variable**.

When the variables in an algebraic expression are replaced by numbers, the result is called the **value of the expression**.

Terms are the parts that are added in an expression, such as 5 and $-x$ in the expression $5 - x$.

A **coefficient** is the number multiplied by a variable in a term.

Two algebraic expressions are **equivalent** if they have the same value for all values of their variable(s).

EXAMPLE 1 *Using Order of Operations*

$$
\begin{aligned}
2(3 + 18 \div 3^2 - 7) &= 2(3 + 18 \div 9 - 7) && \text{Evaluate the power.} \\
&= 2(3 + 2 - 7) && \text{Divide.} \\
&= 2(-2) && \text{Add within parentheses.} \\
&= -4 && \text{Multiply.}
\end{aligned}
$$

Exercises for Example 1

Evaluate the expression.

1. $(-1 + 3) - 4^2$ **2.** $14 - 12 \div 3$ **3.** $(-5)^3$

4. $5 - (-2 + 4)^2$ **5.** $36 \div (-3)^2 - 1$ **6.** -5^2

Practice with Examples

For use with pages 11–17

EXAMPLE 2 *Evaluating an Algebraic Expression*

Evaluate $2t^2 - 3$ when $t = 4$.

SOLUTION

$$2t^2 - 3 = 2(4)^2 - 3 \qquad \text{Substitute 4 for } t.$$
$$= 2(16) - 3 \qquad \text{Evaluate the power.}$$
$$= 32 - 3 \qquad \text{Multiply.}$$
$$= 29 \qquad \text{Subtract.}$$

Exercises for Example 2

Evaluate the expression.

7. $x^2(4 - x)$ when $x = 2$

8. $x - (x + 5)$ when $x = 20$

9. $x^2 + 5$ when $x = -3$

10. $3x^3 + 4$ when $x = -2$

11. $4x - 3y + 2$ when $x = 4$ and $y = -3$

12. $9(m - n)^2$ when $m = 4$ and $n = 1$

Chapter 1

Practice with Examples

For use with pages 11–17

EXAMPLE 3 *Simplifying by Combining Like Terms*

Simplify $6(x - y) - 4(x - y)$.

SOLUTION

$$6(x - y) - 4(x - y) = 6x - 6y - 4x + 4y \qquad \text{Distributive property}$$
$$= (6x - 4x) + (-6y + 4y) \qquad \text{Group like terms.}$$
$$= 2x - 2y \qquad \text{Combine like terms.}$$

Exercises for Example 3

Simplify the expression.

13. $7x - (9x + 5)$

14. $2(n^2 + n) - 5(n^2 - 4n)$

15. $-6x^2 + 4x - x^2 + 15x$

16. $7x - 2y + 3 - 9y + 4 + 5x$

Algebra 2
Practice Workbook with Examples

NAME _____ DATE _____

Practice with Examples

For use with pages 19–24

GOAL **Solve linear equations and use linear equations to answer questions about real-life situations**

VOCABULARY

An **equation** is a statement in which two expressions are equal.

A **linear equation** in one variable is an expression that can be written in the form $ax = b$ where a and b are constants and $a \neq 0$.

A number is a **solution** of an equation if the statement is true when the number is substituted for the variable.

Two equations are **equivalent** if they have the same solutions.

EXAMPLE 1 *Variable on One Side*

Solve $-19 = -2y + 5$.

SOLUTION

$-19 = -2y + 5$	Write original equation.
$-24 = -2y$	To isolate y, subtract 5 from each side.
$12 = y$	Divide each side by -2.

Exercises for Example 1

Solve the equation.

1. $3 = -x - 2$ 　　　　**2.** $-18 = y + 6$ 　　　　**3.** $9 - z = 5$

4. $6 + 6x = -12$ 　　　　**5.** $2x - 5 = 1$ 　　　　**6.** $-\dfrac{x}{3} = 2$

NAME _____ DATE _____

Practice with Examples

For use with pages 19–24

EXAMPLE 2 *Variable on Both Sides*

Solve $4x - 2x = 15 - 3x$.

SOLUTION

$4x - 2x = 15 - 3x$	Write original equation.
$2x = 15 - 3x$	Combine like terms.
$5x = 15$	To collect the variable terms, add $3x$ to each side.
$x = 3$	Divide each side by 5.

Exercises for Example 2

Solve the equation.

7. $15 - 3a = -4a + 16$

8. $-3m + 6 = 24m + 6$

9. $4s - 6 = 7s + 3$

10. $8t - t + 1 = 10 - 2t$

11. $x - 4 = 2x + 7$

12. $4x = 24 + 16x$

EXAMPLE 3 *Using the Distributive Property*

Solve $15(4 - y) = 5(10 + 2y)$.

SOLUTION

$15(4 - y) = 5(10 + 2y)$	Write original equation.
$60 - 15y = 50 + 10y$	Distributive property
$60 = 50 + 25y$	To collect the variable terms, add $15y$ to each side.
$10 = 25y$	Subtract 50 from each side.
$\frac{2}{5} = y$	Divide each side by 25.

NAME _____ DATE _____

Practice with Examples

For use with pages 19–24

Exercises for Example 3

Solve the equation.

13. $5(x - 3) + 12 = -2(x - 2)$

14. $-4(k - 2) + 3(k + 1) = 7$

15. $-2x = 2(x + 1)$

16. $3x - 9 = 2(x - 5)$

EXAMPLE 4 *Solving an Equation with Fractions*

Solve $\frac{2}{3}x + \frac{3}{5} = \frac{4}{15}$.

SOLUTION

$\frac{2}{3}x + \frac{3}{5} = \frac{4}{15}$	Write original equation.
$15\left(\frac{2}{3}x + \frac{3}{5}\right) = 15\left(\frac{4}{15}\right)$	Multiply each side by the LCD, 15.
$10x + 9 = 4$	Distributive property
$10x = -5$	To isolate x, subtract 9 from each side.
$x = -\frac{1}{2}$	Divide each side by 10.

Exercises for Example 4

Solve the equation.

17. $6n = \frac{2}{3}(5n - 2)$

18. $\frac{3}{4}x + 1 = 4$

19. $\frac{1}{2}x - \frac{2}{3} = 4x$

20. $\frac{3}{5}x = \frac{2}{3}x + 1$

Algebra 2
Practice Workbook with Examples

9

Chapter 1

NAME _____ DATE _____

Practice with Examples

For use with pages 26–32

GOAL **Rewrite equations and common formulas with more than one variable**

EXAMPLE 1 *Calculating the Value of a Variable*

Given the equation $-y + 2x = -10$, find the value of y when $x = -4$.

SOLUTION: Method 1

$-y + 2x = -10$	Write original equation.
$-y + 2(-4) = -10$	Substitute -4 for x.
$-y - 8 = -10$	Simplify.
$-y = -2$	To isolate y, add 8 to each side.
$y = 2$	Divide each side by -1.

SOLUTION: Method 2

$-y + 2x = -10$	Write original equation.
$-y = -10 - 2x$	To isolate y, subtract $2x$ from each side.
$y = 10 + 2x$	Divide each side by -1.
$y = 10 + 2(-4)$	Substitute -4 for x.
$y = 2$	Simplify.

Exercises for Example 1

Find the value of *y* for the given value of *x*.

1. $-xy + 2x = 20$; $x = 5$ **2.** $4x - 3y - 10 = 1$; $x = -1$

3. $5x + 7y = -1$; $x = 4$ **4.** $x = 6 + xy$; $x = -3$

NAME _____   DATE _____

Practice with Examples

For use with pages 26–32

EXAMPLE 2   *Using an Equation with More than One Variable*

The formula for calculating the selling price is $S = L - rL$, where L is the list price and r is the rate of discount. An automatic coffee maker is advertised to sell for $53.55, which is a 15% discount. Calculate the list price.

SOLUTION

$S = L - rL$	Formula for selling price.
$S = L(1 - r)$	Factor L out of the terms on the right.
$\dfrac{S}{1 - r} = L$	Divide each side by $1 - r$.
$\dfrac{53.55}{1 - 0.15} = L$	Substitute 53.55 for S and 0.15 for r.
$63 = L$	Simplify.

The list price for the coffee maker is $63.

Exercises for Example 2

5. The cost is $c = 5000 + 0.56x$ where x is the number of items produced. Solve the equation for x, then evaluate x when $c = 8360$.

6. At a delicatessen, ham costs $2.49 per pound and Swiss cheese costs $3.79 per pound. The customer has $9.50 to spend on 2 pounds of ham and some cheese. How much cheese can she purchase? Write an equation and solve it.

Practice with Examples
For use with pages 26–32

EXAMPLE 3 *Rewriting a Common Formula*

The formula for converting from Celsius to Fahrenheit is $F = \frac{9}{5}C + 32$.
Solve for C.

SOLUTION

$F = \frac{9}{5}C + 32$	Formula for conversion from Celsius to Fahrenheit
$F - 32 = \frac{9}{5}C$	To isolate C, subtract 32 from each side.
$\frac{5}{9}(F - 32) = C$	Multiply each side by $\frac{5}{9}$.

Exercises for Example 3

Solve for the indicated variable.

7. Solve for r: $A = 2\pi rh$

8. Solve for w: $V = lwh$

9. Solve for b: $\dfrac{b}{h} = \dfrac{3}{4}$

10. Solve for t: $A = P + Prt$

11. Solve for h: $V = \dfrac{1}{3}b^2h$

12. Solve for x: $p = 12 - \dfrac{x}{1000}$

Practice with Examples

For use with pages 33–40

GOAL   **Use a general problem-solving plan and other strategies to solve real-life problems**

> **VOCABULARY**
>
> A **verbal model** is an expression that uses words to represent a real-life situation.
>
> The verbal model is then used to write a mathematical statement, called an **algebraic model**.

EXAMPLE 1   *Drawing a Diagram*

Two airports, one in California and one in New York, are 3000 miles apart. A plane leaving California is traveling to New York at 200 miles per hour. Another plane leaving New York is traveling to California at 250 miles per hour. When will the two planes pass each other?

SOLUTION

California   3000 miles   New York

		From California		From New York	
Verbal Model	Total distance =	Miles per hour ·	Number of hours	+ Miles per hour ·	Number of hours

Labels
   Total distance = 3000   (miles)

   California rate = 200   (miles per hour)

   California time = t (hours)

   New York rate = 250   (miles per hour)

   New York time = t (hours)

Algebraic $3000 = 200t + 250t$ Write algebraic model.

Model $3000 = 450t$ Combine like terms.

            $6\frac{2}{3} = t$ Divide each side by 450.

After $6\frac{2}{3}$ hours, the two planes will pass each other.

NAME _____ DATE _____

Practice with Examples

For use with pages 33–40

Exercises for Example 1

1. In a football game, the quarterback is 15 yards away from making a first down and is running at 264 yards per minute. After 0.03 of a minute, a linebacker who is 15 yards on the opposite side of the first down marker begins running directly towards the quarterback at 440 yards per minute. Will the linebacker be able to tackle the quarterback before he gets the first down?

2. Two sisters who live 500 miles apart decide to meet at the halfway point for a visit. Joanne leaves at 11:00 and travels at 50 miles per hour. At noon, Sue leaves traveling 60 miles per hour. Who will reach the halfway point first, and how long will she have to wait for her sister?

Algebra 2
Practice Workbook with Examples

NAME _____ DATE _____

Practice with Examples

For use with pages 33–40

EXAMPLE 2 *Guess, Check, and Revise*

Compact discs cost $16.99 each and cassette tapes cost $8.99 each. If the total bill equaled $78.93, how many of each were bought?

SOLUTION

Verbal Model

| Total bill | = | Price per CD | · | Number of CDs | + | Price per tape | · | Number of tapes |

Algebraic Model $78.93 = 16.99c + 8.99t$

Guess different values for c and t. Substitute these values into the equation until you get both sides equal.

The number of CDs was 2, $16.99 \times 2 = 33.98$, and the number of tapes was 5, $8.99 \times 5 = 44.95$, for a total bill of $33.98 + 44.95 = 78.93$.

Exercises for Example 2

3. A farmer has 64 yards of fencing and wants to create a rectangular enclosure for his animals. What is the enclosure with the greatest area?

4. A cylindrical swimming pool 5 feet in depth needs approximately 2292 gallons of water to be full. To the nearest tenth, what is the radius of the pool?

Chapter 1

Practice with Examples

For use with pages 41–47

GOAL **Solve simple inequalities and compound inequalities**

> ### VOCABULARY
>
> Inequalities such as $x \le 1$ and $2n - 3 > 9$ are examples of **linear inequalities** in one variable.
>
> A **solution** of an inequality in one variable is a value of the variable that makes the inequality true.
>
> A **compound inequality** is two simple inequalities joined by "and" or "or."
>
> The **graph** of an inequality in one variable consists of all points on a real number line that corresponds to solutions of the inequality.

EXAMPLE 1 *Solving an Inequality with a Variable on One Side*

Solve $3 - 2x \ge 5$. Then graph the solution.

SOLUTION

$3 - 2x \ge 5$	Write original inequality.
$-2x \ge 2$	To isolate $-2x$, subtract 3 from each side.
$x \le -1$	Divide each side by -2 and reverse the inequality.
	Graph the solution.

Exercises for Example 1

Solve the inequality. Then graph your solution.

1. $-4x \le -4$

2. $3x \ge -6$

3. $-2x > 6$

4. $-x - 1 < -1$

5. $6 \le 3x - 3$

6. $-5 > 2x + 13$

NAME _____ DATE _____

Practice with Examples
For use with pages 41–47

EXAMPLE 2 *Solving an Inequality with a Variable on Both Sides*

Solve $-n + 4 > -5n + 8$. Then graph the solution.

SOLUTION

$-n + 4 > -5n + 8$	Write original inequality.
$4n + 4 > 8$	To collect the variable terms, add $5n$ to each side.
$4n > 4$	Subtract 4 from each side.
$n > 1$	Divide each side by 4.
	Graph the solution.

Exercises for Example 2

Solve the inequality. Then graph your solution.

7. $3x + 5 > x + 7$

8. $-5x + 9 \leq 2(x - 6)$

9. $-x \leq -4x + 3$

EXAMPLE 3 *Solving an "And" Compound Inequality*

Solve $-2 < 1 - 3x < 10$. Then graph the solution.

SOLUTION

$-2 < 1 - 3x < 10$	Write the original inequality.
$-3 < -3x < 9$	To isolate $-3x$, subtract 1 from each expression.
$1 > x > -3$	Divide each expression by -3 and reverse the inequality.
	Graph the solution.

NAME _____ DATE _____

Practice with Examples

For use with pages 41–47

Exercises for Example 3

Solve the inequality. Then graph your solution.

10. $4 < 2x < 8$

11. $2 \le 3 - x \le 8$

12. $-4 < x + 1 < 6$

EXAMPLE 4   *Solving an "Or" Compound Inequality*

Solve $2x - 5 \ge 1$ or $2x - 5 \le -1$. Then graph the solution.

SOLUTION OF FIRST INEQUALITY		**SOLUTION OF SECOND INEQUALITY**	
$2x - 5 \ge 1$	Write first inequality.	$2x - 5 \le -1$	Write second inequality.
$2x \ge 6$	Add 5 to each side.	$2x \le 4$	Add 5 to each side.
$x \ge 3$	Divide each side by 2.	$x \le 2$	Divide each side by 2.

   Graph the solutions.

Exercises for Example 4

Solve the inequality. Then graph your solution.

13. $3x \le -3$ or $x - 1 \ge 0$

14. $5x + 6 \le 11$ or $-3x \le -12$

15. $4x - 3 > 9$ or $-2x > 2$

16. $x > 0$ or $5x - 4 < -14$

NAME _____ DATE _____

Practice with Examples

For use with pages 50–56

GOAL Solve absolute value equations and inequalities and use absolute value equations and inequalities to solve real-life problems

---

VOCABULARY

The **absolute value** of a number x, written $|x|$, is the distance the number is from 0 on a number line. The absolute value of a number is always nonnegative.

EXAMPLE 1 *Solving an Absolute Value Equation*

Solve $\left|\frac{1}{2}x + 5\right| = 7$.

SOLUTION

$\left|\frac{1}{2}x + 5\right| = 7$	Write original equation.
$\frac{1}{2}x + 5 = 7$ or $\frac{1}{2}x + 5 = -7$	Expression can be 7 or -7.
$\frac{1}{2}x = 2$ or $\frac{1}{2}x = -12$	Subtract 5 from each side.
$x = 4$ or $x = -24$	Multiply each side by $\frac{2}{1}$.

The solutions are 4 and -24.

When $x = 4$: $\left|\frac{1}{2}(4) + 5\right| = |7| = 7$

When $x = -24$: $\left|\frac{1}{2}(-24) + 5\right| = |-7| = 7$

Exercises for Example 1

Solve the equation.

1. $|r - 8| = 2$ **2.** $|2m + 5| = 9$ **3.** $|8 - 3n| = 16$

EXAMPLE 2 *Solving an Inequality of the Form $|ax + b| < c$*

Solve $|2x + 3| < 7$.

SOLUTION

$|2x + 3| < 7.$	Write original inequality.
$-7 < 2x + 3 < 7$	Write equivalent compound inequality.
$-10 < 2x < 4$	Subtract 3 from each expression.
$-5 < x < 2$	Divide each expression by 2.

The solutions are all real numbers greater than -5 and less than 2.

NAME _____ DATE _____

Practice with Examples

For use with pages 50–56

Exercises for Example 2

Solve the inequality.

4. $|x - 5| < 3$ **5.** $|2x + 1| \leq 3$ **6.** $|10 - 4x| < 2$

EXAMPLE 3 *Solving an Inequality of the Form* $|ax + b| \geq c$

Solve $\left|\frac{2}{3}t + 2\right| \geq 10$.

SOLUTION OF FIRST INEQUALITY		**SOLUTION OF SECOND INEQUALITY**
$\frac{2}{3}t + 2 \leq -10$	Write inequality.	$\frac{2}{3}t + 2 \geq 10$
$\frac{2}{3}t \leq -12$	Subtract 2 from each side.	$\frac{2}{3}t \geq 8$
$t \leq -18$	Multiply each side by $\frac{3}{2}$.	$t \geq 12$

The solutions are all real numbers less than or equal to -18 or greater than or equal to 12.

Exercises for Example 3

Solve the inequality.

7. $|y + 3| > 5$ **8.** $|x - 4| \geq 14$ **9.** $|4n + 7| > 1$

NAME _____ DATE _____

Practice with Examples

For use with pages 50–56

EXAMPLE 4 *Writing an Absolute Value Model*

The tolerance when machining a certain piece of steel is 0.0005 inch.
One piece of steel is supposed to be 5.25 inches. Write an absolute value
inequality that describes the acceptable lengths for the piece of steel.

SOLUTION

**Verbal
Model** $\left| \boxed{\text{Actual length}} - \boxed{\text{Ideal length}} \right| \leq \boxed{\text{Tolerance}}$

Labels   Actual length $= l$ (inches)

 Ideal length $= 5.25$ (inches)

 Tolerance $= 0.0005$ (inch)

**Algebraic
Model** $|l - 5.25| \leq 0.0005$

Exercises for Example 4

10. The average height range of a golden retriever is 20–24 inches. Write
the average height range as an absolute value inequality.

11. The average life span for a horse is 20 to 40 years. Write the average
life span as an absolute value inequality.

Chapter 1

NAME _____ DATE _____

Practice with Examples

For use with pages 67–74

GOAL **Represent relations and functions and graph and evaluate linear functions**

VOCABULARY

A **relation** is a mapping, or pairing, of input values with output values.

The set of input values is the **domain,** and the set of output values is the **range.**

A relation is a **function** provided there is exactly one output for each input. It is not a function if at least one input has more than one output.

The first number in an ordered pair is the **x-coordinate,** and the second number is the **y-coordinate.**

A **coordinate plane** is formed by two real number lines that intersect at a right angle.

A **quadrant** is one of the four parts into which the axes divide a coordinate plane.

The horizontal axis in a coordinate plane is the **x-axis,** and the vertical axis is the **y-axis.**

The **origin** (0, 0) is the point in a coordinate plane where the axes intersect.

An ordered pair (x, y) is a **solution** of an equation if the equation is true when the values of x and y are substituted into the equation.

The input variable is called the **independent variable,** and the output variable is called the **dependent variable.**

EXAMPLE 1 *Identifying Functions*

Identify the domain and range. Then tell whether the relation is a function.

Input		Output
−3		4
−1		0
2		1
		−2

SOLUTION

The domain consists of −3, −1, and 2, and the range consists of −2, 0, 1, and 4. The relation is not a function because the input −1 is mapped onto both 1 and 4.

Practice with Examples

For use with pages 82–89

EXAMPLE 2 *Graphing with the Standard Form*

Graph $-2x + 3y = -6$.

SOLUTION

1. The equation is already in standard form.

2. $-2x + 3(0) = -6$ Let $y = 0$.

         $x = 3$ Solve for x.

The x-intercept is 3, so plot $(3, 0)$.

3. $-2(0) + 3y = -6$ Let $x = 0$.

         $y = -2$ Solve for y.

The y-intercept is -2, so plot $(0, -2)$.

4. Draw a line through the two points.

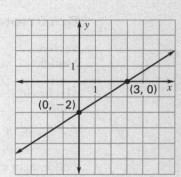

Exercises for Example 2

Graph the equation.

4. $-x + 4y = 8$

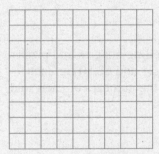

5. $2x + 5y = -10$

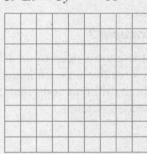

6. $2x - y = 4$

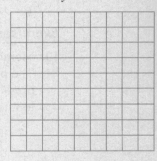

7. $x = -3$

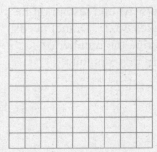

8. $y = -6$

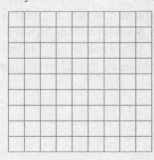

9. $x = 4$

Chapter 2

NAME _____ DATE _____

Practice with Examples

For use with pages 82–89

EXAMPLE 3 *Using the Standard Form*

Sales for the firefighter's benefit dinner were $1980. The cost for a child's dinner was $4.50 and an adult's dinner was $6.00. Describe the number of children and adults who attended to reach this amount.

SOLUTION

Verbal Model | Cost per child | · | Number of children | + | Cost per adult | · | Number of adults | = | Total revenue |

Algebraic Model $4.50c + 6.00a = 1980$

The graph of $4.5c + 6a = 1980$ is a line that intersects the c-axis at $(440, 0)$ and the a-axis at $(0, 330)$. Points with integer coefficients on the line segment joining $(440, 0)$ and $(0, 330)$ represent the numbers of adults and children that could have attended. One way to earn $1980 would be to sell 200 children's tickets and 180 adults' tickets.

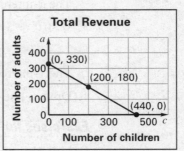

Exercises for Example 3

10. Members of the chorus need to raise $650 selling hoagies and pizzas. The profit they receive on each hoagie is $1.25 and $2.50 for each pizza. Find three different combinations for the numbers of each sold to raise the needed amount.

11. Daniel is employed at two different restaurants. At one restaurant he makes $5.35 per hour and at the other he makes $6.25. Daniel needs to earn $105.30 a week to pay his bills. Describe the number of hours he could work at each restaurant to earn this amount.

Algebra 2
Practice Workbook with Examples

NAME _____ DATE _____

Practice with Examples

For use with pages 91–98

GOAL **Write linear equations and direct variation equations**

> ### VOCABULARY
>
> Two variables x and y show **direct variation** provided $y = kx$ and $k \neq 0$.
>
> The nonzero constant k is called the **constant of variation.**

EXAMPLE 1 *Writing an Equation Given the Slope and y-intercept*

Write an equation of the line that has $m = -\frac{2}{3}$ and $b = -2$.

SOLUTION

$y = mx + b$ Use slope-intercept form.

$y = -\frac{2}{3}x - 2$ Substitute $-\frac{2}{3}$ for m and -2 for b.

An equation of the line is $y = -\frac{2}{3}x - 2$.

Exercises for Example 1

Write an equation of the line that has the given slope and y-intercept.

1. $m = 3, \ b = 0$ **2.** $m = \frac{3}{4}, \ b = 2$ **3.** $m = -2, \ b = -3$

EXAMPLE 2 *Writing an Equation Given the Slope and a Point*

Write an equation of the line that passes through $(-1, -3)$ and has a slope of 4.

SOLUTION

$y - y_1 = m(x - x_1)$ Use point-slope form.

$y + 3 = 4(x + 1)$ Substitute for m, x_1, and y_1.

$y + 3 = 4x + 4$ Distributive property

$y = 4x + 1$ Write in slope-intercept form.

Chapter 2

NAME _____ DATE _____

Practice with Examples

For use with pages 91–98

Exercises for Example 2

Write an equation of the line that passes through the given point and has the given slope.

4. $(2, -1)$, $m = -5$ **5.** $(0, 5)$, $m = \frac{1}{3}$ **6.** $(-3, -2)$, $m = 0$

EXAMPLE 3 *Writing an Equation Given Two Points*

Write an equation of the line that passes through $(-1, -3)$ and $(2, 4)$.

SOLUTION

First, find the slope by letting $(x_1, y_1) = (-1, -3)$ and $(x_2, y_2) = (2, 4)$.

$$m = \frac{y_2 - y_1}{x_2 - x_1} = \frac{4 - (-3)}{2 - (-1)} = \frac{7}{3}$$

Because you know the slope and a point on the line, use the point-slope form to find an equation of the line.

$y - y_1 = m(x - x_1)$	Use point-slope form.
$y + 1 = \frac{7}{3}(x + 3)$	Substitute for m, x_1, and y_1.
$y + 1 = \frac{7}{3}x + 7$	Distributive property
$y = \frac{7}{3}x + 6$	Write in slope-intercept form.

Exercises for Example 3

Write an equation of the line that passes through the given points.

7. $(2, 5)$ and $(4, -1)$ **8.** $(-2, 1)$ and $(4, 7)$ **9.** $(-5, 0)$ and $(0, -1)$

NAME _____ DATE _____

Practice with Examples

For use with pages 91–98

EXAMPLE 4 *Writing and Using a Direct Variation Equation*

The variables x and y vary directly, and $y = 3$ when $x = -4$. Write an equation that relates the variables. Then find y when $x = 4$.

SOLUTION

$y = kx$

$3 = k(-4)$

$-\frac{3}{4} = k$

The direct variation equation is $y = -\frac{3}{4}x$.

When $x = 4$, the value of y is $y = -\frac{3}{4}(4) = -3$.

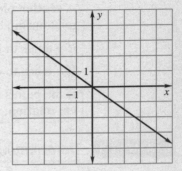

Exercises for Example 4

The variables x and y vary directly. Write an equation that relates the variables. Then find y when $x = -2$.

10. $x = 10,\ y = 100$

11. $x = -3,\ y = 12$

12. $x = 18,\ y = -2$

Chapter 2

NAME _____ DATE _____

Practice with Examples

For use with pages 100–106

GOAL Use a scatter plot to identify the correlation shown by a set of data and approximate the best-fitting line for a set of data

VOCABULARY

A **scatter plot** is a graph used to determine whether there is a relationship between paired data.

If y tends to increase as x increases, then there is a **positive correlation.**

If y tends to decrease as x increases, then there is a **negative correlation.**

If the points show no linear pattern, then there is **relatively no correlation.**

EXAMPLE 1 *Determining Correlation*

Draw a scatter plot of the data and describe the correlation shown by the scatter plot.

x	-5	-3	-2	-1.5	0	1	2	3	4	5
y	6	5	2	3.5	2	0.5	3	0	-1	1

SOLUTION

The scatter plot shows a negative correlation, which means that as the values of x increase, the values of y tend to decrease.

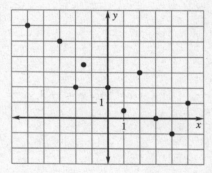

Exercises for Example 1

Draw a scatter plot of the data. Then tell whether the data have a *positive correlation, negative correlation,* or *relatively no correlation.*

1.

x	-2.5	-2	-2	-1	0	0	0	1	2	2
y	-6	-2.5	-4	0	0	-1	-3	3	1	5

Practice with Examples

For use with pages 100–106

2.

x	−3	−3	−2	−1	0	0	2	2	3	5
y	4	0	−1	2	3	−3	−2	4	2	0

EXAMPLE 2 *Fitting a Line to Data*

Approximate the best-fitting line for the data in the table.

x	1	1.5	2	3	4	5	6	7	7.5	8
y	7.5	6	6	5	4.5	5	3	3.5	4	3.5

SOLUTION

To begin, draw a scatter plot of the data. Then sketch the
line that best fits the points, with as many points above
the line as below it.

Now, estimate the coordinates of two points on the line,
not necessarily data points. Use these points to find an
equation of the line.

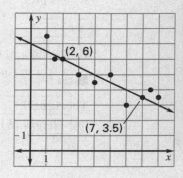

$$m = \frac{y_2 - y_1}{x_2 - x_1} = \frac{3.5 - 6}{7 - 2} = \frac{-2.5}{5} = -\frac{1}{2}$$ Find the slope of the line.

$$y - y_1 = m(x - x_1)$$ Use point-slope form.

$$y - 6 = -\frac{1}{2}(x - 2)$$ Substitute for m, x_1, and y_1.

$$y - 6 = -\frac{1}{2}x + 1$$ Distributive property

$$y = -\frac{1}{2}x + 7$$ Solve for y.

Chapter 2

Practice with Examples

For use with pages 100–106

Exercises for Example 2

Approximate the best-fitting line for the data.

3.

x	-1	-0.5	0.5	1	1.5	2	3	3.5	4	4.2
y	8	8	7	5.5	10	3	3	0.5	0	-2

4. The data in the table shows the age, t (in years), and the corresponding height, h (in inches), for a male from the age of 2 to the age of 19.

Age (t)	2	3	6	8	10	12	14	15	17	18	19
Height (h)	28	33	40	46	52	55	61	64	70	72	72

Algebra 2
Practice Workbook with Examples

Practice with Examples

For use with pages 108–113

GOAL Graph linear inequalities in two variables and use linear inequalities to solve real-life problems

---

VOCABULARY

A **linear inequality** in two variables can be written in one of the following forms: $Ax + By < C$, $Ax + By \leq C$, $Ax + By > C$, $Ax + By \geq C$.

An ordered pair (x, y) is a **solution** of a linear inequality if the inequality is true when the values for x and y are substituted into the inequality.

A **graph** of a linear inequality in two variables is the graph of all solutions of the inequality.

The boundary line of the inequality divides the coordinate plane into two **half-planes;** a shaded region containing the points that are solutions of the inequality, and an unshaded region which contains the points that are not.

EXAMPLE 1 *Checking Solutions of Inequalities*

Check whether the given ordered pair is a solution of $-x + 2y < 6$.

a. $(0, -6)$ **b.** $(2, 4)$ **c.** $(-3, 2)$

SOLUTION

Ordered Pair	Substitute	Conclusion
a. $(0, -6)$	$-(0) + 2(-6) = -12 < 6$	$(0, -6)$ is a solution.
b. $(2, 4)$	$-(2) + 2(4) = 6 \not< 6$	$(2, 4)$ is not a solution.
c. $(-3, 2)$	$-(-3) + 2(2) = 7 \not< 6$	$(-3, 2)$ is not a solution.

Exercises for Example 1

Check whether the given ordered pairs are solutions of the inequality.

1. $x \geq -1$; $(-1, -2)$, $(5, 2)$ **2.** $y \leq x + 1$; $(4, 5)$, $(-2, 1)$

3. $y > 5$; $(2, 6)$, $(0, 2)$ **4.** $4x < -9$; $(3, -2)$, $(-2, -5)$

Chapter 2

Practice with Examples

For use with pages 108–113

EXAMPLE 2 *Graphing Linear Inequalities in One Variable*

Graph (a) $2y > 6$ and (b) $x \geq -5$ in the coordinate plane.

SOLUTION

a. Graph the boundary line $y = 3$. Use a dashed line because $y > 3$.

Test the point $(0, 0)$. Because $(0, 0)$ is *not* a solution of the inequality, shade the half-plane above the line.

b. Graph the boundary line $x = -5$. Use a solid line because $x \geq -5$.

Test the point $(0, 0)$. Because $(0, 0)$ *is* a solution of the inequality, shade the half-plane to the right of the line.

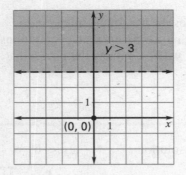

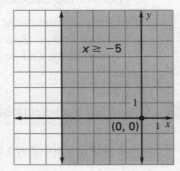

Exercises for Example 2

Graph the inequality in the coordinate plane.

5. $2x \geq -4$ $x \geq -2$

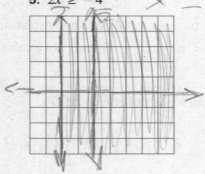

6. $-y < -2$ $y > 2$

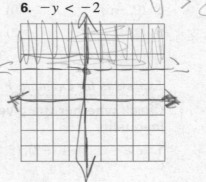

7. $3x \leq 9$ $x \leq 3$

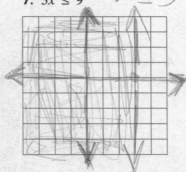

NAME _____ DATE _____

Practice with Examples

For use with pages 108–113

EXAMPLE 3 ### Graphing Linear Inequalities in Two Variables

Graph $y > -2x - 5$.

SOLUTION

Graph the boundary line $y = -2x - 5$. Use a dashed line because
$y > -2x - 5$. Test the point $(0, 0)$. Because $(0, 0)$ *is* a solution of the
inequality, shade the half-plane above the line.

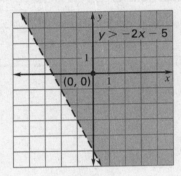

Exercises for Example 3

Graph the inequality.

8. $y \geq -x + 2$

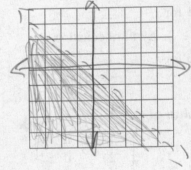

9. $y < -\frac{1}{2}x + 4$

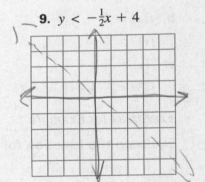

10. $-y \leq x + 3$

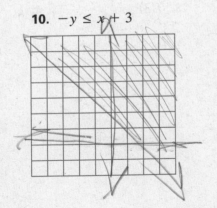

Chapter 2

Practice with Examples

For use with pages 114–120

GOAL **Represent piecewise functions**

VOCABULARY

Piecewise functions are represented by a combination of equations, each corresponding to a part of the domain.

A **step function** has a graph which resembles a set of stair steps. An example of a step function is the *greatest integer function*. This function is denoted by $g(x) = [\![x]\!]$, where for every real number x, $g(x)$ is the greatest integer less than or equal to x.

EXAMPLE 1 *Evaluating a Piecewise Function*

Evaluate $f(x)$ when (a) $x = -1$, (b) $x = 1$, and (c) $x = 3$.

$$f(x) = \begin{cases} 2x + 3, & \text{if } x < 0 \\ 2, & \text{if } 0 \le x < 2 \\ -x + 1, & \text{if } x \ge 2 \end{cases}$$

SOLUTION

a. $f(x) = 2x + 3$ Because $-1 < 0$, use first equation.

    $f(-1) = 2(-1) + 3 = 1$ Substitute -1 for x.

b. $f(x) = 2$ Because $0 \le 1 < 2$, use second equation.

    $f(1) = 2$ Substitute 1 for x.

c. $f(x) = -x + 1$ Because $3 \ge 2$, use third equation.

    $f(3) = -3 + 1 = -2$ Substitute 3 for x.

Exercises for Example 1

Evaluate the function for the given value of x.

$$f(x) = \begin{cases} x + 1, & \text{if } x > 1 \\ -x - 2, & \text{if } x \le 1 \end{cases} \qquad g(x) = \begin{cases} 3x + 2, & \text{if } x < 5 \\ -2x, & \text{if } x \ge 5 \end{cases}$$

1. $g(5)$ **2.** $f(0)$ **3.** $f(3)$ **4.** $g(-2)$

Chapter 2

NAME _____ DATE _____

Practice with Examples

For use with pages 114–120

EXAMPLE 2 *Graphing a Piecewise Function*

Graph the function: $f(x) = \begin{cases} -x, & \text{if } x \leq 3 \\ \frac{2}{3}x - 4, & \text{if } x > 3 \end{cases}$

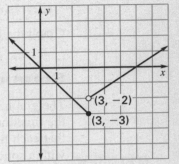

SOLUTION

To the right of $x = 3$, the graph is given by $y = \frac{2}{3}x - 4$. To the left of and including $x = 3$, the graph is given by $y = -x$.

The graph consists of two rays.

Exercises for Example 2

Graph the function.

5. $f(x) = \begin{cases} x + 2, & \text{if } x > 1 \\ -x + 2, & \text{if } x \leq 1 \end{cases}$

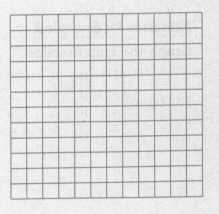

6. $f(x) = \begin{cases} \frac{1}{2}x + 4, & \text{if } x < 2 \\ -2x + 9, & \text{if } x \geq 2 \end{cases}$

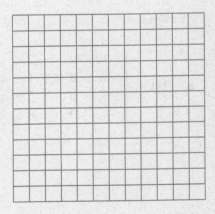

NAME _____ DATE _____

Practice with Examples

For use with pages 114–120

EXAMPLE 3 *Graphing a Step Function*

Graph the function. $f(x) = \begin{cases} -2, & \text{if } 0 \le x < 2 \\ -4, & \text{if } 2 \le x < 4 \\ -6, & \text{if } 4 \le x < 6 \end{cases}$

SOLUTION

The graph is composed of three line segments, because the function has three parts. The intervals of x tell you that each line segment is 2 units in length and begins with a solid dot and ends with an open dot.

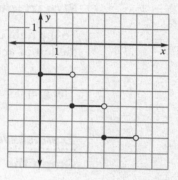

Exercises for Example 3

Graph the step function.

7. $f(x) = \begin{cases} 1, & \text{if } 0 < x \le 1 \\ 3, & \text{if } 1 < x \le 2 \\ 4, & \text{if } 2 < x \le 3 \\ 6, & \text{if } 3 < x \le 4 \end{cases}$

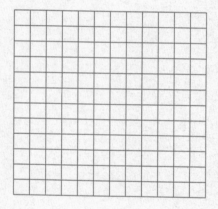

8. $f(x) = \begin{cases} -1, & \text{if } -2 \le x < 1 \\ -2, & \text{if } 1 \le x < 3 \\ -3, & \text{if } 3 \le x < 6 \\ -4, & \text{if } 6 \le x < 8 \end{cases}$

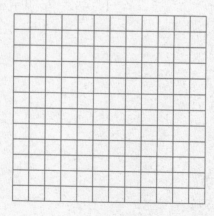

Practice with Examples

For use with pages 122–128

GOAL **Represent absolute value functions and use absolute value functions to model real-life situations**

VOCABULARY

The absolute value function has the standard form of $y = a|x - h| + k$, and its graph has the following characteristics.

- The **vertex** occurs at the point (h, k) and the graph is symmetric in the line $x = h$.

- The graph is V-shaped and opens up if $a > 0$ and down if $a < 0$.

- The graph is wider than the graph of $y = |x|$ if $|a| < 1$ and narrower if $|a| > 1$.

EXAMPLE 1 *Graphing an Absolute Value Function*

Graph $y = 3|x - 2| - 4$.

SOLUTION

First plot the vertex at $(2, -4)$. Then plot another point, such as $(1, -1)$. Use symmetry to plot a third point, $(3, -1)$. Connect these three points with a V-shaped graph. Notice that $a = 3 > 0$ and $|a| > 1$, so the graph opens up and is narrower than $y = |x|$.

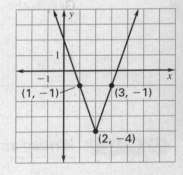

Chapter 2

Algebra 2
Practice Workbook with Examples
43

NAME _____ DATE _____

Practice with Examples

For use with pages 122–128

Exercises for Example 1

Graph the function.

1. $y = -2|x + 1| + 3$

2. $y = |x - 3| + 4$

3. $y = |x| + 5$

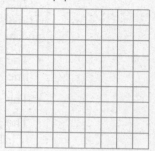

4. $y = 5|x - 2|$

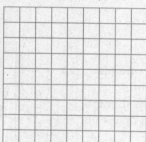

5. $y = -|x - 1| - 3$

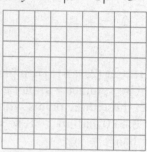

6. $y = -|x| - 2$

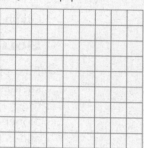

EXAMPLE 2 | **Writing an Absolute Value Function**

Write an equation of the graph shown.

SOLUTION

The vertex is $(-1, 3)$, so the equation has the form
$y = a|x + 1| + 3$.

To find a, substitute the coordinates of the point $(3, 0)$
into the equation and solve.

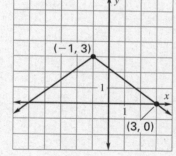

$y = a|x + 1| + 3$	Write equation.
$0 = a|3 + 1| + 3$	Substitute 0 for y and 3 for x.
$0 = 4a + 3$	Simplify.
$-3 = 4a$	Subtract 3 from each side.
$-\frac{3}{4} = a$	Solve for a.

An equation of the graph is $y = -\frac{3}{4}|x + 1| + 3$.

✓ CHECK Notice the graph opens down since $a = -\frac{3}{4} < 0$, and it is
wider than the graph of $y = |x|$ since $|a| = \left|-\frac{3}{4}\right| = \frac{3}{4} < 1$.

NAME _____ DATE _____

Practice with Examples

For use with pages 122–128

Exercises for Example 2

Write an equation of the graph shown.

7.

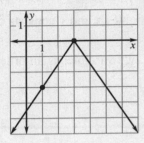

8.

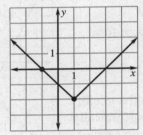

9.

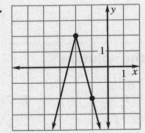

NAME _____ DATE _____

Practice with Examples

For use with pages 139–145

GOAL **Graph and solve systems of linear equations in two variables**

> **VOCABULARY**
>
> A **system of two linear equations** in two variables x and y consists of two equations, $Ax + By = C$ and $Dx + Ey = F$.
>
> A **solution** of a system of linear equations in two variables is an ordered pair (x, y) that satisfies *both* equations.

EXAMPLE 1 *Solving a System Graphically*

Solve the system.

$$x - y = 1 \qquad \textbf{Equation 1}$$
$$2x + y = -4 \qquad \textbf{Equation 2}$$

SOLUTION

Begin by writing each equation in slope-intercept form.

$$y = x - 1 \qquad \textbf{Equation 1}$$
$$y = -2x - 4 \qquad \textbf{Equation 2}$$

Then sketch the graph of each equation. From the graph, the lines appear to intersect at $(-1, -2)$. To algebraically check this, substitute -1 for x and -2 for y into each of the original equations.

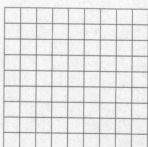

$$-1 - (-2) = 1 \checkmark \qquad \text{Equation 1 checks.}$$
$$2(-1) + (-2) = -4 \checkmark \qquad \text{Equation 2 checks.}$$

The solution is $(-1, -2)$.

Exercises for Example 2

Graph the linear system and estimate the solution. Then check the solution algebraically.

1. $x - 2y = 4$
$y = -x + 4$

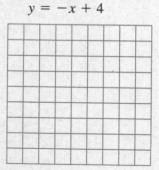

2. $y = -3x + 6$
$2x + 3y = -3$

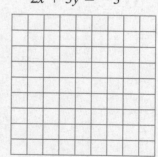

3. $2x - y = -4$
$y = 3$

NAME _____ DATE _____

Practice with Examples

For use with pages 139–145

EXAMPLE 2 *Systems with Many Solutions*

Tell how many solutions the linear system has.

$$6x - 8y = 2$$
$$\frac{9}{2}x - 6y = \frac{3}{2}$$

SOLUTION

Begin by writing each equation in slope-intercept form.
Notice that both equations have the same slope-intercept
form, $y = \frac{3}{4}x - \frac{1}{4}$. The graph of the equations is the same
line. So, each point on the line is a solution, and the
system has infinitely many solutions.

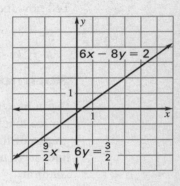

Exercises for Example 2

Graph the linear system and tell how many solutions it has.

4. $x - 2y = -8$

$y = \frac{1}{2}x + 4$

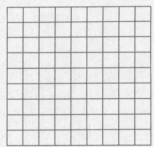

5. $6x + 8y = 8$

$y = -\frac{3}{4}x + 1$

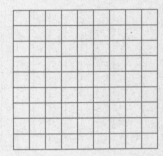

6. $y = -2x - 3$

$4x + 2y = -6$

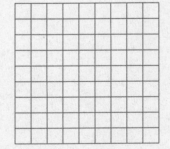

NAME _____ DATE _____

Practice with Examples

For use with pages 139–145

EXAMPLE 3 **Systems with No Solutions**

Tell how many solutions the linear system has.

$$x + 3y = 3$$
$$x + 3y = -3$$

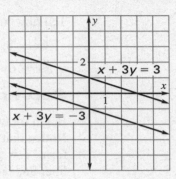

SOLUTION

Begin by writing each equation in slope-intercept form. Notice that both equations have the same slope, $-\frac{1}{3}$. The graphs of the equations are two parallel lines, so the two lines have no point of intersection and the system has no solution.

Exercises for Example 3

Graph the linear system and tell how many solutions it has.

7. $2x + y = 5$
  $-2x - y = 1$

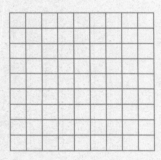

8. $3x + y = 4$
  $-6x - 2y = -12$

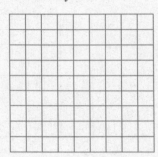

9. $-8x + 2y = -4$
  $-12x + 3y = 9$

Practice with Examples

For use with pages 148–155

GOAL **Use algebraic methods to solve linear systems**

VOCABULARY

Two methods for solving linear systems are given below.

The Substitution Method

Step 1: Solve one of the equations for one of its variables.

Step 2: Substitute the expression from Step 1 into the other equation and solve for the other variable.

Step 3: Substitute the value from Step 2 into the revised equation from Step 1 and solve.

The Linear Combination Method

Step 1: Multiply one or both of the equations by a constant to obtain coefficients that differ only in sign for one of the variables.

Step 2: Add the revised equations from Step 1. Combining like terms will eliminate one of the variables. Solve for the remaining variable.

Step 3: Substitute the value obtained in Step 2 into either of the original equations and solve for the other variable.

EXAMPLE 1 *The Substitution Method*

Use the substitution method to solve the linear system.

$$6x + y = -2 \qquad \textbf{Equation 1}$$
$$4x - 3y = 17 \qquad \textbf{Equation 2}$$

SOLUTION

Solve Equation 1 for y.

$6x + y = -2$	Write Equation 1.
$y = -6x - 2$	Revised Equation 1

Substitute $-6x - 2$ for y in Equation 2 and solve for x.

$4x - 3y = 17$	Write Equation 2.
$4x - 3(-6x - 2) = 17$	Substitute $-6x - 2$ for y.
$4x + 18x + 6 = 17$	Distributive property
$x = \frac{1}{2}$	Solve for x.

Substitute the value of x into the revised Equation 1 and solve for y.

$y = -6x - 2$	Revised Equation 1
$y = -6\left(\frac{1}{2}\right) - 2$	Substitute $\frac{1}{2}$ for x.
$y = -5$	Solve for y.

The solution is $\left(\frac{1}{2}, -5\right)$.

Chapter 3

NAME _____ DATE _____

Practice with Examples

For use with pages 148–155

Exercises for Example 1

Solve the linear system using the substitution method.

1. $2x - y =, 6$
$2x + 2y = -9$

2. $2x + 3y = 7$
$x - 2y = -7$

3. $-2x + y = 0$
$-x + y = 2$

$$\frac{-x \quad +x}{y = -x + 2}$$

$-2x + x + 2 = -6$

$-x + 2 = 0$

$$\frac{-2 \quad -2}{-x = -2}$$

$x = 2$

$y = 2 + 2$

$y = 4$

$(2, 4)$

4. $2x - 5y = 9$
$y = 3x - 7$

5. $-3x + 4y = 1$
$x = 2y + 1$

6. $6x + 2y = 11$
$y = -4x + 6$

$2x - 5(3x - 7) = 9$

$2x - 15x - 35 = 9$

$-13x - 35 = 9$

$$\frac{+35 \quad +35}{}$$

$$\frac{-13x}{-13} = \frac{44}{-13}$$

$x = 2$

$y = -1$

$(2, -1)$

$-3(2y + 1) + 4y = 1$

$-6y - 3 + 4y = 1$

$-2y - 3 = 1$

$$\frac{+3 \quad +3}{}$$

$$\frac{-2y}{-2} = \frac{4}{-2}$$

$y = -2$

$x = 2(-2) + 1$

$x = -3$

$(-3, -2)$

$6x + 2(-4x + 6) = 11$

$6x - 8x + 12 = 11$

$-2x + 12 = 11$

$$\frac{-12 \quad -12}{}$$

$$\frac{-2x}{-2} = \frac{-1}{-2}$$

$x = \frac{1}{2}$

$y = -4(\frac{1}{2}) + 6$

$y = -2 + 6$

$y = 4$

$(\frac{1}{2}, 4)$

NAME _____ DATE _____

Practice with Examples

For use with pages 148–155

EXAMPLE 2 **The Linear Combination Method**

Use the linear combination method to solve the linear system.

$6x + 3y = 3$ **Equation 1**

$8x + 4y = 4$ **Equation 2**

SOLUTION

$24x + 12y = 12$ Multiply Equation 1 by 4.

$-24x - 12y = -12$ Multiply Equation 2 by -3, so the x-coefficients differ only in sign.

$ 0 = 0$ Add the equations.

Because the statement $0 = 0$ is always true, there are infinitely many solutions.

Exercises for Example 2

Solve the linear system using the linear combination method.

7. $9x + 2y = 0$

$(3x - 5y = 17)(-3)$

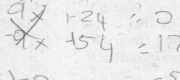

$9x + 24 = 0$
$-9x + 5y = 17$

$9x + 2(-3) = 0$
$9x - 6 = 0$
$ +6 +6$
$9x = 6$
$\overline{9} $

8. $2x - 3y = 5$ (3)

$-6x + 9y = 12$

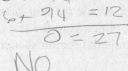

$6x - 9y = 15$
$-6x + 9y = 12$
$\overline{0 = 27}$

$7y = -51$
$y = -3$

NO
Solution

9. $4x + 5y = 13$

$3x + y = -4$

10. $2x - 5y = -4 (-2)$

$4x + 3y = 5$

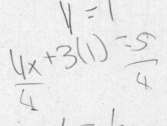

$4x + 4y = 8$
$4x + 3y = 5$
$\overline{3y = 13}$

$y = 1$

$\dfrac{4x + 3(1) = 5}{4}$

$x = -\dfrac{1}{2}$

$(5, -9)$

11. $11x + 6y = 1$

$3x + 2y = -3 (-3)$

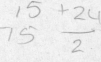

$3(5) 11x + 6y = 1$
$ -9x - 6y = 9$

$2(= 10$

$ 2x = 10$

$\dfrac{32x}{2} = \dfrac{10}{2}$

$39x = 5$

$3(5) + 2y = -3$
$15 + 2y = -3$
$ -15$

$2y = -18$
$y = -9$

12. $6x - 3y = -3 (4)$

$8x - 4y = -4 (-3)$

$24x - 12y = -12$
$-24x + 12y = 12$
$\overline{0 = 0}$

many
Solutions

Chapter 3

NAME _____ DATE _____

Practice with Examples

For use with pages 156–162

GOAL Graph a system of linear inequalities to find the solutions of the system and use systems of linear inequalities to solve real-life problems

VOCABULARY

A **system of linear inequalities** is two or more linear inequalities in the same variables and is also called a system of inequalities.

A **solution** of a system of linear inequalities is an ordered pair that is a solution of each inequality in the system.

The **graph** of a system of linear inequalities is the graph of all solutions of the system.

EXAMPLE 1 *Graphing a System of Two Inequalities*

Graph the system. $x + y \leq 4$ **Inequality 1**

                $2x - y < 4$ **Inequality 2**

SOLUTION

Begin by graphing the line $x + y = 4$ with a solid line. Shade the half-plane that satisfies $x + y \leq 4$, which is below the line. Next, graph the line $2x - y = 4$ with a dashed line. Shade the half-plane that satisfies $2x - y < 4$, which is to the left of the line. The graph of the system is the region shaded by both inequalities.

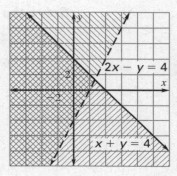

Exercises for Example 1

Graph the system of linear inequalities.

1. $x \geq -2$

    $x < 3$

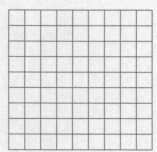

2. $y + 2 < 2x$

    $y < x + 6$

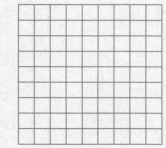

3. $y \leq 4$

    $x > -1$

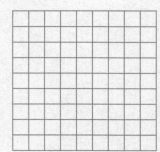

Practice with Examples
For use with pages 156–162

EXAMPLE 2 *Graphing a System of Three Inequalities*

Graph the system. $x + y < -1$ **Inequality 1**

$x < 2$ **Inequality 2**

$y \geq 0$ **Inequality 3**

SOLUTION

Begin by graphing the line $x + y = -1$ with a dashed
line. Shade the half-plane that satisfies $x + y < -1$,
which is to the left of the line. Next, graph the vertical line
$x = 2$ with a dashed line. Shade the half-plane that satisfies $x < 2$, which is to the left of the line. The inequality
$y \geq 0$ restricts the solutions to the second quadrant. The
graph of the system is the triangular region shown.

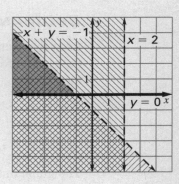

Exercises for Example 2

Graph the system of linear inequalities.

4. $3x + y \leq 5$

$y \geq 1$

$x \leq 1$

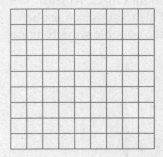

5. $x + 2y \leq 6$

$x - y \geq 3$

$x \geq 0$

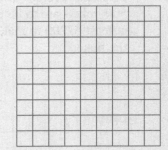

6. $x + y > 2$

$y \leq 2$

$x \geq 2$

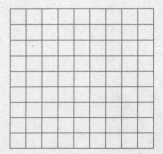

NAME _____ DATE _____

Practice with Examples

EXAMPLE 3 *Writing and Using a System of Inequalities*

A store sells two brands of CD players. To meet customer demands, it is necessary to stock at least twice as many CD players of brand A as of brand B. It is also necessary to have at least 10 of brand B available. In the store there is room for no more than 50 players. Write and graph a system of inequalities to describe the ways to stock the two brands.

SOLUTION

Let x represent brand A and y represent brand B. From the given information, you can write the following three inequalities.

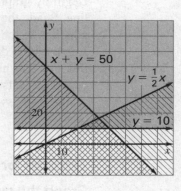

$x \geq 2y$	Brand A must be at least twice brand B.
$y \geq 10$	There must be at least 10 of brand B.
$x + y \leq 50$	The total can at most be 50.

The graph of the system is shown to the right.

Exercises for Example 3

Write and graph a system of linear inequalities to describe the problem.

7. An arena contains 1200 seats. For an upcoming concert, tickets will be priced $12.00 for some seats and $10.00 for others. At least 500 tickets are to be priced at $10.00, and the total sales must be at least $7200 to make a profit. What are the possible ways to price the tickets?

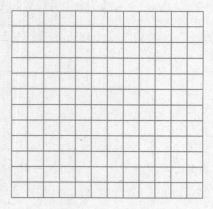

Practice with Examples

For use with pages 163–169

GOAL **Solve linear programming problems**

> **VOCABULARY**
>
> **Optimization** means finding the maximum or minimum value of some quantity.
>
> **Linear programming** is the process of optimizing a linear **objective function** subject to a system of linear inequalities called **constraints.**
>
> The graph of the system of constraints is called the **feasible region.** If an objective function has a maximum or a minimum value, then it must occur at a vertex of the feasible region. Moreover, the objective function will have both a maximum and a minimum value if the feasible region is bounded.

EXAMPLE 1 *Solving a Linear Programming Problem*

Find the minimum and maximum values of the objective function $C = 3x + 2y$ subject to the following constraints.

$$3x + 4y \leq 20$$
$$3x - y \leq 5$$
$$x \geq 0$$
$$y \geq 0$$

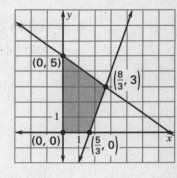

SOLUTION

The feasible region determined by the constraints is shown. The three vertices $(0, 5)$, $(0, 0)$, and $\left(\frac{5}{3}, 0\right)$ are intercepts. The fourth vertex $\left(\frac{8}{3}, 3\right)$ is found by solving the system of equations $3x + 4y = 20$ and $3x - y = 5$. To find the minimum and maximum values of C, evaluate $C = 3x + 2y$ at each of the four vertices.

At $(0, 5)$: $C = 3(0) + 2(5) = 10$

At $(0, 0)$: $C = 3(0) + 2(0) = 0$

At $\left(\frac{5}{3}, 0\right)$: $C = 3\left(\frac{5}{3}\right) + 2(0) = 5$

At $\left(\frac{8}{3}, 3\right)$: $C = 3\left(\frac{8}{3}\right) + 2(3) = 14$

The minimum value of C is 0, which occurs when $x = 0$ and $y = 0$.

The maximum value of C is 14, which occurs when $x = \frac{8}{3}$ and $y = 3$.

Algebra 2
Practice Workbook with Examples

Chapter 3

Practice with Examples

For use with pages 163–169

Exercises for Example 1

Find the minimum and maximum values of the objective function subject to the given constraints.

1. Objective function: $C = 6x - 2y$

Constraints: $x + y \leq 9$

$\quad\quad\quad\quad\quad 4x + y \geq 12$

$\quad\quad\quad\quad\quad x \geq 0$

$\quad\quad\quad\quad\quad y \geq 0$

2. Objective function: $C = x + 3y$

Constraints: $x + y \leq 5$

$\quad\quad\quad\quad\quad x \geq 1$

$\quad\quad\quad\quad\quad y \geq 2$

EXAMPLE 2 *A Region that Is Unbounded*

Find the minimum and maximum values of the objective function $C = 2x + 5y$ subject to the following constraints.

$\quad 3x - 5y \geq 24$

$\quad x - y \geq 6$

$\quad x \geq 0$

$\quad y \leq 0$

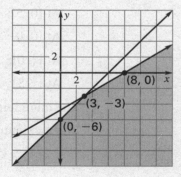

Practice with Examples
For use with pages 163–169

SOLUTION

The feasible region determined by the constraints is shown. The two vertices $(8, 0)$ and $(0, -6)$ are intercepts. The third vertex $(3, -3)$ is found by solving the system of equations $3x - 5y \geq 24$ and $x - y \geq 6$.

Now evaluate $C = 2x + 5y$ at each of the three vertices.

At $(0, -6)$: $C = 2(0) + 5(-6) = -30$

At $(8, 0)$: $C = 2(8) + 5(0) = 16$

At $(3, -3)$: $C = 2(3) + 5(-3) = -9$

Since the feasible region has no lower bound, the objective function has no minimum value. The maximum value of C is 16.

Exercises for Example 2
....

Find the minimum and maximum values of the objective function subject to the given constraints.

3. Objective function: $C = -2x + y$

Constraints: $y - x \leq 0$

$\qquad x \geq 2$

$\qquad y \geq 1$

4. Objective function: $C = 3x - y$

Constraints: $-9x - 4y \geq -16$

$\qquad 5x - 3y \geq 35$

$\qquad x \geq 0$

$\qquad y \leq -5$

Practice with Examples

For use with pages 170–175

GOAL Graph linear equations in three variables, evaluate linear functions in two variables, and use functions of two variables to model real-life situations

> ### VOCABULARY
>
> A **linear equation in three variables** x, y, and z is an equation of the form $ax + by + cz = d$, where a, b, and c are not all zero.
>
> In a **three-dimensional coordinate system,** the xy-plane is in a horizontal position, with the z-**axis** as a vertical line through the origin.
>
> An **ordered triple** is given by (x, y, z), and represents a point in space.

EXAMPLE 1 *Graphing a Linear Equation in Three Variables*

Sketch the graph of $-2x + 4y + 8z = 16$.

SOLUTION

Begin by finding the points where the graph intersects the axes. Let $y = 0$ and $z = 0$, and solve for x to get $x = -8$. The x-intercept is -8, so plot the point $(-8, 0, 0)$. In a similar way, you can find that the y-intercept is 4 and the z-intercept is 2.

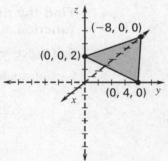

After plotting $(-8, 0, 0)$, $(0, 4, 0)$, and $(0, 0, 2)$, connect these points with lines to form the triangular region of the plane that lies in the second octant.

Exercises for Example 1

Sketch the graph of the equation. Label the three intercepts.

1. $x + y - z = 5$ **2.** $x - 5y + 2z = 10$ **3.** $-2x + 4y - 8z = 8$

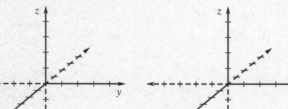

Practice with Examples

For use with pages 170–175

EXAMPLE 2 *Evaluating a Function of Two Variables*

a. Write the linear equation $10x - 3y + 12z = -60$ as a function of x and y.

b. Evaluate the function for $f(3, -2)$.

SOLUTION

a. $10x - 3y + 12z = -60$ Write original equation.

$\qquad\qquad 12z = -60 - 10x + 3y$ Isolate z-term.

$\qquad\qquad z = \frac{1}{12}(-60 - 10x + 3y)$ Solve for z.

$\qquad f(x, y) = \frac{1}{12}(-60 - 10x + 3y)$ Replace z with $f(x, y)$.

b. $f(3, -2) = \frac{1}{12}[-60 - 10(3) + 3(-2)]$ Substitute 3 for x and -2 for y.

$\qquad\qquad = \frac{1}{12}(-96)$ Simplify.

$\qquad\qquad = -8$ Multiply.

The graph of $10x - 3y + 12z = -60$ contains the point $(3, -2, -8)$.

Exercises for Example 2

Write the linear equation as a function of *x* and *y*. Then evaluate the function for the given values.

4. $12x - 2y + 4z = 12, \ f(0, 2)$ **5.** $-3x + 5y - z = 14, \ f(-1, 2)$

6. $4x + 3y + 2z = -12, \ f(-2, -4)$ **7.** $-6x - 2y - 2z = 18, \ f(3, 5)$

Practice with Examples

For use with pages 170–175

EXAMPLE 3 *Modeling a Real-Life Situation*

You own a specialty coffee shop which grinds gourmet coffee beans. The coffee grinder costs $79. Colombian coffee costs $10 per pound and the Kenyan costs $8 per pound. Write a model for the total cost as a function of the number of pounds of the two types of coffee. Evaluate the model for 6 lb of Colombian and 3 lb of Kenyan.

SOLUTION

Verbal Model

$$\boxed{\text{Total cost}} = \boxed{\text{Colombian cost}} \cdot \boxed{\text{Amount of Colombian}} +$$

$$\boxed{\text{Kenyan cost}} \cdot \boxed{\text{Amount of Kenyan}} + \boxed{\text{Grinder cost}}$$

Algebraic Model

$\boxed{c} = 10x + 8y + 79$

$c = 10(6) + 8(3) + 79$ Substitute 6 for x and 3 for y.

$= 163$ Simplify.

Exercises for Example 3

8. You are planting an apple orchard and decide to plant two types of trees: McIntosh and Red Delicious. The McIntosh trees cost $20.85 each and the Red Delicious cost $21.25 each. To plant the trees you need to buy a shovel which costs $30 and peat moss which costs $50. Write a model for the total amount you will spend as a function of the number of each type of tree. Evaluate the model for 25 McIntosh trees and 18 Red Delicious trees.

9. You are planning a cookout for the neighborhood and decide to serve hot dogs and hamburgers. The hot dogs cost $2.79 per pound and the hamburger costs $1.99 per pound. The condiments are $12. Write a model for the total amount you will spend as a function of the number of pounds of hot dogs and hamburger. Evaluate the model for 5 lb of hot dogs and 2.5 lb of hamburger.

Chapter 3

NAME _____ DATE _____

Practice with Examples
For use with pages 177–184

GOAL **Solve systems of linear equations in three variables and use linear systems in three variables to model real-life situations**

VOCABULARY

A **system of three linear equations** includes three equations in the same variables.

A **solution** of a linear system in three variables is an ordered triple (x, y, z) that satisfies all three equations. The linear combination method you learned in Lesson 3.2 can be extended to solve a system of linear equations in three variables.

The Linear Combination Method (3-Variable Systems)

Step 1: Use the linear combination method to rewrite the linear system in three variables as a linear system in *two* variables.

Step 2: Solve the new linear system for both of its variables.

Step 3: Substitute the values found in Step 2 into one of the original equations and solve for the remaining variable.

Note: If you obtain a false equation, such as $0 = 1$, in any step, then the system has no solution. If you do not obtain a false solution, but obtain an identity, such as $0 = 0$, then the system has infinitely many solutions.

EXAMPLE 1 *Using the Linear Combination Method*

Solve the system.

$$x + y + z = 2 \qquad \textbf{Equation 1}$$
$$-x + 3y + 2z = 8 \qquad \textbf{Equation 2}$$
$$4x + y = 4 \qquad \textbf{Equation 3}$$

SOLUTION

Since Equation 3 does not have a z-term, eliminate the z from one of the other equations.

$$\begin{array}{rl} -x + 3y + 2z = & 8 \\ -2x - 2y - 2z = & -4 \\ \hline -3x + y = & 4 \end{array}$$ Add -2 times the first equation to the second.

  New Equation 2

Now solve the system of the new Equation 2 and Equation 3.

$$\begin{array}{rl} -3x + y = 4 & \quad \text{New Equation 2} \\ -4x - y = -4 & \quad \text{Add } -1 \text{ times Equation 3 to Equation 2.} \\ \hline -7x = 0 & \quad \text{Solve for } x: x = 0. \end{array}$$

Substitute 0 for x into Equation 3 and solve for y: $y = 4$.

Substitute $x = 0$ and $y = 4$ into either original Equation 1 or 2 and solve for z: $0 + 4 + z = 2$, so $z = -2$.

The solution is the ordered triple $(0, 4, -2)$.

Practice with Examples

For use with pages 177–184

Exercises for Example 1

Solve the system using any algebraic method.

1. $5x + 2y - z = -7$

$\quad x - 2y + 2z = 0$

$\quad 3y + z = 17$

2. $x - 2y - 3z = -1$

$\quad 2x + y + z = 6$

$\quad x + 3y - 2z = 13$

3. $x + y + z = 6$

$\quad 2x - y + z = 3$

$\quad 3x - z = 0$

EXAMPLE 2 *Solving a System with Many Solutions*

Solve the system.

$2x + y + z = 0$	**Equation 1**
$x - 2y - 2z = 0$	**Equation 2**
$x + y + z = 0$	**Equation 3**

NAME _____ DATE _____

Practice with Examples

For use with pages 177–184

SOLUTION

$x - 2y - 2z = 0$ Equation 2 $2x + y + z = 0$ Equation 1

$\underline{-x - y - z = 0}$ -1 times Equation 3 $\underline{-2x - 2y - 2z = 0}$ -2 times Equation 3

$-3y - 3z = 0$ New Equation 2 $-y - z = 0$ New Equation 1

$-3y - 3z = 0$

$\underline{3y + 3z = 0}$

$0 = 0$

Because $0 = 0$ is always a true equation, the system has infinitely many solutions. To describe the solution, express two of the variables in terms of the third. One way to do this is to express x and y in terms of z. Using the new Equation 2 you get $y = -z$ when you solve for y. Now substitute z for z and $-z$ for y in any of the original equations and solve for x. The solution is any ordered triple of the form $(0, -z, z)$.

Exercises for Example 2

Solve the system using any algebraic method and describe the solution.

4. $x + 3y + z = 0$ **5.** $3x - 2y + 4z = 1$

$x + y - z = 0$ $x + y - 2z = 3$

$x - 2y - 4z = 0$ $2x - 3y + 6z = 8$

6. $x - y + 2z = 4$ **7.** $x - 2y + z = -6$

$x + z = 6$ $2x - 3y = -7$

$2x - 3y + 5z = 4$ $-x + 3y - 3z = 11$

Practice with Examples

For use with pages 199–206

GOAL Add and subtract matrices, multiply a matrix by a scalar, solve matrix equations, and use matrices in real-life situations

> ### VOCABULARY
>
> A **matrix** is a rectangular arrangement of numbers in rows and columns where the numbers are called **entries.**
>
> The **dimensions** of a matrix are given as *the number of rows × the number of columns.*
>
> **Scalar multiplication** is the process of multiplying each entry in a matrix by a **scalar,** a real number.

EXAMPLE 1 *Adding and Subtracting Matrices*

Perform the indicated operation, if possible.

a. $\begin{bmatrix} 2 \\ -1 \\ 7 \end{bmatrix} + \begin{bmatrix} 4 & 0 & -6 \end{bmatrix}$

b. $\begin{bmatrix} 2 & 3 & -5 \\ -1 & 0 & 4 \end{bmatrix} - \begin{bmatrix} 0 & 1 & 3 \\ 3 & -2 & -1 \end{bmatrix}$

SOLUTION

a. To add or subtract matrices, they must have the same dimensions.

Since $\begin{bmatrix} 2 \\ -1 \\ 7 \end{bmatrix}$ is a 3×1 matrix and $\begin{bmatrix} 4 & 0 & -6 \end{bmatrix}$ is a 1×3 matrix, you cannot add them.

b. Since both matrices are 2×3, you can subtract them.

$$\begin{bmatrix} 2 & 3 & -5 \\ -1 & 0 & 4 \end{bmatrix} - \begin{bmatrix} 0 & 1 & 3 \\ 3 & -2 & -1 \end{bmatrix} = \begin{bmatrix} 2-0 & 3-1 & -5-3 \\ -1-3 & 0-(-2) & 4-(-1) \end{bmatrix}$$

$$= \begin{bmatrix} 2 & 2 & -8 \\ -4 & 2 & 5 \end{bmatrix}$$

Exercises for Example 1

Perform the indicated operation, if possible.

1. $\begin{bmatrix} 2 & 5 \\ -1 & -3 \end{bmatrix} + \begin{bmatrix} 4 & -2 \\ 0 & 7 \\ 0 & 0 \end{bmatrix}$

2. $\begin{bmatrix} 5 & 0 \\ -2 & 1 \\ 4 & -3 \end{bmatrix} - \begin{bmatrix} 4 & -6 \\ 2 & -2 \\ -1 & 3 \end{bmatrix}$

Chapter 4

NAME _____ DATE _____

Practice with Examples

For use with pages 199–206

EXAMPLE 2 *Solving a Matrix Equation*

Solve the matrix equation for x and y: $\quad -2x\begin{bmatrix} 5 & 0 & -1 \\ 4 & 2 & 8 \end{bmatrix} = \begin{bmatrix} 20 & 0 & -4 \\ 16 & 8 & y \end{bmatrix}$.

SOLUTION

$-2x\begin{bmatrix} 5 & 0 & -1 \\ 4 & 2 & 8 \end{bmatrix} = \begin{bmatrix} 20 & 0 & -4 \\ 16 & 8 & y \end{bmatrix}$ Write original equation.

$\begin{bmatrix} -10x & 0 & 2x \\ -8x & -4x & -16x \end{bmatrix} = \begin{bmatrix} 20 & 0 & -4 \\ 16 & 8 & y \end{bmatrix}$ Multiply by $-2x$.

$-10x = 20$ $-16x = y$ Equate corresponding entries involving x and y.

$x = -2$ $-16(-2) = y$ Solve the resulting equations.

$32 = y$

Exercises for Example 2

Solve the matrix equation for x and y.

3. $\begin{bmatrix} 3x & 2 & 4 \end{bmatrix} = \begin{bmatrix} 9 & -y & 4 \end{bmatrix}$

4. $\begin{bmatrix} 2y & -1 \\ -6 & 0 \end{bmatrix} + \begin{bmatrix} 5 & 4 \\ x & 8 \end{bmatrix} = \begin{bmatrix} -5 & 3 \\ -7 & 8 \end{bmatrix}$

NAME _____ DATE _____

Practice with Examples

For use with pages 199–206

EXAMPLE 3 *Using Matrix Operations*

Write a matrix that shows the average costs in health care from this year to next year.

	This Year (A)	
	Individual	Family
Comprehensive	$694.32	$1725.36
HMO Standard	$451.80	$1187.76
HMO Plus	$489.48	$1248.12

	Next Year (B)	
	Individual	Family
Comprehensive	$683.91	$1699.48
HMO Standard	$463.10	$1217.45
HMO Plus	$499.27	$1273.08

SOLUTION

Begin by adding matrix A and matrix B to determine the total costs for two years. Then multiply the result by $\frac{1}{2}$, which is equivalent to dividing by 2. Round your answers to the nearest cent to find the average.

$$\frac{1}{2}(A + B) = \frac{1}{2}\left(\begin{bmatrix} 694.32 & 1725.36 \\ 451.80 & 1187.76 \\ 489.48 & 1248.12 \end{bmatrix} + \begin{bmatrix} 683.91 & 1699.48 \\ 463.10 & 1217.45 \\ 499.27 & 1273.08 \end{bmatrix}\right)$$

$$= \frac{1}{2}\begin{bmatrix} 1378.23 & 3424.84 \\ 914.90 & 2405.21 \\ 988.75 & 2521.20 \end{bmatrix} = \begin{bmatrix} \$689.12 & \$1712.42 \\ \$457.45 & \$1202.61 \\ \$494.38 & \$1260.60 \end{bmatrix}$$

Exercises for Example 3

5. Using the matrix B on health care costs, write a matrix C for the following year that shows the costs after a 2% decrease.

6. Write a matrix which will show the monthly payment following a 3% increase in the costs from matrix B.

Practice with Examples

For use with pages 208–213

GOAL **Multiply two matrices**

> **VOCABULARY**
>
> The product of two matrices A and B is defined only if the number of columns in A is equal to the number of rows in B.
>
> If A is an $m \times n$ matrix and B is an $n \times p$ matrix, then the product AB is an $m \times p$ matrix.

EXAMPLE 1 *Finding the Product of Two Matrices*

Find AB and BA if $A = \begin{bmatrix} 2 & 1 \\ -2 & 0 \\ 0 & 3 \end{bmatrix}$ and $B = \begin{bmatrix} 4 & 3 \\ 2 & 0 \end{bmatrix}$.

SOLUTION

$AB = \begin{bmatrix} 2 & 1 \\ -2 & 0 \\ 0 & 3 \end{bmatrix} \begin{bmatrix} 4 & 3 \\ 2 & 0 \end{bmatrix}$

Because the number of columns in A equals the number of rows in B, the product is defined. AB will be a 3×2 matrix.

$= \begin{bmatrix} 2(4) + 1(2) & 2(3) + 1(0) \\ -2(4) + 0(2) & -2(3) + 0(0) \\ 0(4) + 3(2) & 0(3) + 3(0) \end{bmatrix}$

Multiply corresponding entries in the first row of A and the first column of B. Then add. Use a similar procedure to write the other entries.

$= \begin{bmatrix} 10 & 6 \\ -8 & -6 \\ 6 & 0 \end{bmatrix}$

BA is undefined because B is a 2×2 matrix and A is a 3×2 matrix. The number of columns in B does not equal the number of rows in A.

Exercises for Example 1

Find the product. If it is not defined, state the reason.

1. $[2 \quad 3 \quad 4] \begin{bmatrix} -1 & 4 \\ 0 & 1 \\ 5 & 2 \end{bmatrix}$

2. $\begin{bmatrix} 2 & 1 \\ 3 & -2 \end{bmatrix} \begin{bmatrix} -1 & 5 \\ 6 & 2 \end{bmatrix}$

LESSON

4.2

CONTINUED

NAME _____ DATE _____

Practice with Examples

For use with pages 208–213

3. $\begin{bmatrix} 2 & -1 & 0 \\ 0 & 5 & 3 \\ 1 & -2 & -1 \end{bmatrix} \begin{bmatrix} 1 & 0 & -1 \\ 2 & 3 & 3 \end{bmatrix}$

4. $\begin{bmatrix} 0 & 1 \\ 4 & 3 \\ 5 & -1 \end{bmatrix} \begin{bmatrix} 2 & -1 & 0 \\ 3 & 4 & 1 \end{bmatrix}$

EXAMPLE 2 *Using Matrix Operations*

If $A = \begin{bmatrix} 4 & 3 \\ -1 & 0 \end{bmatrix}$, $B = \begin{bmatrix} -3 & 5 \\ 2 & 1 \end{bmatrix}$, and $C = \begin{bmatrix} 1 & -2 \\ 0 & -1 \end{bmatrix}$, simplify each expression.

a. $A(BC)$　　　　　　　　　　　　　　　　　　**b.** $(AB)C$

SOLUTION

a. $A(BC) = \begin{bmatrix} 4 & 3 \\ -1 & 0 \end{bmatrix} \left(\begin{bmatrix} -3 & 5 \\ 2 & 1 \end{bmatrix} \begin{bmatrix} 1 & -2 \\ 0 & -1 \end{bmatrix} \right)$　Substitute the matrices for A, B, and C.

　　　$= \begin{bmatrix} 4 & 3 \\ -1 & 0 \end{bmatrix} \begin{bmatrix} -3 & 1 \\ 2 & -5 \end{bmatrix}$　Multiply B by C first.

　　　$= \begin{bmatrix} -6 & -11 \\ 3 & -1 \end{bmatrix}$　Multiply A by the result.

b. $(AB)C = \left(\begin{bmatrix} 4 & 3 \\ -1 & 0 \end{bmatrix} \begin{bmatrix} -3 & 5 \\ 2 & 1 \end{bmatrix} \right) \begin{bmatrix} 1 & -2 \\ 0 & -1 \end{bmatrix}$　Substitute the matrices for A, B, and C.

　　　$= \begin{bmatrix} -6 & 23 \\ 3 & -5 \end{bmatrix} \begin{bmatrix} 1 & -2 \\ 0 & -1 \end{bmatrix}$　Multiply A by B first.

　　　$= \begin{bmatrix} -6 & -11 \\ 3 & -1 \end{bmatrix}$　Multiply the result by C.

Chapter 4

NAME _____ DATE _____

Practice with Examples

For use with pages 208–213

Exercises for Example 2

Use the given matrices to simplify the expression.

$$A = \begin{bmatrix} -1 & 1 \\ 2 & -1 \end{bmatrix}, \; B = \begin{bmatrix} 4 & -3 \\ 0 & 2 \end{bmatrix}, \; C = \begin{bmatrix} -2 & -3 \\ 1 & 1 \end{bmatrix}$$

5. AA **6.** $A(B + C)$ **7.** $2(CA)$

8. $AB + BC$ **9.** $A(B - C)$ **10.** $-2(BA)$

NAME _____ DATE _____

Practice with Examples

For use with pages 214–221

GOAL **Evaluate determinants of 2 × 2 and 3 × 3 matrices**

VOCABULARY

The **determinant** of a square matrix A is denoted by det A or $|A|$.

Cramer's Rule is a method of solving a system of linear equations using the determinant of the coefficient matrix of the linear system.

The entries in the **coefficient matrix** are the coefficients of the variables in the same order.

The area of a triangle with vertices (x_1, y_2), (x_2, y_2), and (x_3, y_3) is given by

$$\text{Area} = \pm\frac{1}{2}\begin{vmatrix} x_1 & y_1 & 1 \\ x_2 & y_2 & 1 \\ x_3 & y_3 & 1 \end{vmatrix}$$

where the symbol $\pm$ indicates that the appropriate sign should be chosen to yield a positive value.

Determinant of a 2 × 2 Matrix

$$\det\begin{bmatrix} a & b \\ c & d \end{bmatrix} = \begin{vmatrix} a & b \\ c & d \end{vmatrix} = ad - cb$$

The determinant of a 2 × 2 matrix is the difference of the products of the entries on the diagonals.

Determinant of a 3 × 3 Matrix

1. Repeat the first two columns to the right of the determinant.

2. Subtract the sum of the products of the entries on the diagonals going *up* from left to right from the sum of the products of the entries on the diagonals going *down* from left to right.

$$\det\begin{bmatrix} a & b & c \\ d & e & f \\ g & h & i \end{bmatrix} = \begin{vmatrix} a & b & c \\ d & e & f \\ g & h & i \end{vmatrix}\begin{matrix} a & b \\ d & e \\ g & h \end{matrix} = (aei + bfg + cdh) - (gec + hfa + idb)$$

Practice with Examples

For use with pages 214–221

EXAMPLE 1 *The Area of a Triangle*

Find the area of the triangle with the vertices $A(-3, -1)$, $B(2, 0)$, $C(2, -4)$.

SOLUTION

$$\text{Area} = \pm\frac{1}{2}\begin{vmatrix} -3 & -1 & 1 \\ 2 & 0 & 1 \\ 2 & -4 & 1 \end{vmatrix}\begin{matrix} -3 & -1 \\ 2 & 0 \\ 2 & -4 \end{matrix}$$

Write the determinant, repeating the first two columns at the end.

$$= \pm\frac{1}{2}([0 + (-2) + (-8)] - [0 + 12 + (-2)])$$

Find the products of the diagonals.

$$= \pm\frac{1}{2}[-10 - 10]$$

Simplify.

$$= 10$$

Multiply by $-\frac{1}{2}$ to get a positive value.

Exercises for Example 1

Find the area of the triangle with the given vertices.

1. $A(2, 3)$, $B(0, 5)$, $C(-1, -2)$

2. $A(0, 4)$, $B(3, 5)$, $C(-1, 4)$

3. $A(-1, -2)$, $B(2, 1)$, $C(0, 3)$

4. $A(1, 2)$, $B(2, 6)$, $C(3, 2)$

NAME _____ DATE _____

Practice with Examples

For use with pages 214–221

EXAMPLE 2 ***Using Cramer's Rule for a 2 × 2 System***

Use Cramer's Rule to solve this system: $3x - 2y = 22$

$x + 4y = -2$

SOLUTION

$\begin{vmatrix} 3 & -2 \\ 1 & 4 \end{vmatrix} = 12 - (-2) = 14$ Evaluate the determinant of the coefficient matrix.

$x = \dfrac{\begin{vmatrix} 22 & -2 \\ -2 & 4 \end{vmatrix}}{14} = \dfrac{88 - 4}{14} = 6$ Since the determinant is not 0, apply Cramer's Rule.

$y = \dfrac{\begin{vmatrix} 3 & 22 \\ 1 & -2 \end{vmatrix}}{14} = \dfrac{-6 - 22}{14} = -2$

The solution is $(6, -2)$.

✓ Check this solution in the original equations.

$3x - 2y = 22$ $\qquad\qquad$ $x + 4y = -2$

$3(\mathbf{6}) - 2(\mathbf{-2}) \overset{?}{=} 22$ $\qquad$ $\mathbf{6} + 4(\mathbf{-2}) \overset{?}{=} -2$

$22 = 22$ ✓ $\qquad\qquad$ $-2 = -2$ ✓

Exercises for Example 2

Use Cramer's Rule to solve the linear system.

5. $2x + y = 1$

$-x + y = 7$

6. $3x + 4y = 2$

$2x + y = 3$

7. $x + y = 5$

$2x - y = 4$

8. $6x - 3y = 39$

$5x + 9y = -25$

9. $3x - 2y = 8$

$4x - 3y = 10$

10. $5x - 2y = -9$

$-7x + 3y = 14$

Chapter 4

Practice with Examples

For use with pages 223–229

GOAL **Find and use inverse matrices and use inverse matrices in real-life situations**

VOCABULARY

The $n \times n$ **identity matrix** is the matrix that has 1's on the main diagonal and 0's elsewhere.

Two $n \times n$ matrices are **inverses** of each other if their product (in *both* orders) is the $n \times n$ identity matrix.

The inverse of the matrix $A = \begin{bmatrix} a & b \\ c & d \end{bmatrix}$ is

$$A^{-1} = \frac{1}{|A|} \begin{bmatrix} d & -b \\ -c & a \end{bmatrix} = \frac{1}{ad - cb} \begin{bmatrix} d & -b \\ -c & a \end{bmatrix} \text{ provided } ad - cb \neq 0.$$

EXAMPLE 1 *Finding the Inverse of 2 × 2 Matrix*

Find the inverse of $A = \begin{bmatrix} -3 & -7 \\ 2 & 5 \end{bmatrix}$.

SOLUTION

$|A| = (-3)(5) - (2)(-7) = -1$ Evaluate the determinant of A.

$A^{-1} = \frac{1}{-1} \begin{bmatrix} 5 & 7 \\ -2 & -3 \end{bmatrix} = \begin{bmatrix} -5 & -7 \\ 2 & 3 \end{bmatrix}$ Use the formula $A^{-1} = \frac{1}{|A|} \begin{bmatrix} d & -b \\ -c & a \end{bmatrix}$.

Exercises for Example 1

Find the inverse of the matrix.

1. $\begin{bmatrix} 2 & 3 \\ 3 & 4 \end{bmatrix}$ **2.** $\begin{bmatrix} 2 & 5 \\ 4 & 11 \end{bmatrix}$ **3.** $\begin{bmatrix} 2 & 1 \\ 1 & 2 \end{bmatrix}$

NAME _____ DATE _____

Practice with Examples

For use with pages 223–229

EXAMPLE 2 *Solving a Matrix Equation*

$$\overbrace{\begin{bmatrix} 3 & 2 \\ 4 & 3 \end{bmatrix}}^{A} X = \overbrace{\begin{bmatrix} 12 & 2 \\ 17 & 3 \end{bmatrix}}^{B}$$

Solve the matrix equation $\begin{bmatrix} 3 & 2 \\ 4 & 3 \end{bmatrix} X = \begin{bmatrix} 12 & 2 \\ 17 & 3 \end{bmatrix}$ for the 2×2 matrix X.

SOLUTION

$A^{-1} = \dfrac{1}{9-8}\begin{bmatrix} 3 & -2 \\ -4 & 3 \end{bmatrix} = \begin{bmatrix} 3 & -2 \\ -4 & 3 \end{bmatrix}$ Find the inverse of A, A^{-1}.

To solve for X, multiply both sides of the equation by A^{-1} on the *left*.

$\begin{bmatrix} 3 & -2 \\ -4 & 3 \end{bmatrix}\begin{bmatrix} 3 & 2 \\ 4 & 3 \end{bmatrix} X = \begin{bmatrix} 3 & -2 \\ -4 & 3 \end{bmatrix}\begin{bmatrix} 12 & 2 \\ 17 & 3 \end{bmatrix}$ $A^{-1}AX = A^{-1}B$

$\begin{bmatrix} 1 & 0 \\ 0 & 1 \end{bmatrix} X = \begin{bmatrix} 2 & 0 \\ 3 & 1 \end{bmatrix}$

$X = \begin{bmatrix} 2 & 0 \\ 3 & 1 \end{bmatrix}$

$\begin{bmatrix} 3 & 2 \\ 4 & 3 \end{bmatrix}\begin{bmatrix} 2 & 0 \\ 3 & 1 \end{bmatrix} = \begin{bmatrix} 12 & 2 \\ 17 & 3 \end{bmatrix} = B$ Check by multiplying A and X to see if you get B.

Exercises for Example 2

Solve the matrix equation.

4. $\begin{bmatrix} 2 & 2 \\ 1 & 3 \end{bmatrix} X = \begin{bmatrix} 12 & 2 \\ 16 & -5 \end{bmatrix}$

5. $\begin{bmatrix} 4 & -6 \\ 3 & -4 \end{bmatrix} X = \begin{bmatrix} 6 & 0 \\ 5 & 1 \end{bmatrix}$

Chapter 4

Practice with Examples

For use with pages 223–229

EXAMPLE 3 *Encoding a Message*

Use $A = \begin{bmatrix} 3 & 0 \\ -1 & 2 \end{bmatrix}$ to encode the message GO NORTH.

SOLUTION

First, convert the letters to row matrices, inserting a 0 for spaces between words.

$$[7 \quad 15][0 \quad 14][15 \quad 18][20 \quad 8]$$

Then multiply each of the uncoded row matrices by matrix A on the *right* to obtain coded row matrices.

__ = 0	F = 6	L = 12	R = 18	X = 24
A = 1	G = 7	M = 13	S = 19	Y = 25
B = 2	H = 8	N = 14	T = 20	Z = 26
C = 3	I = 9	O = 15	U = 21	
D = 4	J = 10	P = 16	V = 22	
E = 5	K = 11	Q = 17	W = 23	

$$[7 \quad 15]\begin{bmatrix} 3 & 0 \\ -1 & 2 \end{bmatrix} = [6 \quad 30] \qquad [15 \quad 18]\begin{bmatrix} 3 & 0 \\ -1 & 2 \end{bmatrix} = [27 \quad 36]$$

$$[0 \quad 14]\begin{bmatrix} 3 & 0 \\ -1 & 2 \end{bmatrix} = [-14 \quad 28] \qquad [20 \quad 8]\begin{bmatrix} 3 & 0 \\ -1 & 2 \end{bmatrix} = [52 \quad 16]$$

The coded message is 6, 30, __, 14, 28, 27, 36, 52, 16.

Exercises for Example 3

Use the code above and the matrix to encode the message.

6. HELLO

$$A = \begin{bmatrix} -2 & 1 \\ 3 & -3 \end{bmatrix}$$

7. CALL ME

$$A = \begin{bmatrix} 4 & -3 \\ 2 & 0 \end{bmatrix}$$

8. I WON

$$A = \begin{bmatrix} -1 & 5 \\ 3 & -2 \end{bmatrix}$$

Practice with Examples

For use with pages 230–236

GOAL Solve systems of linear equations using inverse matrices and use systems of linear equations to solve real-life problems

VOCABULARY

For a linear system of equations written as a matrix equation $AX = B$, the matrix A is the coefficient matrix of the system, X is the **matrix of variables,** and B is the **matrix of constants.** If the determinant of A is nonzero, then the linear system has exactly one solution, which is $X = A^{-1}B$.

EXAMPLE 1 *Solving a Linear System*

Use matrices to solve the linear system. $5x + 2y = 3$ **Equation 1**

$4x + 2y = 4$ **Equation 2**

SOLUTION

$$\begin{matrix} A & X & B \end{matrix}$$

$$\begin{bmatrix} 5 & 2 \\ 4 & 2 \end{bmatrix}\begin{bmatrix} x \\ y \end{bmatrix} = \begin{bmatrix} 3 \\ 4 \end{bmatrix}$$

Write the matrix equation for the system.

$$A^{-1} = \frac{1}{10 - 8}\begin{bmatrix} 2 & -2 \\ -4 & 5 \end{bmatrix} = \begin{bmatrix} 1 & -1 \\ -2 & \frac{5}{2} \end{bmatrix}$$

Find the inverse of matrix A.

$$\begin{bmatrix} x \\ y \end{bmatrix} = \begin{bmatrix} 1 & -1 \\ -2 & \frac{5}{2} \end{bmatrix}\begin{bmatrix} 3 \\ 4 \end{bmatrix} = \begin{bmatrix} -1 \\ 4 \end{bmatrix}$$

To find X, multiply B by A^{-1} on the **left.**

The solution is $(-1, 4)$.

Exercises for Example 1

Use an inverse matrix to solve the linear system.

1. $2x - y = 1$

$-3x + 2y = 0$

2. $3x + 4y = -4$

$4x + 5y = -7$

3. $6x - 5y = 3$

$3x - 2y = 3$

NAME _____ DATE _____

Practice with Examples
For use with pages 230–236

EXAMPLE 2 *Writing and Using a Linear System*

A chemist wants to use three different solutions to create a 50-liter mixture containing 32% acid. The first solution contains 10% acid, the second 30%, and the third 50%. He needs to use twice as much of the 50% solution as the 30% solution. How many liters of each solution should be used?

SOLUTION

Verbal Model

| Amount of 10% | + | Amount of 30% | + | Amount of 50% | = | Total amount |

0.10 | Amount of 10% | $+ \ 0.30$ | Amount of 30% | $+ \ 0.50$ | Amount of 50% | $= 0.32$ | Total amount |

| Amount of 50% | $= 2$ | Amount of 30% |

Labels   Amount of 10% = f Amount of 50% = t

Amount of 30% = s Total amount = 50

Algebraic $f + s + t = 50$ Equation 1

Model $0.10f + 0.30s + 0.50t = 0.32(50)$ Equation 2

$t = 2s$ Equation 3

$f + s + t = 50$

$0.10f + 0.30s + 0.50t = 16$

$-2s + t = 0$

$$\begin{matrix} & A & & X & & B \end{matrix}$$

$$\begin{bmatrix} 1 & 1 & 1 \\ 0.1 & 0.3 & 0.5 \\ 0 & -2 & 1 \end{bmatrix} \begin{bmatrix} f \\ s \\ t \end{bmatrix} = \begin{bmatrix} 50 \\ 16 \\ 0 \end{bmatrix}$$

Using a graphing calculator, enter the coefficient matrix A and the matrix of constants B. To find X, multiply A^{-1} by B.

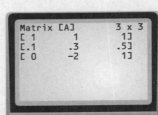
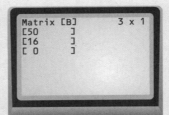

The chemist should use 17 liters of 10% solution, 11 liters of 30% solution and 22 liters of 50% solution.

Chapter 4

Practice with Examples

For use with pages 230–236

Exercises for Example 2

4. You can purchase peanuts for $3 per pound, almonds for $4 per pound, and cashews for $8 per pound. You want to create 140 pounds of a mixture that costs $6 per pound. If twice as many peanuts are used than almonds, how many pounds of each type should be used?

5. Suppose the chemist in Example 2 wants to create a 600-liter mixture containing 25% acid. This time, the first solution contains 30% acid, the second 20%, and the third 15%. If the mixture is to contain 100 more liters of the 15% solution than the 20% solution, how many liters of each solution should be used?

5.1

NAME _Olivia Smith_   DATE _____

Practice with Examples

For use with pages 249–255

GOAL   **Graph quadratic functions**

> ### VOCABULARY
>
> A **quadratic function in standard form** is written as
> $y = ax^2 + bx + c$, where $a \neq 0$.
>
> A **parabola** is the U-shaped graph of a quadratic function.
>
> The **vertex** of a parabola is the lowest point of a parabola that opens up, and the highest point of a parabola that opens down.
>
> The vertical line passing through the vertex of a parabola, which divides the parabola into two symmetrical parts that are mirror images of each other, is called the **axis of symmetry**.

EXAMPLE 1   *Graphing a Quadratic Function*

Graph $y = x^2 - 4x + 3$.

SOLUTION

The coefficients are $a = 1$, $b = -4$, and $c = 3$. Since $a > 0$, the parabola opens up.

To find the *x*-coordinate of the vertex, substitute 1 for *a* and -4 for *b* in the formula:

$$x = -\frac{b}{2a} = -\frac{(-4)}{2(1)} = 2$$

To find the *y*-coordinate of the vertex, substitute 2 for *x* in the original equation, and solve for *y*.

$$y = x^2 - 4x + 3 = (2)^2 - 4(2) + 3 = 4 - 8 + 3 = -1$$

The vertex is $(2, -1)$. Plot two points, such as $(1, 0)$ and $(0, 3)$. Then use symmetry to plot two more points $(3, 0)$ and $(4, 3)$. Draw the parabola.

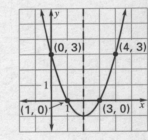

Exercises for Example 1

Graph the quadratic function.

1. $y = x^2 + 2x + 1$ **2.** $y = -2x^2 - 8x - 5$ **3.** $y = -x^2 + 4$

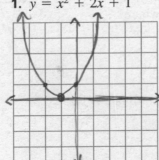
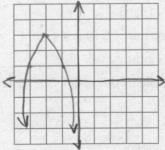
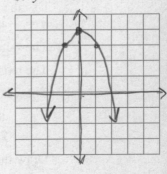

Handwritten work (left margin):

$x = -\frac{2}{2(1)} \; -\frac{2}{2} \; -1$

$y = -1^2 + 2(-1) + 1$
$y = 1 + 2 + 1$
$y - 1 + 2 + 1$
$y = 2$ $4 + -4 + 1$

x	y
0	1
-1	0
-2	1

NAME _____ DATE _____

Practice with Examples

For use with pages 249–255

Practice
For use with pages

EXAMPLE 2 *Graphing a Quadratic Function in Vertex Form*

Graph $y = 2(x - 3)^2 - 4$.

SOLUTION

Use the form $y = a(x - h)^2 + k$, where $a = 2$, $h = 3$, and $k = -4$. Since $a > 0$, the parabola opens up.

Plot the vertex $(h, k) = (3, -4)$.

Plot two points, such as $(2, -2)$ and $(1, 4)$.

Use symmetry to plot two more points, $(4, -2)$ and $(5, 4)$.

Draw the parabola.

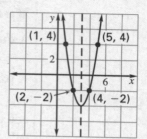

Exercises for Example 2

Graph the quadratic function in vertex form.

4. $y = (x + 2)^2 - 3$ UP   5. $y = -(x - 1)^2 + 2$ down   6. $y = (x + 3)^2 - 1$ UP

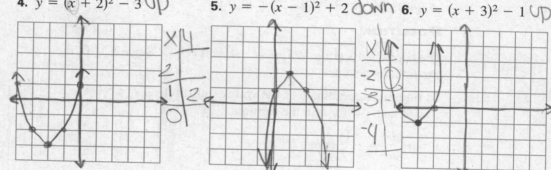

EXAMPLE 3 *Graphing a Quadratic Function in Intercept Form*

Graph $y = -\frac{1}{2}(x - 1)(x + 3)$.

SOLUTION

Use the intercept form $y = a(x - p)(x - q)$, where $a = -\frac{1}{2}$, $p = 1$, and $q = -3$.

The x-intercepts are $(1, 0)$ and $(-3, 0)$.

The axis of symmetry is $x = -1$.

The x-coordinate of the vertex is -1. The y-coordinate is

$$y = -\frac{1}{2}(-1 - 1)(-1 + 3) = 2$$

Draw the parabola.

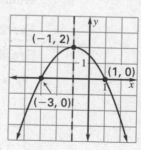

Practice with Examples

For use with pages 249–255

Exercises for Example 3

Graph the quadratic function in intercept form.

7. $y = (x + 3)(x - 5)$

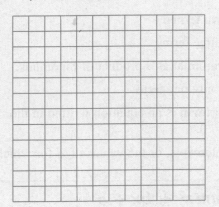

8. $y = -(x - 1)(x + 3)$

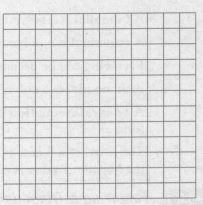

EXAMPLE 4 **Writing Quadratic Functions in Standard Form**

Write $y = 2(x - 3)(x + 8)$ in standard form. 3 and -8 $\dfrac{3-8}{2} = \dfrac{-5}{2}$

$-2\frac{1}{2}$

SOLUTION

$y = 2(x - 3)(x + 8)$	Write original equation.
$= 2(x^2 + 5x - 24)$	Multiply using FOIL.
$= 2x^2 + 10x - 48$	Use distributive property.

Exercises for Example 4

Write the quadratic function in standard form.

9. $y = (x + 1)^2 - 8$

$y = (x+1)(x+1)$ ⟵ vertex

$y = x^2 + x + x + 1 - 8$

$\boxed{y = x^2 + 2x - 7}$ Standard.

10. $y = -4(x + 2)(x - 2)$

$y = -4x^2 - 2x + 2x - 4$

$y = -4x^2 - 4$

$y = -4x^2 + 16$

NAME _____ DATE _____

Practice with Examples

For use with pages 256–263

GOAL Factor quadratic expressions, solve quadratic equations by factoring, and find zeros of quadratic functions

VOCABULARY

A **binomial** is a polynomial with two terms.

A **trinomial** is a polynomial with three terms.

Factoring can be used to write a trinomial as a product of binomials.

A **monomial** is a polynomial with only one term.

A **quadratic equation in standard form** is an equation written in the form $ax^2 + bx + c = 0$, where $a \neq 0$.

The **zeros** of a function are the x-intercepts, or the values of x, for which the function's value is zero.

EXAMPLE 1 *Factoring a Trinomial of the Form $x^2 + bx + c$*

Factor $x^2 - 14x + 24$.

SOLUTION

You want $x^2 - 14x + 24 = (x + m)(x + n)$, where $mn = 24$ and $m + n = -14$.

Factors of 24	1, 24	−1, −24	2, 12	−2, −12	3, 8	−3, −8	4, 6	−4, −6
Sum of factors	25	−25	14	−14	11	−11	10	−10

Since the sum of the factors is -14 when $m = -2$ and $n = -12$,
$x^2 - 14x + 24 = (x - 2)(x - 12)$.

Exercises for Example 1

Factor the trinomial.

1. $x^2 - 5x - 6$

$(x-6)(x+1)$

2. $y^2 - 9y + 18$

$(y-6)(y-3)$

3. $r^2 + 15r + 14$

$(r+14)(r+1)$

4. $q^2 + 4q - 12$

$(q+6)(q-2)$

5. $x^2 + 3x + 2$

$(x+1)(x+2)$

6. $z^2 - z - 2$

$(z-2)(z+1)$

LESSON

5.2

CONTINUED

NAME _____ DATE _____

Practice with Examples

For use with pages 256–263

EXAMPLE 2 *Factoring a Trinomial of the Form $ax^2 + bx + c$*

Factor $2x^2 - 11x - 6$.

SOLUTION

The possible factorizations are:

$(2x + 3)(x - 2) = 2x^2 - x - 6$ $(2x + 2)(x - 3) = 2x^2 - 4x - 6$

$(2x + 6)(x - 1) = 2x^2 + 4x - 6$ $(2x + 1)(x - 6) = 2x^2 - 11x - 6$

The correct factorization is $2x^2 - 11x - 6 = (2x + 1)(x - 6)$.

Exercises for Example 2

Factor the trinomial. If the trinomial cannot be factored, say so.

7. $2x^2 + 13x + 6$ **8.** $4x^2 + 3x + 1$ **9.** $3x^2 + 2x - 8$

 $2x+1 \ x+6$ Can not be factored

EXAMPLE 3 *Factoring Monomials First*

Factor $2x^2 - 12x + 18$.

SOLUTION

$2x^2 - 12x + 18 = 2(x^2 - 6x + 9)$

$ = 2(x^2 - 2(x)(3) + 3^2)$

$ = 2(x - 3)^2$

Exercises for Example 3

Factor the quadratic expression.

10. $2x^2 - 50$ **11.** $5x^2 + 10x + 5$ **12.** $4y^2 + 4y$

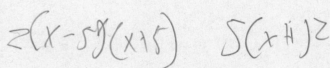 $2(x-5)(x+5)$ 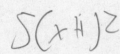 $5(x+1)^2$ 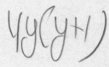 $4y(y+1)$

Algebra 2
Practice Workbook with Examples

LESSON
5.2
CONTINUED

Practice with Examples

For use with pages 256–263

EXAMPLE 4 *Finding the Zeros of a Quadratic Function*

Find the zeros of $y = x^2 - 6x$.

SOLUTION

First, check to see if the terms have a common monomial factor.

The terms have an x in common.

$x^2 - 6x = x(x - 6)$

The zeros of the function are 0 and 6.

Check by graphing $y = x^2 - 6x$. The graph passes through $(0, 0)$ and $(6, 0)$.

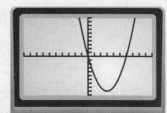

Exercises for Example 4

Find the zeros of the function.

13. $y = x^2 + x - 20$

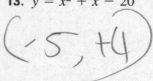

$(-5, +4)$

14. $y = x^2 - 1$

$(1, -1)$

15. $y = x^2 + 3x - 10$

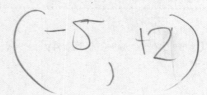

$(-5, +2)$

Algebra 2
Practice Workbook with Examples

NAME _____ DATE _____

Practice with Examples

For use with pages 264–270

GOAL Solve quadratic equations by finding square roots and use quadratic equations to solve real-life problems

---

VOCABULARY

If $b^2 = a$, then b is a **square root** of a. A positive number a has two square roots, $\sqrt{a}$ and $-\sqrt{a}$. The symbol $\sqrt{}$ is a **radical sign,** a is the **radicand,** and $\sqrt{a}$ is a **radical.**

Rationalizing the denominator is the process of eliminating square roots in the denominator of a fraction.

EXAMPLE 1 *Using Properties of Square Roots*

Simplify the expression.

a. $\sqrt{99} = \sqrt{9} \cdot \sqrt{11} = 3\sqrt{11}$ **b.** $\sqrt{6} \cdot \sqrt{8} = \sqrt{48} = \sqrt{16} \cdot \sqrt{3} = 4\sqrt{3}$

c. $\sqrt{\dfrac{3}{25}} = \dfrac{\sqrt{3}}{\sqrt{25}} = \dfrac{\sqrt{3}}{5}$ **d.** $\sqrt{\dfrac{36}{5}} = \dfrac{\sqrt{36}}{\sqrt{5}} = \dfrac{6}{\sqrt{5}} \cdot \dfrac{\sqrt{5}}{\sqrt{5}} = \dfrac{6\sqrt{5}}{5}$

Exercises for Example 1

Simplify the expression.

1. $\sqrt{60}$

2. $\sqrt{2} \cdot \sqrt{18}$

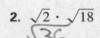

3. $\sqrt{\dfrac{81}{121}}$

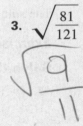

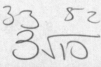

EXAMPLE 2 *Solving a Quadratic Equation*

Solve $\dfrac{x^2}{6} - 4 = 10$.

SOLUTION

$\dfrac{x^2}{6} - 4 = 10$ Write original equation.

$\dfrac{x^2}{6} = 14$ Add 4 to each side.

$x^2 = 84$ Multiply both sides by 6.

$x = \pm\sqrt{84}$ Take square roots of both sides.

$x = \pm 2\sqrt{21}$ Simplify.

The solutions are $2\sqrt{21}$ and $-2\sqrt{21}$.

NAME _____ DATE _____

Practice with Examples

For use with pages 264–270

Exercises for Example 2

Solve the equation.

4. $4x^2 - 5 = -1$

5. $12 - 2y^2 = 4$

6. $\dfrac{p^2}{4} - 3 = 33$

± 1

± 2

± 12

EXAMPLE 3 *Solving a Quadratic Equation*

Solve $5(x - 7)^2 = 135$.

$5(x - 7)^2 = 135$	Write original equation.
$(x - 7)^2 = 27$	Divide both sides by 5.
$x - 7 = \pm\sqrt{27}$	Take the square roots of both sides.
$x - 7 = \pm 3\sqrt{3}$	Simplify.
$x = 7 \pm 3\sqrt{3}$	Add 7 to both sides.

The solutions are $7 + 3\sqrt{3}$ and $7 - 3\sqrt{3}$.

Exercises for Example 3

Solve the equation.

7. $(y + 3)^2 = 9$

8. $(w - 1)^2 = 196$

9. $-2(x - 3)^2 = -12$

$0, 6$

$15, -13$

$3 \pm \sqrt{6}$

10. $(r - 8)^2 = 50$

11. $5(x - 3)^2 = 50$

12. $\frac{1}{3}(z + 3)^2 = 5$

$8 \pm 5\sqrt{2}$

$3 \pm \sqrt{10}$

$-3 \pm \sqrt{15}$

Practice with Examples

For use with pages 264–270

EXAMPLE 4 *Modeling a Falling Object's Height with a Quadratic Function*

A person is trapped in a building 120 feet above the ground and wants to land on a rescue team's air cushion. How long before the person reaches safety?

SOLUTION

Use the falling object model $h = -16t^2 + h_0$, where h is the height (in feet) of the object after t seconds and h_0 is the object's initial height.

$0 = -16t^2 + 120$	Substitute 120 for h_0 and 0 for h.
$-120 = -16t^2$	Subtract 120 from each side.
$\dfrac{120}{16} = t^2$	Divide each side by -16.
$\sqrt{\dfrac{120}{16}} = t$	Take positive square root.
$2.7 \approx t$	Use a calculator.

The person will reach safety in about 2.7 seconds.

Exercises for Example 4

13. A coyote is standing on a cliff 254 feet above a roadrunner. If the coyote drops a boulder from the cliff, how much time does the roadrunner have to move out of its way?

14. An apple falls from a branch on a tree 30 feet above a man sleeping underneath. When will the apple strike the man?

Chapter 5

Practice with Examples

For use with pages 272–280

GOAL Solve quadratic equations with complex solutions and perform operations with complex numbers

VOCABULARY

The **imaginary unit** i is defined as $i = \sqrt{-1}$.

A **complex number** written in **standard form** is a number $a + bi$, where a and b are real numbers.

If $b \neq 0$, then $a + bi$ is an **imaginary number.**

If $a = 0$ and $b \neq 0$, then $a + bi$ is a **pure imaginary number.**

Sum of complex numbers:

$$(a + bi) + (c + di) = (a + c) + (b + d)i$$

Difference of complex numbers:

$$(a + bi) - (c + di) = (a - c) + (b - d)i$$

In the **complex plane,** the horizontal axis is called the **real axis** and the vertical axis is called the **imaginary axis.**

The expressions $a + bi$ and $a - bi$ are called **complex conjugates.** The product of complex conjugates is always a real number.

EXAMPLE 1 *Solving a Quadratic Equation*

Solve $2x^2 - 12 = -40$

SOLUTION

$2x^2 - 12 = -40$	Write original equation.
$2x^2 = -28$	Add 12 to each side.
$x^2 = -14$	Divide each side by 2.
$x = \pm\sqrt{-14}$	Take square roots of each side.
$x = \pm i\sqrt{14}$	Write in terms of i.

Exercises for Example 1

Solve the equation.

1. $x^2 = -16$

2. $5y^2 = -40$

3. $r^2 - 4 = -8$

4. $-2t^2 - 8 = 46$

5. $3x^2 + 1 = -35$

6. $y^2 + 25 = 0$

Practice with Examples

For use with pages 272–280

EXAMPLE 2 Adding and Subtracting Complex Numbers

Write $(6 + 3i) - (-4 - 2i) - 7i$ as a complex number in standard form.

$(6 + 3i) - (-4 - 2i) - 7i = (6 + 4) + (3 + 2 - 7)i$ Definition of complex addition

$= 10 - 2i$ Simplify and use standard form.

Exercises for Example 2

Write the expression as a complex number in standard form.

7. $(5 + 4i) + (7 + 2i)$ **8.** $(-6 + 3i) + (5 + i)$ **9.** $i - (5 - 6i)$

10. $(12 - 8i) - (6 - 6i)$ **11.** $(6 - 7i) + (-3 - i)$ **12.** $12 - (8 - 10i)$

EXAMPLE 3 Multiplying Complex Numbers

Write $(7 - 3i)(1 - 4i)$ as a complex number in standard form.

SOLUTION

$(7 - 3i)(1 - 4i) = 7 - 28i - 3i + 12i^2$ Use FOIL.

$= 7 - 31i + 12(-1)$ Simplify and use $i^2 = -1$.

$= -5 - 31i$ Standard form

Exercises for Example 3

Write as a complex number in standard form.

13. $-2i(5 + i)$ **14.** $4i(3 - 5i)$ **15.** $(2 + 3i)(2 - 3i)$

16. $(4 - i)(-2 + 6i)$ **17.** $(5 + 3i)^2$ **18.** $(8 + i)(2 + i)$

Practice with Examples

For use with pages 272–280

EXAMPLE 4 *Dividing Complex Numbers*

Write the quotient $\dfrac{7 - 4i}{2 + i}$ in standard form.

SOLUTION

$$\dfrac{7 - 4i}{2 + i} = \dfrac{7 - 4i}{2 + i} \cdot \dfrac{2 - i}{2 - i}$$ Multiply by $2 - i$, the conjugate of $2 + i$.

$$= \dfrac{14 - 7i - 8i + 4i^2}{4 - 2i + 2i - i^2}$$ Use FOIL.

$$= \dfrac{14 - 15i - 4}{4 + 1}$$ Simplify and use $i^2 = -1$.

$$= \dfrac{10 - 15i}{5}$$ Simplify.

$$= 2 - 3i$$ Standard form

Exercises for Example 4

Write as a complex number in standard form.

19. $\dfrac{6}{1 - i}$

20. $\dfrac{5i}{2 + i}$

21. $\dfrac{2 - 3i}{5i}$

22. $\dfrac{1 - i}{1 + i}$

NAME _____ DATE _____

Practice with Examples

For use with pages 282–289

GOAL Solve quadratic equations by completing the square, and use completing the square to write quadratic functions in vertex form

---

VOCABULARY

Completing the square is the process of rewriting an expression of the form $x^2 + bx$ as the square of the binomial. To complete the square for $x^2 + bx$, you need to add $\left(\frac{b}{2}\right)^2$. This leads to the rule

$x^2 + bx + \left(\frac{b}{2}\right)^2 = \left(x + \frac{b}{2}\right)^2$.

EXAMPLE 1 *Completing the Square*

Find the value of c that makes $x^2 + 1.6x + c$ a perfect square trinomial. Then write the expression as the square of a binomial.

SOLUTION

Use the form $x^2 + bx + \left(\frac{b}{2}\right)^2$ and that $b = 1.6$.

$$c = \left(\frac{b}{2}\right)^2 = \left(\frac{1.6}{2}\right)^2 = (0.8)^2 = 0.64$$

$x^2 + 1.6x + c = x^2 + 1.6x + 0.64$ Perfect square trinomial

$\qquad\qquad\qquad = (x + 0.8)^2$ Square of a binomial: $\left(x + \frac{b}{2}\right)^2$

Exercises for Example 1

Find the value of *c* that makes the expression a perfect square trinomial. Then write the expression as the square of a binomial.

  1. $x^2 + 6x + c$ **2.** $x^2 - 12x + c$

  3. $x^2 + 2x + c$

Practice with Examples

For use with pages 282–289

EXAMPLE 2 *Solving a Quadratic Equation if the Coefficient of x² is 1*

Solve $x^2 - 2x - 2 = 0$ by completing the square.

SOLUTION

$x^2 - 2x - 2 = 0$	Write original equation.
$x^2 - 2x = 2$	To isolate the terms containing x, add 2 to each side.
$x^2 - 2x + (-1)^2 = 2 + 1$	Add $\left(\frac{-2}{2}\right)^2 = (-1)^2 = 1$ to each side.
$(x - 1)^2 = 3$	Write the left side as a binomial squared.
$x - 1 = \pm\sqrt{3}$	Take square roots of each side.
$x = 1 \pm \sqrt{3}$	To solve for x, add 1 to each side.

The solutions are $1 + \sqrt{3}$ and $1 - \sqrt{3}$.

Exercises for Example 2

Solve the equation by completing the square.

4. $x^2 - x = 1$ **5.** $x^2 + 6x + 5 = 0$

6. $x^2 = 4x - 13$

EXAMPLE 3 *Solving a Quadratic Equation if the Coefficient of x² is Not 1*

Solve $4x^2 - 6x + 1 = 0$ by completing the square.

SOLUTION

$4x^2 - 6x + 1 = 0$	Write original equation.
$x^2 - \frac{3}{2}x + \frac{1}{4} = 0$	Divide by 4 to make the coefficient of x^2 be 1.
$x^2 - \frac{3}{2}x = -\frac{1}{4}$	Write the left side in the form $x^2 + bx$.
$x^2 - \frac{3}{2}x + \left(-\frac{3}{4}\right)^2 = -\frac{1}{4} + \frac{9}{16}$	Add $\left(\frac{-3}{4}\right)^2 = \frac{9}{16}$ to each side.
$\left(x - \frac{3}{4}\right)^2 = \frac{5}{16}$	Write the left side as the square of a binomial.
$x - \frac{3}{4} = \pm\frac{\sqrt{5}}{4}$	Take square roots of each side.
$x = \frac{3}{4} \pm \frac{\sqrt{5}}{4}$	To solve for x, add $\frac{3}{4}$ to each side.

The solutions are $\frac{3}{4} + \frac{\sqrt{5}}{4}$ and $\frac{3}{4} - \frac{\sqrt{5}}{4}$.

NAME _____ DATE _____

Practice with Examples

For use with pages 282–289

Exercises for Example 3

Solve the equation by completing the square.

7. $4x^2 + 24x - 8 = 0$

8. $3x^2 + 12x - 9 = 0$

EXAMPLE 4 *Writing a Quadratic Function in Vertex Form*

Write $y = -2x^2 - 4x - 7$ in vertex form.

SOLUTION

$y = -2x^2 - 4x - 7$	Write original function.
$y + \underline{\ ?\ } = -2(x^2 - 2x + \underline{\ ?\ }) - 7$	Prepare to complete the square for $x^2 - 2x$.
$y - 2 = -2(x^2 - 2x + 1) - 7$	Add $-2\left(\frac{-2}{2}\right)^2 = -2$ to each side.
$y - 2 = -2(x - 1)^2 - 7$	Write $x^2 - 2x + 1$ as a binomial squared.
$y = -2(x - 1)^2 - 5$	Solve for y.

The vertex form is $y = -2(x - 1)^2 - 5$. The vertex is $(1, -5)$.

Exercises for Example 4

Write the function in vertex form.

9. $y = x^2 + 8x + 2$

10. $y = x^2 - 4x + 10$

11. $y = x^2 - 2x - 5$

Practice with Examples

For use with pages 291–298

GOAL **Solve quadratic equations using the quadratic formula**

> ### VOCABULARY
>
> The **quadratic formula,**
>
> $$x = \frac{-b \pm \sqrt{b^2 - 4ac}}{2a},$$
>
> is used to find the solutions of the quadratic equation $ax^2 + bx + c = 0$, when $a \neq 0$.
>
> The expression $b^2 - 4ac$, where a, b, and c are coefficients of the quadratic equation $ax^2 + bx + c = 0$, is called the **discriminant.**
>
> If $b^2 - 4ac > 0$, then the equation has two real solutions.
> If $b^2 - 4ac = 0$, then the equation has one real solution.
> If $b^2 - 4ac < 0$, then the equation has two imaginary solutions.

EXAMPLE 1 *Solving a Quadratic Equation with Two Real Solutions*

Solve $-8x^2 - 5x = -x^2 - 1$.

SOLUTION

$-8x^2 - 5x = -x^2 - 1$	Write original equation.
$-7x^2 - 5x + 1 = 0$	Write in standard form.
$x = \dfrac{5 \pm \sqrt{(-5)^2 - 4(-7)(1)}}{2(-7)}$	Quadratic formula with $a = -7$, $b = -5$, and $c = 1$.
$x = \dfrac{5 \pm \sqrt{53}}{-14}$	Simplify.

The solutions are

$$x = \frac{5 + \sqrt{53}}{-14} \approx -0.88 \quad \text{and} \quad x = \frac{5 - \sqrt{53}}{-14} \approx 0.16.$$

Exercises for Example 1

Use the quadratic formula to solve the equation.

1. $x^2 - 9x + 5 = 0$

2. $5x^2 + 3x - 1 = 0$

3. $-x^2 + 2x + 4 = 0$

Practice with Examples

For use with pages 291–298

EXAMPLE 2 *Solving a Quadratic Equation with One Real Solution*

Solve $2x^2 - 5x + 7 = x^2 - 3x + 6$.

SOLUTION

$2x^2 - 5x + 7 = x^2 - 3x + 6$	Write original equation.
$x^2 - 2x + 1 = 0$	Write in standard form.
$x = \dfrac{2 \pm \sqrt{(-2)^2 - 4(1)(1)}}{2(1)}$	Quadratic formula with $a = 1$, $b = -2$, and $c = 1$.
$x = \dfrac{2 \pm \sqrt{0}}{2}$	Simplify.
$x = 1$	Simplify.

The solution is 1.

Exercises for Example 2

Use the quadratic formula to solve the equation.

4. $x^2 - 6x + 9 = 0$

5. $x^2 + 4x + 4 = 0$

6. $x^2 + 10x + 25 = 0$

NAME _____ DATE _____

Practice with Examples
For use with pages 291–298

EXAMPLE 3 *Solving a Quadratic Equation with Two Imaginary Solutions*

Solve $3x^2 - 3x + 5 = 0$.

SOLUTION

$3x^2 - 3x + 5 = 0$　　　　　　　Write original equation.

$x = \dfrac{3 \pm \sqrt{(-3)^2 - 4(3)(5)}}{2(3)}$　　Quadratic formula with $a = 3$, $b = -3$, and $c = 5$.

$x = \dfrac{3 \pm \sqrt{-51}}{6}$　　　　　　Simplify.

$x = \dfrac{3 \pm i\sqrt{51}}{6}$　　　　　　Write using the imaginary unit i.

The solutions are $\dfrac{1}{2} + \dfrac{\sqrt{51}}{6}i$ and $\dfrac{1}{2} - \dfrac{\sqrt{51}}{6}i$.

Exercises for Example 3

Use the quadratic formula to solve the equation.

7. $x^2 - 6x = -10$

8. $x^2 = -x - 1$

9. $x^2 - 2x + 3 = 0$

NAME _____ DATE _____

Practice with Examples

For use with pages 299–305

GOAL **Graph quadratic inequalities in two variables and solve quadratic inequalities in one variable**

VOCABULARY

A **quadratic inequality in two variables** can be written as follows:

$$y < ax^2 + bx + c \qquad y \leq ax^2 + bx + c$$

$$y > ax^2 + bx + c \qquad y \geq ax^2 + bx + c$$

A **quadratic inequality in one variable** can be written as follows:

$$ax^2 + bx + c < 0 \qquad ax^2 + bx + c \leq 0$$

$$ax^2 + bx + c > 0 \qquad ax^2 + bx + c \geq 0$$

EXAMPLE 1 *Graphing a Quadratic Inequality*

Graph $y \geq -x^2 + 4$.

SOLUTION

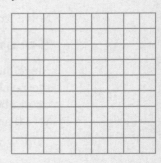

1 Graph $-x^2 + 4$. Since the inequality symbol is $\geq$, make the parabola solid.

2 Test a point inside the parabola, such as $(0, 0)$.

$$y \geq -x^2 + 4$$

$$0 \geq -(0)^2 + 4$$

$$0 \ngeq 4$$

So, $(0, 0)$ is not a solution of the inequality.

3 Shade the region outside the parabola.

Exercises for Example 1

Graph the inequality.

1. $y \leq x^2 + 2$ **2.** $y > -x^2 + 2x$ **3.** $y \geq 2x^2$

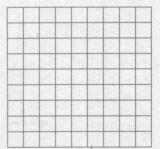
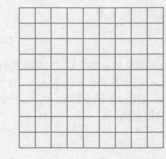
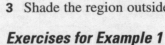

Practice with Examples

For use with pages 299–305

EXAMPLE 2 *Graphing a System of Quadratic Inequalities*

Graph $y > x^2 - 4x + 4$ and $y < \frac{1}{4}x^2 - x + 3$.

SOLUTION

Graph $y > x^2 - 4x + 4$. The region inside the dashed parabola is shaded.

Graph $y < \frac{1}{4}x^2 - x + 3$. The region outside the dashed parabola is shaded.

The region where the two graphs overlap is the graph of the system.

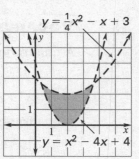

Exercises for Example 2

Graph the system of inequalities.

4. $y \leq -x^2$

$y \geq x^2 - 4$

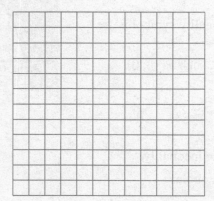

5. $y \geq x^2$

$y \leq 4x - x^2$

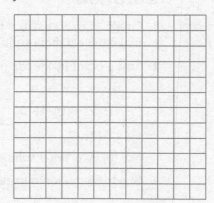

EXAMPLE 3 *Solving a Quadratic Inequality by Graphing*

Solve $3x^2 + 2x - 1 \geq 0$.

SOLUTION

Since the inequality symbol is $\geq$, the solution consists of the x-values for which the graph $y = 3x^2 + 2x - 1$ lies on or above the x-axis. Find the x-intercepts by letting $y = 0$ and solving for x.

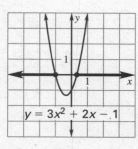

$$0 = 3x^2 + 2x - 1$$

$$0 = (3x - 1)(x + 1)$$

$$x = \tfrac{1}{3} \text{ or } -1$$

The graph lies on and above the x-axis when $x \leq -1$ or $x \geq \frac{1}{3}$.

NAME _____ DATE _____

Practice with Examples

For use with pages 299–305

Exercises for Example 3

Solve the inequality by graphing.

6. $0 \geq 2x^2 + x - 3$

7. $0 \leq -x^2 + 2x + 8$

8. $0 > 2x^2 - 6x - 20$

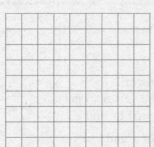

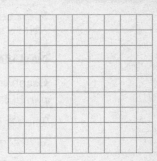

EXAMPLE 4 *Solving a Quadratic Inequality Algebraically*

Solve $x^2 + 3x > 4$.

SOLUTION

The corresponding equation $x^2 + 3x - 4 = 0$ can be factored as
$(x + 4)(x - 1) = 0$. The solutions -4 and 1 are the *critical x-values*.
Since the inequality symbol is $>$, open circles appear at -4 and 1.
Test an x-value in each interval.

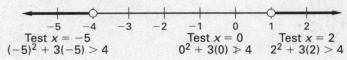

The solution is $x < -4$ or $x > 1$.

Exercises for Example 4

Solve the inequality algebraically.

9. $x^2 - 3x - 10 < 0$

10. $x^2 + 3x \geq 18$

11. $2x^2 + 5x \leq 12$

Practice with Examples

For use with pages 306–312

GOAL **Write quadratic functions given certain characteristics of their graphs**

EXAMPLE 1 *Writing a Quadratic Function in Vertex Form*

Write a quadratic function for the parabola shown.

SOLUTION

Since you are given the vertex, use the vertex form
$y = a(x - h)^2 + k$. Substitute the values for the vertex to get
$y = a(x + 3)^2 - 1$. Use the given point $(-5, -5)$ to find a.

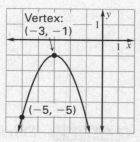

$\quad -5 = a(-5 + 3)^2 - 1 \qquad$ Substitute -5 for x and -5 for y.

$\quad -5 = 4a - 1 \qquad\qquad$ Simplify.

$\quad -1 = a \qquad\qquad\qquad$ Solve for a.

A quadratic function for the parabola is $y = -(x + 3)^2 - 1$.

Exercises for Example 1

Write a quadratic function in vertex form for the parabola.

1.

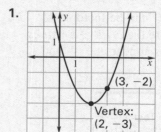

2.

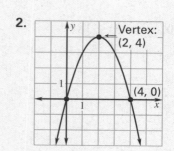

Algebra 2
Practice Workbook with Examples

NAME _____ DATE _____

Practice with Examples

For use with pages 306–312

EXAMPLE 2 *Writing a Quadratic Function in Intercept Form*

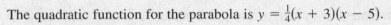

Write a quadratic function for the parabola shown.

SOLUTION

Since you are given the x-intercepts, use the intercept form
$y = a(x - p)(x - q)$. Substitute the values for the x-intercepts
to get $y = a(x + 3)(x - 5)$.

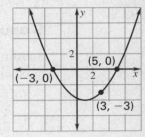

Use the given point $(1, -4)$ to find a.

$-4 = a(1 + 3)(1 - 5)$ Substitute 1 for x and -4 for y.

$-4 = -16a$ Simplify.

$\frac{1}{4} = a$ Solve for a.

The quadratic function for the parabola is $y = \frac{1}{4}(x + 3)(x - 5)$.

Exercises for Example 2

Write a quadratic function in intercept form for the parabola.

3.

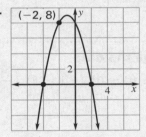

4.

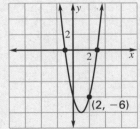

Practice with Examples

For use with pages 306–312

EXAMPLE 3 *Finding a Quadratic Model for a Data Set*

Write a quadratic function which contains the data $(0, -6)$, $(-2, 8)$, and $(5, -6)$.

SOLUTION

Substitute the coordinates of the points into the model $y = ax^2 + bx + c$ to obtain a system of three linear equations.

$(0, -6)$	$\rightarrow$	$0a + 0b + c = -6$
$(-2, 8)$	$\rightarrow$	$4a - 2b + c = 8$
$(5, -6)$	$\rightarrow$	$25a + 5b + c = -6$

From the first equation, you can conclude that $c = -6$.

Solve the remaining system of two linear equations in two variables.

The solution is $a = 1$ and $b = -5$.

Substitute the values for a, b, and c into the model $y = ax^2 + bx + c$.

The quadratic model for the data is $y = x^2 - 5x - 6$.

Exercises for Example 3

Write a quadratic function that contains the data.

5. $(1, 3), (-3, -5), (0, -2)$ **6.** $(0, -6), (-1, -5), (-2, 4)$

NAME _____ DATE _____

Practice with Examples

For use with pages 323–328

GOAL How to use properties of exponents to evaluate and simplify expressions involving powers and to use exponents and scientific notation to solve real-life problems

---

VOCABULARY

The following are properties of exponents.

Let a and b be real numbers and let m and n be integers.

Product of Powers Property $\qquad a^m \cdot a^n = a^{m+n}$

Power of a Power Property $\qquad (a^m)^n = a^{mn}$

Power of a Product Property $\qquad (ab)^m = a^m b^m$

Negative Exponent Property $\qquad a^{-m} = \dfrac{1}{a^m}, a \neq 0$

Zero Exponent Property $\qquad a^0 = 1, a \neq 0$

Quotient of Powers Property $\qquad \dfrac{a^m}{a^n} = a^{m-n}, a \neq 0$

Power of a Quotient Property $\qquad \left(\dfrac{a}{b}\right)^m = \dfrac{a^m}{b^m}, b \neq 0$

A number is expressed in **scientific notation** if it is in the form $c \times 10^n$ where $1 \leq c < 10$ and n is an integer.

EXAMPLE 1 *Evaluating Numerical Expressions*

a. $\dfrac{3^6}{3^2} = 3^{6-2}$ $\qquad$ Quotient of powers property

$\qquad = 3^4$ $\qquad$ Simplify exponent

$\qquad = 81$ $\qquad$ Evaluate power.

b. $(-6)(-6)^{-1} = (-6)^{1+(-1)}$ $\qquad$ Product of powers property

$\qquad = (-6)^0$ $\qquad$ Simplify exponent.

$\qquad = 1$ $\qquad$ Zero exponent property

Exercises for Example 1

Evaluate the expression.

1. $(2^3)^2$ $\qquad\qquad$ **2.** $8^3 \cdot 8$ $\qquad\qquad$ **3.** $(3^2)^4$

4. $\left(\dfrac{2}{3}\right)^3$ $\qquad\qquad$ **5.** $\left(\dfrac{1}{5}\right)^{-2}$ $\qquad\qquad$ **6.** $\dfrac{3^3}{3^2}$

Chapter 6

Practice with Examples

For use with pages 323–328

EXAMPLE 2 *Simplifying Algebraic Expressions*

Remember that simplified algebraic expressions contain only positive exponents.

a. $\dfrac{x^7 y^4}{x^{-1} y^{-2}} = x^{7-(-1)} y^{4-(-2)}$ Quotient of powers property

     $= x^8 y^6$ Simplify exponents.

b. $(3x^{-2} y^4)^2 = 3^2 (x^{-2})^2 (y^4)^2$ Power of a product property

     $= 9x^{-4} y^8$ Power of a power property

     $= \dfrac{9y^8}{x^4}$ Negative exponent property

c. $(-2x^5 y^3)^{-2} = (-2)^{-2} (x^5)^{-2} (y^3)^{-2}$ Power of a product property

     $= (-2)^{-2} x^{-10} y^{-6}$ Power of a power property

     $= \dfrac{1}{4x^{10} y^6}$ Negative exponent property

Exercises for Example 2

Simplify the expression.

7. $(2x^2)^5$

8. $\dfrac{y^{-2}}{y^3}$

9. $3^3 \cdot 3^{-5}$

10. $(x^2 y^4)^{-3}$

11. $\dfrac{x^4 y^{10}}{xy^3}$

Chapter 6

Practice with Examples
For use with pages 323–328

EXAMPLE 3 *Writing Numbers in Scientific Notation*

Alaska is the largest state in the United States, with an area of 1,530,693 square kilometers. Express Alaska's area in scientific notation.

SOLUTION

Recall that a number expressed in scientific notation has the form $c \times 10^n$.

1.530693×10^6 Place the decimal point between the 1 and 5 since $1 \le c < 10$.

The power of 10 is 6 since the decimal point was shifted 6 places to the left.

The area of Alaska is about 1.5 million square kilometers.

Exercises for Example 3

12. On average, the planet Pluto's distance from the sun is about 3,670,000,000 miles. Express the distance in scientific notation.

13. The Pacific Ocean is the world's largest ocean, covering 70,000,000 square miles of the Earth's surface. Express this area in scientific notation.

Chapter 6

NAME _____ DATE _____

Practice with Examples

For use with pages 329–336

GOAL **How to evaluate and graph a polynomial function**

> ### VOCABULARY
>
> A **polynomial function** has the form $f(x) = a_n x^n + a_{n-1} x^{n-1} + \cdots + a_1 x + a_0$, where $a_n \neq 0$ and the exponents are all whole numbers. For this polynomial function a_n is the **leading coefficient**, a_0 is the **constant term,** and n is the **degree.**
>
> A polynomial function is in **standard form** if its terms are written in descending order of exponents from left to right.
>
> **Synthetic substitution** is another method of evaluating a polynomial function, which is equivalent to evaluating the polynomial in nested form.
>
> The **end behavior** of a polynomial function's graph is the behavior of the graph as x approaches positive infinity or negative infinity.

EXAMPLE 1 *Identifying Polynomial Functions*

Decide whether the function is a polynomial function. If it is, write the function in standard form and state its degree, type, and leading coefficient.

a. $f(x) = 3x^{1/2} - 2x^2 + 5$ **b.** $f(x) = 3$ **c.** $f(x) = \sqrt{5} - x$

SOLUTION

a. The function is not a polynomial function because the term $3x^{1/2}$ has an exponent that is not a whole number.

b. The function is a polynomial function. It is already in standard form. It has degree 0, so it is a constant function. The leading coefficient is 3.

c. The function is a polynomial function. Its standard form is $f(x) = -x + \sqrt{5}$. It has degree 1, so it is a linear function. The leading coefficient is -1.

Exercises for Example 1

Decide whether the function is a polynomial function. If it is, write the function in standard form and state the degree, type, and leading coefficient.

1. $f(x) = x + 5x^3$

2. $f(x) = 6 - 4x + \pi x^4$

3. $f(x) = 1 + 3x - \frac{1}{2}x^{-2}$

NAME _____ DATE _____

Practice with Examples

For use with pages 329–336

EXAMPLE 2 *Using Synthetic Substitution*

Use synthetic substitution to evaluate $f(x) = 4x^4 + 2x^3 - x + 7$ when $x = -2$.

SOLUTION

Begin by writing the polynomial in standard form, inserting terms with coefficients of 0 for missing terms. Then write the coefficients of $f(x)$ in a row. Bring down the leading coefficients and multiply by -2. Write the result in the next column. Add the numbers in the column and bring down the result. Continue until you reach the end of the row.

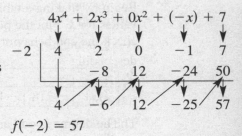

$f(-2) = 57$

Exercises for Example 2

Use synthetic substitution to evaluate the polynomial function for the given value of x.

4. $f(x) = x^3 + 5x^2 + 4x + 6, x = 2$

5. $f(x) = 2x^3 + x^4 + 5x^2 - x, x = -3$

6. $f(x) = x^3 - x^5 + 3, x = -1$

7. $f(x) = 5x^3 - 4x^2 - 2, x = 0$

Chapter 6

NAME _____ DATE _____

Practice with Examples

For use with pages 329–336

EXAMPLE 3 *Graphing Polynomial Functions*

Graph (a) $f(x) = x^5 + 2x^2 - x + 4$ (b) $f(x) = -x^3 + 3x^2 + 6x - 2$

SOLUTION

Begin by making a table of values, including positive, negative, and zero values for x. Plot the points and connect them with a smooth curve. Then check the end behavior.

a.

x	-3	-2	-1	0	1	2	3
$f(x)$	-218	-18	6	4	6	42	262

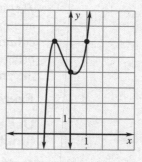

The degree is odd and the leading coefficient is positive, so $f(x) \to -\infty$ as $x \to -\infty$ and $f(x) \to +\infty$ as $x \to +\infty$.

b.

x	-3	-2	-1	0	1	2	3
$f(x)$	34	6	-4	-2	6	14	16

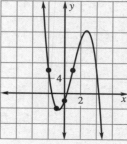

The degree is odd and the leading coefficient is negative, so $f(x) \to +\infty$ as $x \to -\infty$ and $f(x) \to -\infty$ as $x \to +\infty$.

Exercises for Example 3

Graph the polynomial function.

8. $f(x) = -x^5$

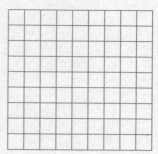

9. $f(x) = -x^4 + 1$

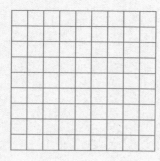

10. $f(x) = x^3 - 5$

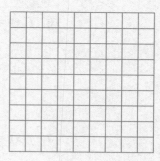

GOAL **Add, subtract, and multiply polynomials**

VOCABULARY

Special Product Patterns

Sum and Difference   **Example**

$(a + b)(a - b) = a^2 - b^2$ $(x + 3)(x - 3) = x^2 - 9$

Square of a Binomial

$(a + b)^2 = a^2 + 2ab + b^2$ $(y + 4)^2 = y^2 + 8y + 16$

$(a - b)^2 = a^2 - 2ab + b^2$ $(3t^2 - 2)^2 = 9t^4 - 12t^2 + 4$

Cube of a Binomial

$(a + b)^3 = a^3 + 3a^2b + 3ab^2 + b^3$ $(x + 1)^3 = x^3 + 3x^2 + 3x + 1$

$(a - b)^3 = a^3 - 3a^2b + 3ab^2 - b^3$ $(p - 2)^3 = p^3 - 6p^2 + 12p - 8$

EXAMPLE 1 *Adding Polynomials Horizontally and Vertically*

───

Add the polynomials.

a. $(2x^2 + 8x + 4) + (x^2 - 8x - 2) = 2x^2 + x^2 + 8x - 8x + 4 - 2$

$$= 3x^2 + 2$$

b. $2x^3 - 3x^2 + x - 3$

  $+ \quad\quad -x^2 + 2x + 4$

  ────────────────────────

  $2x^3 - 4x^2 + 3x + 1$

Exercises for Example 1

Find the sum.

1. $(5x^2 + 2x + 1) + (4x^2 + 3x - 8)$ **2.** $(9x^3 - 5) + (-11x^3 + 4)$

3. $(4x^2 + x + 6) + (7x - 10)$ **4.** $(14 - 6x) + (8x - 5)$

Chapter 6

Practice with Examples

For use with pages 338–344

EXAMPLE 2 *Subtracting Polynomials Horizontally and Vertically*

a. $(3x^3 - 2x^2 + x) - (x^2 + 2x - 3) = 3x^3 - 2x^2 + x - x^2 - 2x + 3$ Add the opposite.

$$= 3x^3 - 3x^2 - x + 3$$

b.
$$\begin{array}{r} 4x^2 + x - 3 \\ -\,(2x^2 - 5x + 1) \end{array} \rightarrow \begin{array}{r} 4x^2 + x - 3 \\ -\,2x^2 + 5x - 1 \\ \hline 2x^2 + 6x - 4 \end{array}$$ Add the opposite.

Exercises for Example 2

Find the difference.

5. $(5x^2 - 6x - 1) - (4x^2 - 2x + 1)$

6. $(5x^3 + 7x + 8) - (x^3 - 6x + 4)$

7. $(-8x^2 + x + 5) - (2x^2 - 3)$

8. $(x^2 - 2x + 7) - (-5x^2 - 3)$

EXAMPLE 3 *Multiplying Polynomials Horizontally and Vertically*

Find the product of the polynomials.

a. $(x - 3)(x^2 + 3x + 2) = (x - 3)x^2 + (x - 3)3x + (x - 3)2$

$$= x^3 - 3x^2 + 3x^2 - 9x + 2x - 6$$

$$= x^3 - 7x - 6$$

b.
$$\begin{array}{r} 3x^2 - 2x + 1 \\ \times \quad\quad\quad x + 2 \\ \hline 6x^2 - 4x + 2 \\ 3x^3 - 2x^2 + \ x \\ \hline 3x^3 + 4x^2 - 3x + 2 \end{array}$$

Multiply $3x^2 - 2x + 1$ by 2.

Multiply $3x^2 - 2x + 1$ by x.

Combine like terms.

NAME _____ DATE _____

Practice with Examples

For use with pages 338–344

Exercises for Example 3

Find the product of the polynomials.

9. $3x(x^2 + x - 2)$

10. $-2x(1 - x - x^2)$

11. $(x - 2)(x^2 + 2x + 4)$

12. $(2x + 1)(x^2 - x - 3)$

EXAMPLE 4 *Using Special Product Patterns*

Multiply the polynomials.

a. $(5x + 3)(5x - 3) = (5x)^2 - 3^2$ Sum and difference
$$= 25x^2 - 9$$

b. $(2x + y)^2 = (2x)^2 + 2(2x)(y) + (y)^2$ Square of a binomial
$$= 4x^2 + 4xy + y^2$$

c. $(2x - 1)^3 = (2x)^3 - 3(2x)^2(1) + 3(2x)(1)^2 - (1)^3$ Cube of a binomial
$$= 8x^3 - 12x^2 + 6x - 1$$

Exercises for Example 4

Find the product.

13. $(x + 5)(x - 5)$

14. $(2x + 7)(2x - 7)$

15. $(x + 6)^2$

16. $(x - 3)^2$

17. $(x - 1)^3$

18. $(x + 2)^3$

Practice with Examples

For use with pages 345–351

GOAL How to factor polynomial expressions and use factoring to solve polynomial equations

---

VOCABULARY

Two special factoring patterns are given below.

Sum of Two Cubes

Difference of Two Cubes

$a^3 + b^3 = (a + b)(a^2 - ab + b^2)$ $a^3 - b^3 = (a - b)(a^2 + ab + b^2)$

To **factor by grouping,** group pairs of terms that have a common monomial factor together, factor out this common factor and look for a pattern. An expression of the form $au^2 + bu + c$ where u is any expression in x is said to be in **quadratic form.**

EXAMPLE 1 *Factoring the Sum or Difference of Cubes*

Factor each polynomial.

a. $64x^3 + 1 = (4x)^3 + 1^3$ Sum of two cubes

$\qquad\qquad = (4x + 1)(16x^2 - 4x + 1)$

b. $54x^3 - 16 = 2(27x^3 - 8)$ Factor common monomial.

$\qquad\qquad = 2[(3x)^3 - 2^3]$ Difference of two cubes

$\qquad\qquad = 2(3x - 2)(9x^2 + 6x + 4)$

Exercises for Example 1

Factor the polynomial.

1. $x^3 + 125$ **2.** $x^3 - 343$ **3.** $64x^3 - 1$

4. $8x^3 + 27$ **5.** $3x^3 - 24$ **6.** $1000x^3 - 729$

Practice with Examples
For use with pages 345–351

EXAMPLE 2 *Factoring By Grouping*

Factor the polynomial $x^3 + x^2 - 4x - 4$.

SOLUTION

$$\begin{aligned}
x^3 + x^2 - 4x - 4 &= (x^3 + x^2) - (4x + 4) & \text{Group terms.}\\
&= x^2(x + 1) - 4(x + 1) & \text{Factor out common monomial factor.}\\
&= (x^2 - 4)(x + 1) & \text{Factor out } (x + 1).\\
&= (x + 2)(x - 2)(x + 1) & \text{Difference of two squares}
\end{aligned}$$

Exercises for Example 2

Factor the polynomial by grouping.

7. $x^3 - x^2 - 9x + 9$

8. $x^3 - x + 5x^2 - 5$

9. $x^3 - 3x^2 - 16x + 48$

EXAMPLE 3 *Factoring Polynomials in Quadratic Form*

Factor each polynomial.

a. $36x^4 - 9x^2$

b. $x^4 + 6x^2 + 9$

SOLUTION

a. $\begin{aligned}[t]
36x^4 - 9x^2 &= 9x^2(4x^2 - 1)\\
&= 9x^2[(2x)^2 - 1^2]\\
&= 9x^2(2x + 1)(2x - 1)
\end{aligned}$

b. $\begin{aligned}[t]
x^4 + 6x^2 + 9 &= (x^2)^2 + 2(x^2)(3) + 3^2\\
&= (x^2 + 3)^2
\end{aligned}$

Exercises for Example 3

Factor the polynomial.

10. $25x^4 - 9$

11. $x^4 - x^2 + 6$

12. $x^4 - 16x^2 + 64$

13. $49x^4 - 4$

Chapter 6

Practice with Examples

For use with pages 345–351

EXAMPLE 4 *Solving a Polynomial Equation*

Solve $3x^3 + 21x = 24x^2$.

SOLUTION

$3x^3 + 21x = 24x^2$	Write original equation.
$3x^3 - 24x^2 + 21x = 0$	Rewrite in standard form.
$3x(x^2 - 8x + 7) = 0$	Factor common monomial.
$3x(x - 7)(x - 1) = 0$	Factor trinomial.
$x = 0, x = 7, x = 1$	Set each factor equal to 0 and solve for x.

The solutions are 0, 1, and 7.

Exercises for Example 4

Find the real-number solutions of the equation.

14. $3x^2 = 9x$

15. $x^2 = 2x + 15$

16. $4x^3 = 16x$

17. $x^2 + 2x = 24$

NAME _____ DATE _____

Practice with Examples

For use with pages 352–358

GOAL How to divide polynomials and relate the result to the remainder theorem and the factor theorem

---

VOCABULARY

In **polynomial long division,** when you divide a polynomial $f(x)$ by a divisor $d(x)$, you get a quotient polynomial $q(x)$ and a remainder polynomial $r(x)$. This can be written as $\dfrac{f(x)}{d(x)} = q(x) + \dfrac{r(x)}{d(x)}$. According to the remainder theorem, if a polynomial $f(x)$ is divided by $x - k$, then the remainder is $r = f(k)$.

In **synthetic division,** you only use the coefficients of the polynomial and the divisor must be in the form $x - k$. According to the factor theorem, a polynomial $f(x)$ has a factor $x - k$ if and only if $f(k) = 0$.

EXAMPLE 1 *Using Polynomial Long Division*

Divide $x^4 - 3x^3 - 2x + 1$ by $x^2 + 1$.

SOLUTION

$$
\begin{array}{r}
x^2 - 3x - 1 \\
x^2 + 1 \overline{\smash{)}\,x^4 - 3x^3 + 0x^2 - 2x + 1} \\
\end{array}
$$

$x^2 + 1 \,)\,x^4 - 3x^3 + 0x^2 - 2x + 1$	Include $0x^2$ for the missing term.
$\underline{x^4 \qquad\quad + x^2}$	$x^2(x^2 + 1)$
$-3x^3 - x^2 - 2x$	Subtract.
$\underline{-3x^3 \qquad\quad - 3x}$	$-3x(x^2 + 1)$
$-x^2 + x + 1$	Subtract.
$\underline{-x^2 \qquad\quad - 1}$	$-1(x^2 + 1)$
$x + 2$	remainder

$$\frac{x^4 - 3x^3 - 2x + 1}{x^2 + 1} = x^2 - 3x - 1 + \frac{x + 2}{x^2 + 1}$$

Exercises for Example 1

Divide using polynomial long division.

1. $(2x^2 - 3x + 1) \div (x + 5)$ **2.** $(3x^2 - x + 4) \div (x - 1)$

Chapter 6

NAME _____ DATE _____

Practice with Examples
For use with pages 352–358

3. $(x^2 - 2x + 6) \div (x + 2)$

4. $(x^2 - 5x - 7) \div (x - 8)$

EXAMPLE 2 *Using Synthetic Division*

Divide $x^3 - 10x - 24$ by $x - 3$.

SOLUTION

Since $x - 3$ is in the form $x - k$, $k = 3$.

$$
\begin{array}{r|rrrr}
3 & 1 & 0 & -10 & -24 \\
  &   & 3 & 9 & -3 \\
\hline
  & 1 & 3 & -1 & \boxed{-27}
\end{array}
$$ ⟵ remainder

Include a 0 for the x^2-term.

$$\frac{x^3 - 10x - 24}{x - 3} = x^2 + 3x - 1 + \frac{-27}{x - 3}$$

Exercises for Example 2

Divide using synthetic division.

5. $(x^2 - 4x + 3) \div (x - 1)$

6. $(2x^2 - 5x - 3) \div (x - 3)$

7. $(x^2 + 2x - 15) \div (x + 4)$

8. $(3x^2 + 10x + 8) \div (x + 2)$

Algebra 2
Practice Workbook with Examples

NAME _____ DATE _____

Practice with Examples
For use with pages 352–358

EXAMPLE 3 *Factoring a Polynomial*
_____

Factor $f(x) = 3x^3 - 11x^2 - 6x + 8$ given that $f(4) = 0$.

SOLUTION

Because $f(4) = 0$, $x - 4$ is a factor of $f(x)$. Use synthetic division to find the other factors.

$$
\begin{array}{r|rrrr}
4 & 3 & -11 & -6 & 8 \\
  &   & 12 & 4 & -8 \\
\hline
  & 3 & 1   & -2 & 0
\end{array}
$$

$3x^3 - 11x^2 - 6x + 8 = (x - 4)(3x^2 + x - 2)$ Write $f(x)$ as the product of two factors.

$\qquad\qquad\qquad\qquad = (x - 4)(3x - 2)(x + 1)$ Factor trinomial.

Exercises for Example 3

Factor the polynomial given that $f(k) = 0$.

9. $f(x) = x^3 + 2x^2 - 9x - 18; k = 3$

10. $f(x) = x^3 + x^2 - 10x + 8; k = -4$

Chapter 6

Practice with Examples

For use with pages 359–365

GOAL **How to find the rational zeros of a polynomial function**

> ### VOCABULARY
>
> According to the rational zero theorem, if $f(x) = a_n x^n + \cdots + a_1 x + a_0$ has *integer* coefficients, then every rational zero of f has the form:
>
> $\dfrac{p}{q} = \dfrac{\text{factor of constant term } a_0}{\text{factor of leading coefficient } a_n}$

EXAMPLE 1 *Using the Rational Zero Theorem*

Find the rational zeros of $f(x) = 3x^3 - 4x^2 - 17x + 6$.

SOLUTION

Begin by listing the possible rational zeros. The leading coefficient is 3 and the constant term is 6

$x = \dfrac{\pm 1, \pm 2, \pm 3, \pm 6}{\pm 1, \pm 3}$ Factors of constant term, 6
Factors of leading coefficient, 3

Test these zeros using synthetic division.

Test $x = 1$:

$$
\begin{array}{r|rrrr}
1 & 3 & -4 & -17 & 6 \\
  &   & 3 & -1 & -18 \\
\hline
  & 3 & -1 & -18 & -12
\end{array}
$$

Test $x = -1$:

$$
\begin{array}{r|rrrr}
-1 & 3 & -4 & -17 & 6 \\
   &   & -3 & 7 & 10 \\
\hline
   & 3 & -7 & -10 & 16
\end{array}
$$

Test $x = 2$:

$$
\begin{array}{r|rrrr}
2 & 3 & -4 & -17 & 6 \\
  &   & 6 & 4 & -26 \\
\hline
  & 3 & 2 & -13 & -20
\end{array}
$$

Test $x = -2$:

$$
\begin{array}{r|rrrr}
-2 & 3 & -4 & -17 & 6 \\
   &   & -6 & 20 & -6 \\
\hline
   & 3 & -10 & 3 & 0
\end{array}
$$

Since the remainder for $x = -2$ is 0, $x + 2$ is a factor of f.

$f(x) = (x + 2)(3x^2 - 10x + 3)$

$ = (x + 2)(3x - 1)(x - 3)$ Factor trinomial.

The zeros of f are $-2, \frac{1}{3}$, and 3.

Exercises for Example 1

Find the rational zeros of the function.

1. $f(x) = x^3 - 7x + 6$

2. $f(x) = 2x^3 + 2x^2 - 8x - 8$

NAME _____ DATE _____

Practice with Examples

For use with pages 359–365

3. $f(x) = x^3 + x^2 - 10x + 8$

4. $f(x) = 2x^3 - 3x^2 - 8x - 3$

EXAMPLE 2 *Using the Rational Zero Theorem*

Find all real zeros of $f(x) = 3x^4 + x^3 - 8x^2 - 2x + 4$.

SOLUTION

Begin by listing the possible rational zeros.

$$x = \frac{\pm 1, \pm 2, \pm 4}{\pm 1, \pm 3} \quad \begin{array}{l}\text{Factors of constant term, 4.} \\ \text{Factors of leading coefficient, 3.}\end{array}$$

Then test these zeros using synthetic division.

Test $x = 1$:

$$\begin{array}{r|rrrrr} 1 & 3 & 1 & -8 & -2 & 4 \\ & & 3 & 4 & -4 & -6 \\ \hline & 3 & 4 & -4 & -6 & -2 \end{array}$$

Test $x = -1$:

$$\begin{array}{r|rrrrr} -1 & 3 & 1 & -8 & -2 & 4 \\ & & -3 & 2 & 6 & -4 \\ \hline & 3 & -2 & -6 & 4 & 0 \end{array}$$

Since the remainder for $x = -1$ is 0, $x + 1$ is a factor of f.

$$f(x) = (x + 1)(3x^3 - 2x^2 - 6x + 4)$$

Repeat this process for $g(x) = 3x^3 - 2x^2 - 6x + 4$. The possible rational zeros are $\pm 1, \pm 2, \pm 4, \pm\frac{1}{3}, \pm\frac{2}{3}, \pm\frac{4}{3}$.

To save time, graph the function f and estimate where it crosses the x-axis. A reasonable choice from the list of possibilities is $x = \frac{2}{3}$.

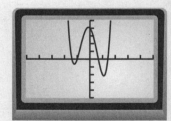

$$\begin{array}{r|rrrr} \frac{2}{3} & 3 & -2 & -6 & 4 \\ & & 2 & 0 & -4 \\ \hline & 3 & 0 & -6 & 0 \end{array}$$

Again, since the remainder is 0, $x - \frac{2}{3}$ is a factor of g.

So, $f(x) = (x + 1)\left(x - \frac{2}{3}\right)(3x^2 - 6)$

$\phantom{\text{So, } f(x)} = 3(x + 1)\left(x - \frac{2}{3}\right)(x^2 - 2)$ Factor out a 3.

$\phantom{\text{So, } f(x)} = 3(x + 1)\left(x - \frac{2}{3}\right)(x + \sqrt{2})(x - \sqrt{2})$ Difference of two squares

The real zeros of f are $-1, \frac{2}{3}, -\sqrt{2}$, and $\sqrt{2}$.

Practice with Examples

For use with pages 359–365

Exercises for Example 2

Find all the real zeros of the function.

5. $f(x) = x^3 + 3x^2 - 5x - 15$

6. $f(x) = x^4 - \frac{3}{2}x^3 - 7x^2 + 9x + 6$

7. $f(x) = x^3 - 5x^2 + 5x - 1$

8. $f(x) = x^3 - x^2 - 3x - 1$

NAME _____ DATE _____

Practice with Examples

For use with pages 366–371

GOAL How to use the fundamental theorem of algebra to determine the number of zeros of a polynomial function and how to use technology to approximate the real zeros of a polynomial function

> **VOCABULARY**
>
> A factor that appears twice in a factored equation is called a **repeated solution.**

EXAMPLE 1 **Finding the Number of Solutions or Zeros**

Equations have solutions, whereas functions have zeros.

a. The equation $x^4 - 2x^3 + 10x^2 - 18x + 9 = 0$ has four solutions, since its degree is 4 : 1, 1, 3i and $-3i$. Notice 1 is a repeated solution.

b. The function $f(x) = x^3 + 7x^2 + 7x - 15$ has three zeros, since its degree is 3 : -3, 1, and -5.

Exercises for Example 1

Find the number of zeros of the polynomial function.

1. $f(x) = x^4 - x^3 - x^2 - x - 2$ **2.** $f(x) = x^3 - 8x^2 + 19x - 12$

3. $f(x) = x^3 - 2x^2 + 5x - 10$ **4.** $f(x) = x^4 + 3x^3 - 4x^2 - 12x$

NAME _____ DATE _____

Practice with Examples

For use with pages 366–371

EXAMPLE 2 *Finding the Zeros of a Polynomial Function*

Find all the zeros of $f(x) = x^4 - 2x^3 + 10x^2 - 18x + 9$.

SOLUTION

The possible rational zeros are $\pm 1, \pm 3,$ and ± 9. Using synthetic division, you can determine that 1 is a repeated zero. The function in factored form is:

$$f(x) = (x - 1)(x - 1)(x^2 + 9)$$

Use the quadratic formula to factor the sum of two squares in order to factor completely.

$$x = \frac{-b \pm \sqrt{b^2 - 4ac}}{2a} = \frac{-0 \pm \sqrt{0^2 - 4(1)(9)}}{2(1)}$$

$$= \frac{\pm\sqrt{-36}}{2} = \frac{\pm 6i}{2} = \pm 3i$$

$$f(x) = (x - 1)(x - 1)(x + 3i)(x - 3i)$$

This factorization gives the four zeros of 1, 1, 3i, and −3i.

Exercises for Example 2

Find all the zeros of the polynomial function.

5. $f(x) = x^4 - x^3 - x^2 - x - 2$

6. $f(x) = x^3 - 8x^2 + 19x - 12$

7. $f(x) = x^3 - 2x^2 + 5x - 10$

8. $f(x) = x^4 + 3x^3 - 4x^2 - 12x$

EXAMPLE 3 *Using Zeros to Write Polynomial Functions*

Write a polynomial function f of least degree that has real coefficients, a leading coefficient of 1, and the zeros −1, 5, and 6.

SOLUTION

Using the three zeros and the factor theorem, write $f(x)$ as a product of three factors.

$f(x) = (x + 1)(x - 5)(x - 6)$	Write $f(x)$ in factored form.
$= (x^2 - 5x + x - 5)(x - 6)$	Multiply $(x + 1)(x - 5)$.
$= (x^2 - 4x - 5)(x - 6)$	Combine like terms.
$= x^3 - 4x^2 - 5x - 6x^2 + 24x + 30$	Multiply.
$= x^3 - 10x^2 + 19x + 30$	Combine like terms.

Chapter 6

NAME _____ DATE _____

Practice with Examples

For use with pages 366–371

Exercises for Example 3

Write a polynomial function of least degree that has real coefficients, the given zeros, and a leading coefficient of 1.

9. $2, -1, 5$

10. $4, -3, 6$

11. $-1, 1, 7$

12. $3, -3, -2$

EXAMPLE 4 *Approximating Real Zeros*

Approximate the real zeros of $f(x) = x^3 + 2x^2 - 5x + 1$.

SOLUTION

First, enter the function in a graphing calculator. Then use the *Zero* (or *Root*) feature as shown.

From this screen, you can see that one of the real zeros is about -3.51.

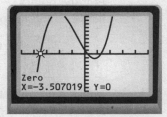

Zero
X=-3.507019 Y=0

Exercises for Example 4

Use a graphing calculator to graph the polynomial function. Then use the *Zero* (or *Root*) feature of the calculator to find the real zeros of the function.

13. $f(x) = x^3 - 6x + 2$

14. $f(x) = x^3 - x^2 + x - 1$

15. $f(x) = x^3 - 3x^2 + 4x + 3$

16. $f(x) = x^3 - 3x - 1$

NAME _____ DATE _____

Practice with Examples

For use with pages 373–378

GOAL How to analyze the graph of a polynomial function and how to use the graph to answer questions about real-life situations

> ### VOCABULARY
>
> The *y*-coordinate of a turning point is a **local maximum** of the function if the point is higher than all nearby points.
>
> The *y*-coordinate of a turning point is a **local minimum** of the function if the point is lower than all nearby points.

EXAMPLE 1 ## *Using x-Intercepts to Graph a Polynomial Function*

Graph the function $f(x) = \frac{1}{3}(x + 1)^2(x - 3)^2$.

SOLUTION

First, plot the *x*-intercepts. Since $x + 1$ and $x - 3$ are factors of $f(x)$, -1 and 3 are the *x*-intercepts of the graph. Plot the points $(-1, 0)$ and $(3, 0)$. Second, plot points between and beyond the *x*-intercepts.

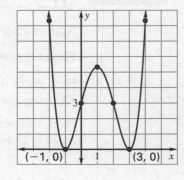

x	−3	−2	0	1	2	4	5
y	48	$8\frac{1}{3}$	3	$5\frac{1}{3}$	3	$8\frac{1}{3}$	48

Third, determine the end behavior of the graph. Since the degree is even and the leading coefficient is positive, $f(x) \to +\infty$ as $x \to -\infty$ and $f(x) \to +\infty$ as $x \to +\infty$.

Finally, draw a smooth curve that passes through the plotted points and has the appropriate end behavior.

Exercises for Example 1

Graph the function.

1. $f(x) = (x - 1)^2(x + 2)$ **2.** $f(x) = (x - 1)(x + 2)^3$ **3.** $f(x) = (x + 3)^2(x + 5)^2$

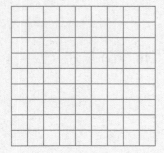   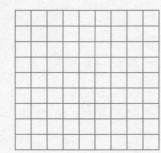   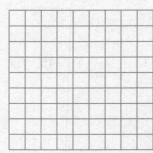

NAME _____ DATE _____

Practice with Examples

For use with pages 373–378

EXAMPLE 2 *Finding Turning Points*

Graph $f(x) = x^5 - 3x^2 - 4x$ using a graphing calculator. Identify the
x-intercepts and the local maximums and local minimums.

SOLUTION

Notice that the graph of the function has three x-intercepts
and two turning points. Using the graphing calculator's
Zero (or *Root*) feature, the x-intercepts are $x = -1$, $x = 0$,
and $x \approx 1.74$. Using the graphing calculator's *Maximum*
and *Minimum* features, the approximate local minimum
occurs at $(1.23, -6.64)$ and the local maximum occurs at
$(-0.43, 1.15)$.

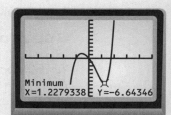

Exercises for Example 2

**Use a graphing calculator to graph the polynomial function.
Identify the x-intercepts and the points where the local
maximums and local minimums occur.**

4. $f(x) = -x^4 - 2x^3 + 3x^2 + 3x + 4$ **5.** $f(x) = x^3 - 3x^2 + 2x - 1$

6. $f(x) = x^4 - x^3 + x^2 - x - 1$ **7.** $f(x) = 2x^3 - 3x + 4$

Chapter 6

NAME _____ DATE _____

Practice with Examples

For use with pages 373–378

EXAMPLE 3 *Maximizing a Polynomial Model*

You are designing a rain gutter made from a piece of sheet
metal 1 foot by 5 feet. The gutter will be formed by turning
up two sides. You want the rain gutter to have the greatest
volume possible. How much should you turn up? What is
the maximum volume?

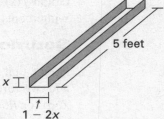

5 feet

x

$1 - 2x$

SOLUTION

Verbal Model: | Volume | = | Width | · | Length | · | Height |

Labels: Volume $= V$ (cubic feet)

               Width $= 1 - 2x$ (feet)

               Length $= 5$ (feet)

               Height $= x$ (feet)

Algebraic Model: $V = (1 - 2x)(5)(x) = 5x - 10x^2$

Graph the polynomial using a graphing calculator. Then find the
maximum volume using the *Maximum* feature. The maximum occurs at
about (0.25, 0.63). Therefore, you should turn up the sides 0.25 foot, or 3
inches. The maximum volume is about 0.63 cubic foot.

Exercises for Example 3

8. You are designing an open box to be made of a piece of cardboard
that is 8 inches by 12 inches. The box will be formed by cutting and
folding up the sides so that the flaps are square. You want the box to
have the greatest volume possible. How many inches should you cut?
What is the maximum volume?

9. What are the dimensions of the box in Exercise 8?

NAME _____ DATE _____

Practice with Examples

For use with pages 380–386

GOAL **How to use finite differences to determine the degree of a polynomial function that will fit a set of data and how to use technology to find polynomial models for real-life data**

VOCABULARY

Finding **finite differences** is a process which uses triangular numbers to decide whether *y*-values for equally spaced *x*-values can be modeled by a polynomial function. The properties of finite differences are listed below.

1. If a polynomial function $f(x)$ has degree *n*, then the *n*th-order differences of function values for equally spaced *x*-values are nonzero and constant.

2. Conversely, if the *n*th-order differences of equally spaced data are nonzero and constant, then the data can be represented by a polynomial function of degree *n*.

EXAMPLE 1 *Writing a Cubic Function*

Write the cubic function whose graph is shown.

SOLUTION

Begin by using the three *x*-intercepts to write the function in factored form:

$$f(x) = a(x + 1)(x - 2)(x - 3)$$

Then solve for *a* by substituting the coordinates of the point $(1, 8)$.

$$8 = a(1 + 1)(1 - 2)(1 - 3)$$

$$8 = 4a$$

$$2 = a$$

The cubic function is $f(x) = 2(x + 1)(x - 2)(x - 3)$.

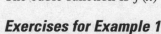

Exercises for Example 1

Write the cubic function whose graph is shown.

1.
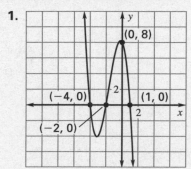

Chapter 6

NAME _____ DATE _____

Practice with Examples

For use with pages 380–386

2.

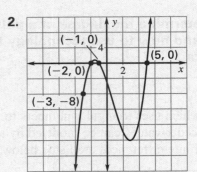

EXAMPLE 2 **Finding Finite Differences**

Show that the third-order differences for the function
$f(x) = x^3 - 2x^2 + x$ are nonzero and constant.

SOLUTION

Begin by evaluating the function for the first several values of x. For
example, $f(1) = 1^3 - 2(1)^2 + 1 = 0$

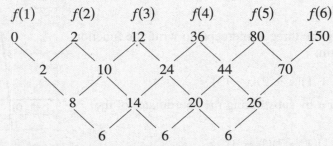

$f(1)$	$f(2)$	$f(3)$	$f(4)$	$f(5)$	$f(6)$	
0	2	12	36	80	150	Function values
	2	10	24	44	70	First-order differences
		8	14	20	26	Second-order differences
			6	6	6	Third-order differences

Notice that the third-order differences are nonzero and constant.

Exercises for Example 2

Show that the *n*th-order differences for the given function of
degree *n* are nonzero and constant.

   3. $f(x) = 4x^2 - x + 5$ **4.** $f(x) = x^3 + x^2 - 3$

Algebra 2
Practice Workbook with Examples

Practice with Examples

For use with pages 380–386

EXAMPLE 3 *Modeling with Cubic Regression*
_____

Find a polynomial model that fits the data below.

x	1	2	3	4	5	6
$f(x)$	-1	5	33	95	203	369

SOLUTION

Enter the data in a graphing calculator. Use cubic regression to obtain a model.

$$f(x) = 2x^3 - x^2 - 5x + 3$$

Exercises for Example 3

Use a graphing calculator to find a polynomial function that fits the data.

5.

x	1	2	3	4	5	6
$f(x)$	8	10	10	8	4	-2

6.

x	1	2	3	4	5	6
$f(x)$	-12	-11	-2	21	64	133

NAME _____ DATE _____

Practice with Examples

For use with pages 401–406

GOAL Evaluate *n*th roots of real numbers using both radical notation and rational exponent notation

---

VOCABULARY

For an integer n greater than 1, if $b^n = a$, then b is an **nth root of a**. An nth root of a is written $\sqrt[n]{a}$, where n is the **index** of the radical.

EXAMPLE 1 *Finding nth Roots*

Find the indicated real nth root(s) of a.

a. $n = 2, a = -25$ **b.** $n = 4, a = 0$

SOLUTION

a. Because n is even and $a < 0$, -25 has no real nth roots.

b. Because n is even and $a = 0$, 0 has one fourth root. Because $(0)^4 = 0$, you can write:

$$\sqrt[4]{0} = 0$$

Exercises for Example 1
....

Find the indicated real *n*th root(s) of *a*.

1. $n = 2, a = 16$ **2.** $n = 3, a = -1$ **3.** $n = 4, a = -16$

4. $n = 3, a = 125$ **5.** $n = 3, a = 0$ **6.** $n = 2, a = 49$

Practice with Examples

For use with pages 401–406

EXAMPLE 2 *Evaluating Expressions with Rational Exponents*

a. $16^{3/4} = \left(\sqrt[4]{16}\right)^3 = 2^3 = 8$ Using radical notation

     $16^{3/4} = (16^{1/4})^3 = 2^3 = 8$ Using rational exponent notation

b. $27^{-4/3} = \dfrac{1}{27^{4/3}} = \dfrac{1}{\left(\sqrt[3]{27}\right)^4} = \dfrac{1}{3^4} = \dfrac{1}{81}$ Using radical notation

     $27^{-4/3} = \dfrac{1}{27^{4/3}} = \dfrac{1}{(27^{1/3})^4} = \dfrac{1}{3^4} = \dfrac{1}{81}$ Using rational exponent notation.

Exercises for Example 2

Evaluate the expression without using a calculator.

7. $27^{2/3}$ **8.** $343^{1/3}$ **9.** $81^{-3/4}$

10. $\sqrt[5]{32}$ **11.** $\sqrt[3]{-8}$ **12.** $\left(\sqrt{36}\right)^3$

EXAMPLE 3 *Approximating a Root with a Calculator*

Use a graphing calculator to approximate $\left(\sqrt[3]{-7}\right)^2$.

SOLUTION

Begin by rewriting $\left(\sqrt[3]{-7}\right)^2$ as $(-7)^{2/3}$. Then enter the following:

Keystrokes: `(` `(-)` `7` `)` `^` `(` `2` `÷` `3` `)` `ENTER`   **Display:** `3.65930571`

$\left(\sqrt[3]{-7}\right)^2 \approx 3.66$

Notice that the negative radicand of -7 was enclosed in parentheses. If parentheses were not used, only the 7 would have been raised to the two-thirds power, and the result would have been negative.

Chapter 7

Practice with Examples

For use with pages 401–406

Exercises for Example 3

Evaluate the expressions using a calculator. Round the result to two decimal places.

13. $\sqrt[4]{252}$

14. $\sqrt[3]{-2111}$

15. $\left(\sqrt[3]{56}\right)^4$

16. $\left(\sqrt[3]{-140}\right)^6$

17. $\sqrt[8]{25{,}102}$

18. $\left(\sqrt[3]{5}\right)^3$

EXAMPLE 4 **Solving Equations Using nth Roots**

Solve the equation.

a. $-5x^2 = -30$

$\qquad x^2 = 6$ Divide each side by -5.

$\qquad x = \pm\sqrt{6}$ Take square root of each side.

$\qquad x \approx \pm 2.45$ Round result.

b. $(x + 4)^3 = 27$

$\qquad x + 4 = \sqrt[3]{27}$ Take cube root of each side.

$\qquad x + 4 = 3$ Simplify.

$\qquad x = -1$ Subtract 4 from each side.

Exercises for Example 4

Solve the equation. Round your answer to two decimal places when appropriate.

19. $x^4 = 87$

20. $2x^3 = 92$

21. $(x - 1)^5 = 12$

NAME _____ DATE _____

Practice with Examples

For use with pages 407–414

GOAL **Use properties of rational exponents to evaluate and simplify expressions**

VOCABULARY

For a radical to be in **simpliest form,** you must apply the properties of radicals, remove any perfect nth powers (other than 1) and rationalize any denominators. Two radical expressions are **like radicals** if they have the same index and the same radicand.

EXAMPLE 1 *Using Properties of Rational Exponents*

Use the properties of rational exponents to simplify the expression.

a. $x^{2/3} \cdot x^{1/9} = x^{(2/3+1/9)} = x^{(6/9+1/9)} = x^{7/9}$

b. $(2^3 x^6)^{1/3} = (2^3)^{1/3} \cdot (x^6)^{1/3} = 2^{(3 \cdot 1/3)} \cdot x^{(6 \cdot 1/3)} = 2^1 \cdot x^2 = 2x^2$

c. $\dfrac{x^{3/4}}{x} = x^{(3/4-1)} = x^{(3/4-4/4)} = x^{-1/4} = \dfrac{1}{x^{1/4}}$

Exercises for Example 1

Use the properties of rational exponents to simplify the expression.

1. $x \cdot x^{1/2}$ 　　　　　　　**2.** $y^{-2/3}$ 　　　　　　　**3.** $(4^{2/3})^6$

4. $\dfrac{y^{2/3}}{y^{1/3}}$ 　　　　　　　**5.** $\dfrac{1}{64^{-1/3}}$ 　　　　　　　**6.** $z^{2/3} \cdot z^{1/2}$

EXAMPLE 2 *Using Properties of Radicals*

Use the properties of radicals to simplify the expression.

a. $\sqrt{8} \cdot \sqrt{2} = \sqrt{8 \cdot 2} = \sqrt{16} = 4$ 　　Use the product property.

b. $\dfrac{\sqrt[3]{320}}{\sqrt[3]{5}} = \sqrt[3]{\dfrac{320}{5}} = \sqrt[3]{64} = 4$ 　　Use the quotient property.

NAME _____ DATE _____

Practice with Examples

For use with pages 407–414

Exercises for Example 2

Use the properties of radicals to simplify the expression.

7. $\sqrt[3]{16} \cdot \sqrt[3]{4}$

8. $\sqrt{6} \cdot \sqrt{6}$

9. $\dfrac{\sqrt[4]{32}}{\sqrt[4]{2}}$

10. $\dfrac{\sqrt[3]{250}}{\sqrt[3]{2}}$

EXAMPLE 3 *Writing Radicals and Variable Expressions in Simplest Form*

Write the expression in simplest form. Assume all variables are positive.

a. $\sqrt[4]{96} = \sqrt[4]{16 \cdot 6}$ Factor out perfect fourth power.

     $= \sqrt[4]{16} \cdot \sqrt[4]{6}$ Use the product property.

     $= 2\sqrt[4]{6}$ Simplify $\sqrt[4]{16} = \sqrt[4]{2^4} = 2$.

b. $\sqrt[3]{\dfrac{12}{25}} = \sqrt[3]{\dfrac{12 \cdot 5}{25 \cdot 5}}$ Make the denominator a perfect cube.

     $= \sqrt[3]{\dfrac{60}{125}}$ Simplify.

     $= \dfrac{\sqrt[3]{60}}{\sqrt[3]{125}}$ Quotient property

     $= \dfrac{\sqrt[3]{60}}{5}$ Simplify $\sqrt[3]{125} = \sqrt[3]{5^3} = 5$.

c. $\sqrt{28y^5} = \sqrt{2^2 \cdot 7y^4 y}$ Factor out perfect square.

     $= \sqrt{2^2 y^4} \cdot \sqrt{7y}$ Product property

     $= 2y^2 \sqrt{7y}$ Simplify $\sqrt{2^2(y^2)^2} = 2y^2$.

d. $\sqrt[5]{\dfrac{x^5}{y^3}} = \sqrt[5]{\dfrac{x^5 y^2}{y^3 y^2}}$ Make the denominator a perfect fifth power.

     $= \dfrac{\sqrt[5]{x^5 y^2}}{\sqrt[5]{y^5}}$ Simplify and use quotient property.

     $= \dfrac{x\sqrt[5]{y^2}}{y}$ Simplify.

Practice with Examples
For use with pages 407–414

Exercises for Example 3

Write the expression in simplest form. Assume all variables are positive.

11. $\sqrt[3]{32}$

12. $\sqrt[4]{\dfrac{2}{9}}$

13. $\sqrt[4]{256x^8y}$

14. $\sqrt{\dfrac{4x^2y}{9z^2}}$

EXAMPLE 4 ## Adding and Subtracting Roots, Radicals, and Variable Expressions

Perform the indicated operation. Assume all variables are positive.

a. $4(3)^{1/3} - 2(3)^{1/3} = (4 - 2)(3)^{1/3} = 2(3)^{1/3}$

b. $\sqrt{27} + \sqrt{12} = \sqrt{9 \cdot 3} + \sqrt{4 \cdot 3}$ ⟶ Factor out perfect squares.

$\qquad\qquad = \sqrt{9} \cdot \sqrt{3} + \sqrt{4} \cdot \sqrt{3}$ ⟶ Product property

$\qquad\qquad = 3\sqrt{3} + 2\sqrt{3}$ ⟶ Simplify.

$\qquad\qquad = (3 + 2)\sqrt{3}$ ⟶ Distributive property

$\qquad\qquad = 5\sqrt{3}$ ⟶ Simplify.

c. $\sqrt[3]{y} + 4\sqrt[3]{y} = (1 + 4)\sqrt[3]{y} = 5\sqrt[3]{y}$

Exercises for Example 4

Perform the indicated operation. Assume all variables are positive.

15. $2\sqrt[5]{3} - \sqrt[5]{3}$

16. $7(2^{1/8}) + 4(2^{1/8})$

17. $4\sqrt{x} + 2\sqrt{x}$

Practice with Examples

For use with pages 415–420

GOAL **Perform operations with functions, including power functions**

VOCABULARY

A **power function** has the form $y = ax^b$, where a is a real number and b is a rational number.

The **composition** of the function f with the function g is given by $h(x) = f(g(x))$, where the domain of h is the set of all x-values such that x is in the domain of g, and $g(x)$ is in the domain of f.

EXAMPLE 1 *Adding and Subtracting Functions*

Let $f(x) = -2x$ and $g(x) = x + 3$. Perform the indicated operation and state the domain.

a. $f(x) + g(x) = -2x + (x + 3) = -x + 3$

b. $f(x) - g(x) = -2x - (x + 3) = -2x + (-x - 3) = -3x - 3$

The functions f and g each have the same domain–all real numbers. So, the domains of $f + g$ and $f - g$ also consist of all real numbers.

Exercises for Example 1

Let $f(x) = 2 - x$ and $g(x) = 3x$. Perform the indicated operation and state the domain.

1. $f(x) + g(x)$

2. $f(x) - g(x)$

3. $g(x) - f(x)$

4. $g(x) + g(x)$

Chapter 7

Practice with Examples

For use with pages 415–420

EXAMPLE 2 *Multiplying and Dividing Functions*

Let $f(x) = 5x^3$ and $g(x) = x - 1$. Perform the indicated operation and state the domain.

a. $f(x) \cdot g(x) = 5x^3(x - 1) = (5x^3)(x) - (5x^3)(1) = 5x^4 - 5x^3$

The functions f and g each have the same domain–all real numbers. So, the domain of $f \cdot g$ also consists of all real numbers.

b. $\dfrac{f(x)}{g(x)} = \dfrac{5x^3}{x - 1}$

Since $x = 1$ will make the denominator zero, the domain is all real numbers except $x = 1$.

Exercises for Example 2

Perform the indicated operation and state the domain.

5. $f \cdot g; f(x) = x^{1/2}, g(x) = 3x^3$

6. $f \cdot g; f(x) = x + 3, g(x) = 2x^2$

7. $\dfrac{f}{g}; f(x) = 4x^{2/3}, g(x) = 2x$

8. $\dfrac{f}{g}; f(x) = -7x + 1, g(x) = x$

NAME _____ DATE _____

Practice with Examples

For use with pages 415–420

EXAMPLE 3 *Finding the Composition of Functions*

Let $f(x) = 3x - 2$ and $g(x) = x^2$. Find the following.

a. $f(g(x))$ **b.** $g(f(x))$ **c.** $f(f(x))$

d. the domain of each composition

SOLUTION

a. To find $f(g(x))$, substitute x^2 for x in the function f.

$f(g(x)) = f(x^2) = 3(x^2) - 2 = 3x^2 - 2$

b. To find $g(f(x))$, substitute $3x - 2$ for x in the function g.

$g(f(x)) = g(3x - 2) = (3x - 2)^2 = 9x^2 - 12x + 4$

c. To find $f(f(x))$, substitute $3x - 2$ for x in the function f.

$f(f(x)) = f(3x - 2) = 3(3x - 2) - 2 = 9x - 6 - 2 = 9x - 8$

d. The functions f and g each have the same domain–all real numbers. So the domain of each composition also consists of all real numbers.

Exercises for Example 3

Let $f(x) = 2x^{-1}$ and $g(x) = x - 2$. Perform the indicated operation and state the domain.

9. $f(g(x))$ **10.** $g(f(x))$

11. $f(f(x))$ **12.** $g(g(x))$

Chapter 7

LESSON 7.4

Practice with Examples

For use with pages 422–429

GOAL **Find inverses of linear and nonlinear functions**

VOCABULARY

An **inverse relation** maps the output values back to their original input values. Two functions f and g are called **inverse functions** provided $f(g(x)) = x$ and $g(f(x)) = x$. According to the **horizontal line test,** if no horizontal line intersects the graph of a function f more than once, then the inverse of f is itself a function.

EXAMPLE 1 *Finding an Inverse Relation*

Find an equation for the inverse of the relation $y = \frac{1}{3}x + 2$.

SOLUTION

$y = \frac{1}{3}x + 2$	Write original relation.
$x = \frac{1}{3}y + 2$	Switch x and y.
$x - 2 = \frac{1}{3}y$	Subtract 2 from each side.
$3x - 6 = y$	Multiply each side by 3, the reciprocal of $\frac{1}{3}$.

The inverse relation is $y = 3x - 6$.

Exercises for Example 1

Find an equation for the inverse relation.

1. $y = 4x + 8$

2. $y = -3x + 12$

3. $y = \frac{2}{3}x - 4$

Chapter 7

NAME _____ DATE _____

Practice with Examples

For use with pages 422–429

EXAMPLE 2 **Verifying Inverse Functions**

Verify that $f(x) = \frac{1}{2}x - 2$ and $f^{-1}(x) = 2x + 4$ are inverses.

SOLUTION

You need to show that $f(f^{-1}(x)) = x$ and $f^{-1}(f(x)) = x$.

$$f(f^{-1}(x)) = f(2x + 4) \qquad\qquad f^{-1}(f(x)) = f^{-1}\left(\frac{1}{2}x - 2\right)$$
$$= \frac{1}{2}(2x + 4) - 2 \qquad\qquad\qquad = 2\left(\frac{1}{2}x - 2\right) + 4$$
$$= x + 2 - 2 \qquad\qquad\qquad\qquad = x - 4 + 4$$
$$= x \checkmark \qquad\qquad\qquad\qquad\qquad = x \checkmark$$

Exercises for Example 2

Verify that *f* and *g* are inverse functions.

4. $f(x) = x - 3$, $g(x) = x + 3$ **5.** $f(x) = \frac{1}{2}x + 3$, $g(x) = 2x - 6$

EXAMPLE 3 **Finding an Inverse Power Function**

Find the inverse of the function $f(x) = x^5$

SOLUTION

$f(x) = x^5$ Write original function.

$y = x^5$ Replace $f(x)$ with y.

$x = y^5$ Switch x and y.

$\sqrt[5]{x} = y$ Take fifth roots of each side.

The inverse function is $f^{-1}(x) = \sqrt[5]{x}$.

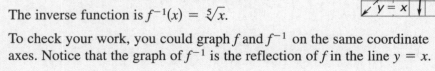

To check your work, you could graph f and f^{-1} on the same coordinate axes. Notice that the graph of f^{-1} is the reflection of f in the line $y = x$.

Practice with Examples

For use with pages 422–429

Exercises for Example 3

Find the inverse power function.

6. $f(x) = -x^2, x \geq 0$ **7.** $f(x) = -27x^3$ **8.** $f(x) = x^4, x \leq 0$

EXAMPLE 4 *Finding an Inverse Function*

Consider the function $f(x) = -x^2 + 5$. Determine whether the inverse of f is a function.

SOLUTION

Begin by graphing the function. The function is a parabola which opens down and is vertically shifted five units up. Notice that a horizontal line, such as $y = 1$, intersects the graph more than once. This tells you that the inverse of f is not a function.

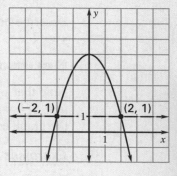

Exercises for Example 4

Graph the function *f*. Then use the graph to determine whether the inverse of *f* is a function. If it is, find the inverse.

9. $f(x) = 3x - 4$ **10.** $f(x) = x^4 + 2$ **11.** $f(x) = x^3 - 4$

12. $f(x) = 5x^2$ **13.** $f(x) = -x^3$ **14.** $f(x) = |x|$

Chapter 7

NAME _____ DATE _____

Practice with Examples

For use with pages 431–436

GOAL Graph square root and cube root functions

VOCABULARY

The graphs of $y = \sqrt{x}$ and $y = \sqrt[3]{x}$ are examples of **radical functions**. To graph $y = a\sqrt{x - h} + k$ or $a\sqrt[3]{x - h} + k$, follow these steps.

Step 1: Sketch the graph of $y = a\sqrt{x}$ or $a\sqrt[3]{x}$.

Step 2: Shift graph h units horizontally and k units vertically.

EXAMPLE 1 *Comparing Two Graphs*

Describe how to obtain the graph of $y = \sqrt[3]{x - 2} + 4$ from the graph of $y = \sqrt[3]{x}$.

SOLUTION

Note that $y = \sqrt[3]{x - 2} + 4$ is in the form $y = a\sqrt[3]{x - h} + k$, where $a = 1$, $h = 2$, and $k = 4$. To obtain the graph of $y = \sqrt[3]{x - 2} + 4$, shift the graph of $y = \sqrt[3]{x}$ right 2 units and up 4 units.

Exercises for Example 1

Describe how to obtain the graph of *g* from the graph of *f*.

1. $g(x) = \sqrt{x} + 3, f(x) = \sqrt{x}$

2. $g(x) = \sqrt[3]{x} + 5, f(x) = \sqrt[3]{x}$

3. $g(x) = \sqrt{x - 1} - 4, f(x) = \sqrt{x}$

4. $g(x) = \sqrt[3]{x + 1} + 6, f(x) = \sqrt[3]{x}$

Practice with Examples

For use with pages 431–436

EXAMPLE 2 *Graphing a Square Root Function*

Graph $y = -2\sqrt{x + 3} + 5$.

SOLUTION

Begin by sketching the graph of $y = -2\sqrt{x}$ (shown as a dashed curve). Notice that the graph begins at the origin and passes through the points $(1, -2)$ and $(4, -4)$.

Note that for $y = -2\sqrt{x + 3} + 5$, $h = -3$ and $k = 5$. So, shift the graph left 3 units and up 5 units. Notice that the graph begins at $(-3, 5)$ and passes through the points $(1 - 3, -2 + 5) = (-2, 3)$ and $(4 - 3, -4 + 5) = (1, 1)$.

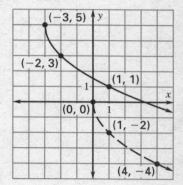

Exercises for Example 2

Graph the square root function.

5. $y = 4\sqrt{x}$

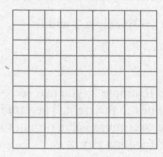

6. $y = 4\sqrt{x + 3}$

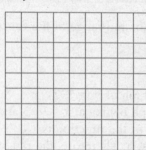

7. $y = 4\sqrt{x} - 5$

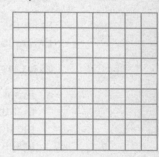

EXAMPLE 3 *Graphing a Cube Root Function*

Graph $y = -\sqrt[3]{x - 1} + 4$.

SOLUTION

Begin by sketching the graph of $y = -\sqrt[3]{x}$ (shown as a dashed curve). Notice that it passes through the origin and the points $(1, -1)$ and $(-1, 1)$. Note that for $y = -\sqrt[3]{x - 1} + 4$, $h = 1$ and $k = 4$. So, shift the graph right 1 unit and up 4 units. Notice that the graph passes through the points $(1, 4)$, $(2, 3)$, and $(0, 5)$.

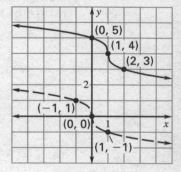

Chapter 7

NAME _____ DATE _____

Practice with Examples

For use with pages 431–436

Exercises for Example 3

Graph the cubic function.

8. $y = 3\sqrt[3]{x}$

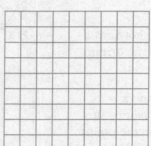

9. $y = 3\sqrt[3]{x} - 2$

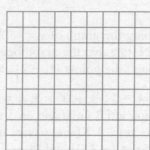

10. $y = 3\sqrt[3]{x} + 2$

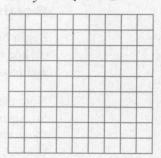

EXAMPLE 4 *Finding Domain and Range*

State the domain and range of the function in (a) Example 2 and (b) Example 3.

SOLUTION

a. From the graph of $y = -2\sqrt{x + 3} + 5$ in Example 2, you can see that the graph begins at $x = -3$ and continues to the right. Therefore, the domain of the function is $x \geq -3$. The maximum value of y in the graph is $y = 5$. Therefore, the range of the function is $y \leq 5$.

b. From the graph of $y = -\sqrt[3]{x - 1} + 4$ in Example 3, you can see that the domain and range of the function are both all real numbers.

Exercises for Example 4

Using the graphs from Exercises 11–16, state the domain and range of the function.

11. $y = 4\sqrt{x}$

12. $y = 4\sqrt{x + 3}$

13. $y = 4\sqrt{x} - 5$

14. $y = 3\sqrt[3]{x}$

15. $y = 3\sqrt[3]{x} - 2$

16. $y = 3\sqrt[3]{x} + 2$

NAME _____ DATE _____

Practice with Examples

For use with pages 437–444

GOAL **Solve equations that contain radicals or rational exponents**

VOCABULARY

The **powers property of equality** states that if $a = b$, then $a^n = b^n$. In other words, you can raise each side of an equation to the same power. An **extraneous solution** is a trial solution that does not satisfy the original equation.

EXAMPLE 1 ### *Solving a Simple Radical Equation*

Solve $\sqrt{x} + 5 = 9$.

SOLUTION

$\sqrt{x} + 5 = 9$	Write original equation.
$\sqrt{x} = 4$	Isolate the radical by subtracting 5 from each side.
$\left(\sqrt{x}\right)^2 = 4^2$	Square each side.
$x = 16$	Simplify.

The solution is 16. You can check this substituting 16 for x in the original equation to get $\sqrt{16} + 5 = 4 + 5 = 9$.

Exercises for Example 1

Solve the equation. Check your solution.

1. $\sqrt[3]{x} + 2 = 0$

2. $-\sqrt{x} - 5 = -6$

3. $\sqrt[4]{x} = 3$

Chapter 7

Practice with Examples

For use with pages 437–444

EXAMPLE 2 **Solving an Equation with Rational Exponents**

Solve $3x^{3/4} = 192$.

SOLUTION

$3x^{3/4} = 192$	Write original equation.
$x^{3/4} = 64$	Isolate the power by dividing each side by 3.
$(x^{3/4})^{4/3} = 64^{4/3}$	Raise each side to $\frac{4}{3}$ power, the reciprocal of $\frac{3}{4}$.
$x = (64^{1/3})^4$	Apply properties of roots.
$x = 4^4 = 256$	Simplify.

The solution is 256. You can check this by substituting 256 for x in the original equation to get $3(256)^{3/4} = 3[(256)^{1/4}]^3 = 3(4)^3 = 3(64) = 192$.

Exercises for Example 2

Solve the equation. Check your solution.

4. $2x^{1/2} = 18$

5. $5x^{3/2} = 40$

6. $x^{3/4} = \frac{1}{8}$

EXAMPLE 3 **Solving an Equation with One Radical**

Solve $\sqrt[3]{8x + 3} - 5 = -2$.

SOLUTION

$\sqrt[3]{8x + 3} - 5 = -2$	Write original equation.
$\sqrt[3]{8x + 3} = 3$	Isolate the radical, by adding 5 to each side.
$(\sqrt[3]{8x + 3})^3 = 3^3$	Cube each side.
$8x + 3 = 27$	Simplify.
$8x = 24$	Subtract 3 from each side.
$x = 3$	Divide each side by 8.

The solution is 3. Check this in the original equation.

Chapter 7

NAME _____ DATE _____

Practice with Examples

For use with pages 437–444

Exercises for Example 3

Solve the equation. Check your solution.

7. $\sqrt{4 + 3x} = 10$　　　　**8.** $\sqrt{2x + 1} = 7$　　　　**9.** $\sqrt[3]{4x - 1} = 3$

EXAMPLE 4　　*Solving an Equation with Two Radicals*

Solve $\sqrt[3]{2x + 4} = 2\sqrt[3]{3 - x}$.

SOLUTION

$\sqrt[3]{2x + 4} = 2\sqrt[3]{3 - x}$　　　　Write original equation.

$\left(\sqrt[3]{2x + 4}\right)^3 = \left(2\sqrt[3]{3 - x}\right)^3$　　　　Cube each side.

$2x + 4 = 8(3 - x)$　　　　Simplify.

$2x + 4 = 24 - 8x$　　　　Distributive property

$10x + 4 = 24$　　　　Add $8x$ to each side.

$10x = 20$　　　　Subtract 4 from each side.

$x = 2$　　　　Divide each side by 10.

The solution is 2. Check this in the original equation.

Exercises for Example 4

Solve the equation. Check your solution.

10. $\sqrt{7x - 8} = \sqrt{5x}$　　　　**11.** $\sqrt{3x + 5} = \sqrt{x + 15}$　　　　**12.** $\sqrt[3]{x + 14} = 2\sqrt[3]{x}$

Practice with Examples
For use with pages 445–452

GOAL Use measures of central tendency and measures of dispersion to describe data sets

VOCABULARY

The **mean**, or average, of n numbers is the sum of the numbers divided by n. The mean is denoted by $\bar{x}$ and is represented by

$$\frac{x_1 + x_2 + \cdots + x_n}{n}.$$

The **median** of n numbers is the middle number when the numbers are written in order. (If n is even, the median is the mean of the two middle numbers.) The **mode** of n numbers is the number or numbers that occur most frequently. There may be one mode, no mode, or more than one mode. The **range** is the difference between the greatest and least data values. The **standard deviation** describes the typical difference (or deviation) between the mean and a data value, and is represented by

$$\sigma = \sqrt{\frac{(x_1 - \bar{x})^2 + (x_2 - \bar{x})^2 + \cdots + (x_n - \bar{x})^2}{n}}.$$

EXAMPLE 1 *Finding Measures of Central Tendency*

Test Scores
32, 72, 81, 95, 98, 58, 77, 75, 83, 97, 45, 89, 93, 57, 82, 97, 52, 75

Find the mean, median, and mode of the data set listed above.

SOLUTION

To find the mean, divide the sum of the scores by the number of scores.

Mean:

$$\bar{x} = \frac{32 + 72 + 81 + 95 + 98 + 58 + 77 + 75 + 83 + 97 + 45 + 89 + 93 + 57 + 82 + 97 + 52 + 75}{18}$$

$$= \frac{1358}{18} \approx 75.4$$

To find the median, order the 18 numbers first. Because there is an even number of scores, the median is the average of the two middle scores.

32, 45, 52, 57, 58, 72, 75, 75, 77, 81, 82, 83, 89, 93, 95, 97, 97, 98

$$\text{Median} = \frac{77 + 81}{2} = 79$$

There are two modes, 75 and 97, because these numbers occur most frequently.

NAME _____ DATE _____

Practice with Examples

For use with pages 445–452

Exercises for Example 1

Find the mean, median, and mode of the data set.

1. 15, 11, 19, 15, 14, 14, 13, 17, 11, 12, 17, 15, 14, 15

2. 79, 78, 99, 98, 54, 75, 85, 61, 55, 86, 74

EXAMPLE 2 *Finding Measures of Dispersion*

Find the range and the standard deviation of the test scores from Example 1.

SOLUTION

To find the range, subtract the lowest score from the highest score.

Range = 98 − 32 = 66

To find the standard deviation, substitute the scores and the mean of 75.4 from Example 1 into the formula:

$$\sigma = \sqrt{\frac{(32 - 75.4)^2 + (45 - 75.4)^2 + (52 - 75.4)^2 + \cdots + (98 - 75.4)^2}{18}}$$

$$\approx \sqrt{\frac{6466}{18}} \approx \sqrt{359} \approx 18.9$$

NAME _____ DATE _____

Practice with Examples

Exercises for Example 2

3. Find the range and standard deviation of the data set in Exercise 1.

4. Find the range and standard deviation of the data set in Exercise 2.

Practice with Examples

For use with pages 465–472

GOAL Graph exponential growth functions and use exponential growth functions to model real-life situations

---

VOCABULARY

An **exponential function** involves the expression b^x where the **base** b is a positive number other than 1. If $a > 0$ and $b > 1$, the function $y = ab^x$ is an exponential growth function.

An **asymptote** is a line that a graph approaches as you move away from the origin. In the exponential growth model $y = a(1 + r)^t$, y is the quantity after t years, a is the initial amount, r is the percent increase expressed as a decimal, and the quantity $1 + r$ is called the **growth factor.**

Compound Interest Consider an initial principal P deposited in an account that pays interest at an annual rate r (expressed as a decimal), compounded n times per year. The amount A in the account after t years can be modeled by this equation: $A = P\left(1 + \dfrac{r}{n}\right)^{nt}$

EXAMPLE 1 *Graphing Exponential Functions*

Graph the function (a) $y = -2 \cdot 3^x$ and (b) $y = 2 \cdot 3^x$.

SOLUTION

Begin by plotting two points on the graph. To find these two points, evaluate the function when $x = 0$ and $x = 1$.

a. $y = -2 \cdot 3^0 = -2 \cdot 1 = -2$
$y = -2 \cdot 3^1 = -2 \cdot 3 = -6$

Plot $(0, -2)$ and $(1, -6)$. Then, from left to right, draw a curve that begins just below the x-axis, passes through the two points, and moves down to the right.

b. $y = 2 \cdot 3^0 = 2 \cdot 1 = 2$
$y = 2 \cdot 3^1 = 2 \cdot 3 = 6$

Plot $(0, 2)$ and $(1, 6)$. Then, from left to right, draw a curve that begins just above the x-axis, passes through the two points, and moves up to the right.

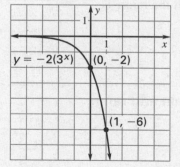

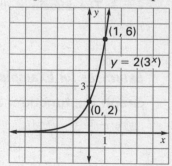

Chapter 8

Algebra 2
Practice Workbook with Examples

151

Practice with Examples

For use with pages 465–472

Exercises for Example 1

Graph the function.

1. $y = 2^x$

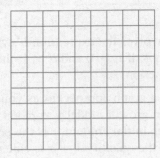

2. $y = -4^x$

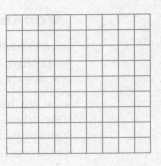

3. $y = -3 \cdot 2^x$

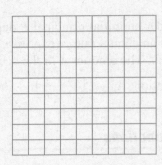

4. $y = 4 \cdot 2^x$

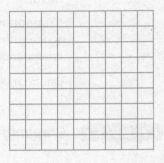

EXAMPLE 2 *Graphing a General Exponential Function*

Graph $y = -2 \cdot 4^{x+1} + 3$. State the domain and range.

SOLUTION

Begin by lightly sketching the graph of $y = -2 \cdot 4^x$, which passes through $(0, -2)$ and $(1, -8)$. Then because $h = -1$ and $k = 3$, translate the graph 1 unit to the left and 3 units up. Notice that the graph passes through $(-1, 1)$ and $(0, -5)$. The graph's asymptote is $y = 3$. The domain is all real numbers and the range is $y < 3$.

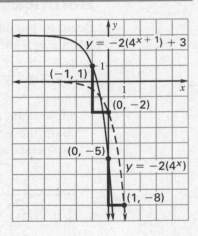

Exercises for Example 2

Graph the function. State the domain and range.

5. $y = -3 \cdot 2^{x+4}$

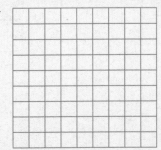

6. $y = 5 \cdot 2^{x-1}$

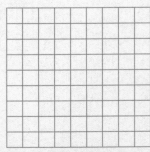

Practice with Examples

For use with pages 465–472

7. $y = 3^{x-2} + 4$

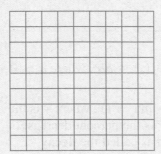

8. $y = 4^{x+2} - 3$

EXAMPLE 3 ___ *Modeling Exponential Growth* _____

A diamond ring was purchased twenty years ago for $500. The value of the ring increased by 8% each year. What is the value of the ring today?

SOLUTION

The initial amount is $a = 500$, the percent increase expressed in decimal form is $r = 0.08$, and the time in years is $t = 20$.

$$y = a(1 + r)^t \qquad \text{Write exponential growth model.}$$

$$= 500(1 + 0.08)^{20} \qquad \text{Substitute } a = 500, r = 0.08, \text{ and } t = 20.$$

$$= 500 \cdot 1.08^{20} \qquad \text{Simplify.}$$

$$\approx 2330.48 \qquad \text{Use a calculator.}$$

The value of the ring today is about $2330.48.

Exercises for Example 3

9. A customer purchases a television set for $800 using a credit card. The interest is charged on any unpaid balance at the rate of 18% per year compounded monthly. If the customer makes no payment for one year, how much is owed at the end of the year?

10. A house was purchased for $90,000 in 1995. If the value of the home increases by 5% per year, what is it worth in the year 2020?

Chapter 8

NAME _____ DATE _____

Practice with Examples

For use with pages 474–479

GOAL Graph exponential decay functions and use exponential decay functions to model real-life situations

---

VOCABULARY

An **exponential decay function** has the form $f(x) = ab^x$, where $a > 0$ and $0 < b < 1$.

An exponential decay model has the form $y = a(1 - r)^t$, where y is the quantity after t years, a is the initial amount, r is the percent decrease expressed as a decimal, and the quantity $1 - r$ is called the **decay factor.**

EXAMPLE 1 *Recognizing Exponential Growth and Decay*

State whether $f(x)$ is an exponential growth or exponential decay function.

a. $f(x) = 4\left(\frac{1}{3}\right)^x$ **b.** $f(x) = 5\left(\frac{3}{4}\right)^{-x}$ **c.** $f(x) = 2(0.15)^x$

SOLUTION

a. Because $b = \frac{1}{3}$, and $0 < b < 1$, f is an exponential decay function.

b. Rewrite the function without negative exponents as $f(x) = 5 \cdot \left(\frac{4}{3}\right)^x$. Because $b = \frac{4}{3}$, and $b > 1$, f is an exponential growth function.

c. Because $b = 0.15$, and $0 < b < 1$, f is an exponential decay function.

Exercises for Example 1
....

State whether the function represents *exponential growth* or *exponential decay*.

1. $f(x) = 3 \cdot 4^x$ **2.** $f(x) = 2 \cdot (0.75)^x$ **3.** $f(x) = 4\left(\frac{1}{3}\right)^x$

4. $f(x) = 4\left(\frac{6}{5}\right)^x$ **5.** $f(x) = 3\left(\frac{1}{4}\right)^{-x}$ **6.** $f(x) = 7\left(\frac{5}{2}\right)^{-x}$

NAME _____ DATE _____

Practice with Examples

For use with pages 474–479

EXAMPLE 2 **Graphing Exponential Functions**

Graph the function (a) $y = -2\left(\frac{1}{3}\right)^x$ and (b) $y = 3\left(\frac{2}{3}\right)^x$.

SOLUTION

Begin by plotting two points on the graph. To find these two points, evaluate the function when $x = 0$ and $x = 1$.

a. $y = -2\left(\frac{1}{3}\right)^0 = -2$

$y = -2\left(\frac{1}{3}\right)^1 = -\frac{2}{3}$

Plot $(0, -2)$ and $\left(1, -\frac{2}{3}\right)$. Then, from *right* to *left,* draw a curve that begins just below the x-axis, passes through the two points, and moves down to the left.

b. $y = 3\left(\frac{2}{3}\right)^0 = 3$

$y = 3\left(\frac{2}{3}\right)^1 = 2$

Plot $(0, 3)$ and $(1, 2)$. Then, from *right* to *left* draw a curve that begins just above the x-axis, passes through the two points, and moves up to the left.

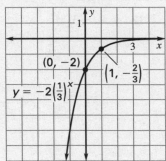

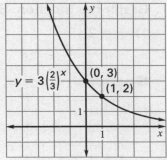

Exercises for Example 2

Graph the function.

7. $y = 2\left(\frac{1}{4}\right)^x$

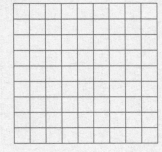

8. $y = -3\left(\frac{1}{2}\right)^x$

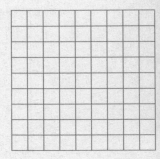

9. $y = 4\left(\frac{3}{4}\right)^x$

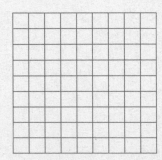

10. $y = -5\left(\frac{2}{3}\right)^x$

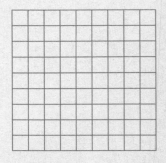

NAME _____ DATE _____

Practice with Examples

For use with pages 474–479

EXAMPLE 3 *Graphing a General Exponential Function*

Graph $y = 2\left(\frac{1}{3}\right)^{x-4} - 5$. State the domain and range.

SOLUTION

Begin by lightly sketching the graph of $y = 2\left(\frac{1}{3}\right)^{x}$, which

passes through $(0, 2)$ and $\left(1, \frac{2}{3}\right)$. Then, because $h = 4$ and
$k = -5$, translate the graph 4 units to the right and 5 units
down. Notice that the graph passes through $(4, -3)$
and $\left(5, -4\frac{1}{3}\right)$. The graph's asymptote is the line $y = -5$.
The domain is all real numbers and the range is $y > -5$.

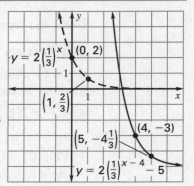

Exercises for Example 3

Graph the function. State the domain and range.

11. $y = 2\left(\frac{1}{2}\right)^{x+3}$

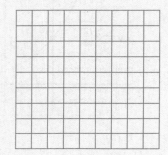

12. $y = -3\left(\frac{2}{3}\right)^{x-4}$

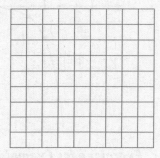

13. $y = -\left(\frac{1}{4}\right)^{x} + 2$

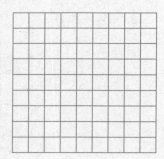

14. $y = 4\left(\frac{1}{2}\right)^{x+4} - 3$

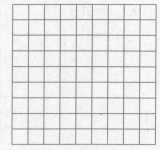

Practice with Examples

For use with pages 480–485

GOAL   **Use the number e as the base of exponential functions**

VOCABULARY

The **natural base** e is irrational. It is defined as follows:

As n approaches $+\infty$, $\left(1 + \dfrac{1}{n}\right)^n$ approaches $e \approx 2.718281828459$.

EXAMPLE 1   *Simplifying Natural Base Expressions*

Simplify the expression.

a. $2e \cdot e^{-4}$ **b.** $\dfrac{6e^{5x}}{2e^{3x}}$ **c.** $(-5e^2)^3$

SOLUTION

a. $2e \cdot e^{-4} = 2e^{1+(-4)}$ **b.** $\dfrac{6e^{5x}}{2e^{3x}} = 3e^{5x-3x}$ **c.** $(-5e^2)^3 = (-5)^3 e^{(2)(3)}$

$= 2e^{-3}$ $= 3e^{2x}$ $= -125e^6$

$= \dfrac{2}{e^3}$

Exercises for Example 1

Simplify the expression.

1. $e^{-2} \cdot e^6$ **2.** $5e^3 \cdot 4e^2$ **3.** $e^{2x} \cdot e^{4x}$

4. $(2e^3)^3$ **5.** $\dfrac{e^5}{e^2}$ **6.** $\dfrac{10e^2}{2e^4}$

Chapter 8

NAME _____ DATE _____

Practice with Examples

For use with pages 480–485

EXAMPLE 2 *Evaluating Natural Base Expressions*

Use a calculator to evaluate the expression (a) $e^{2/3}$ and (b) e^{-2}.

SOLUTION

	Expression	Keystrokes	Display
a.	$e^{2/3}$	2nd $[e^x]$ 2 ÷ 3) ENTER	1.947734041
b.	e^{-2}	2nd $[e^x]$ (-) 2) ENTER	0.1353352832

Exercises for Example 2

Use a calculator to evaluate the expression. Round the result to three decimal places.

7. e^4

8. $e^{1/3}$

9. $e^{1.2}$

10. $2e^{-1/5}$

Chapter 8

NAME _____ DATE _____

Practice with Examples

For use with pages 480–485

EXAMPLE 3 *Graphing Natural Base Functions*

Graph the function. State the domain and range.

a. $y = 3e^{-2x}$ **b.** $y = \frac{1}{2}e^x - 5$

SOLUTION

a. Because $a = 3$ is positive and $r = -2$ is negative, the function is an exponential decay function. Plot points $(0, 3)$ and $(1, 0.41)$ and draw the curve.

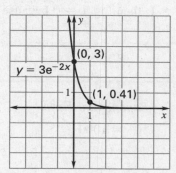

The domain is all real numbers, and the range is $y > 0$.

b. Because $a = \frac{1}{2}$ is positive and $r = 1$ is positive, the function is an exponential growth function. Translate the graph of $y = \frac{1}{2}e^x$ down 5 units.

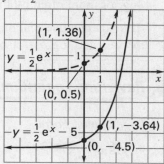

The domain is all real numbers, and the range is $y > -5$.

Exercises for Example 3

Graph the function. State the domain and range.

11. $y = 2e^{-x}$

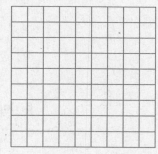

12. $y = e^{x-3}$

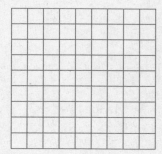

13. $y = 4e^x - 3$

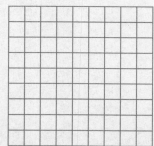

14. $y = e^{-2x} + 1$

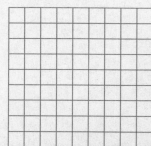

Practice with Examples

For use with pages 486–492

GOAL Evaluate logarithmic functions, and graph logarithmic functions

---

VOCABULARY

Let b and y be positive numbers, $b \neq 1$. The **logarithm of y with base b** is denoted by $\log_b y$ and is defined as follows: $\log_b y = x$ if and only if $b^x = y$. The expression $\log_b y$ is read as "log base b of y."

The logarithm with base 10 is called the **common logarithm,** denoted by $\log_{10}$ or simply by log.

The logarithm with base e is called the **natural logarithm,** denoted by $\log_e$ or more often by ln.

If b is a positive real number such that $b \neq 1$, then $\log_b 1 = 0$ because $b^0 = 1$ and $\log_b b = 1$ because $b^1 = b$.

EXAMPLE 1 *Rewriting Logarithmic Equations*

Logarithmic Form	*Exponential Form*
a. $\log_{10} 1000 = 3$	$10^3 = 1000$
b. $\log_4 1 = 0$	$4^0 = 1$
c. $\log_9 \frac{1}{81} = -2$	$9^{-2} = \frac{1}{81}$

Exercises for Example 1

Rewrite the equation in exponential form.

1. $\log_4 64 = 4$ **2.** $\log_5 125 = 3$ **3.** $\log_7 1 = 0$

4. $\log_2 \frac{1}{8} = -3$ **5.** $\log_8 8 = 1$ **6.** $\log_{1/3} 3 = -1$

NAME _____ DATE _____

Practice with Examples

For use with pages 486–492

EXAMPLE 2 *Evaluating Logarithmic Expressions*

Evaluate the expressions (a) $\log_{27} 3$ and (b) $\log_6 216$.

SOLUTION

To evaluate a logarithm, you are finding an exponent. To help you evaluate $\log_b y$, ask yourself what power of b gives you y.

a. 27 to what power gives 3?

$27^{1/3} = 3$, so $\log_{27} 3 = \frac{1}{3}$.

b. 6 to what power gives 216?

$6^3 = 216$, so $\log_6 216 = 3$.

Exercises for Example 2

Evaluate the expression without using a calculator.

7. $\log_3 243$

8. $\log_2 2$

9. $\log_5 1$

10. $\log_{16} 4$

11. $\log_{1/3} 9$

12. $\log_{1/2} \frac{1}{32}$

EXAMPLE 3 *Using Inverse Properties*

Simplify the expressions (a) $5^{\log_5 4}$ and (b) $\log_2 8^x$.

SOLUTION

a. $5^{\log_5 4} = 4$ Use the inverse property $b^{\log_b x} = x$.

b. $\log_2 8^x = \log_2 (2^3)^x$ Rewrite 8 as a power of the base 2.

$= \log_2 2^{3x}$ Use power rule of exponents.

$= 3x$ Use the inverse property $\log_b b^x = x$.

Exercises for Example 3

Simplify the expression.

13. $4^{\log_4 x}$

14. $8^{\log_8 10}$

15. $\log_6 6^x$

16. $\log_3 81^x$

NAME _____ DATE _____

Practice with Examples

For use with pages 486–492

EXAMPLE 4 *Graphing Logarithmic Functions*

Graph the function. State the domain and range.

a. $y = \log_3 x + 1$

b. $y = \ln (x - 2)$

SOLUTION

a. Because $h = 0$, the vertical line $x = 0$ is an asymptote. Plot the points $(1, 1)$ and $(3, 2)$. Because $b > 1$, from left to right, draw a curve that starts just to the right of the line $x = 0$ and moves up.

b. Because $h = 2$, the vertical line $x = 2$ is an asymptote. Plot the points $(3, 0)$ and $(5, 1.10)$. Because $b > 1$, from left to right, draw a curve that starts just to the right of the line $x = 2$ and moves up.

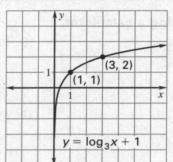

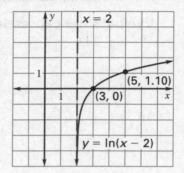

The domain is $x > 0$, and the range is all real numbers.

The domain is $x > 2$, and the range is all real numbers.

Exercises for Example 4

Graph the function. State the domain and range.

17. $y = \log_2 x$

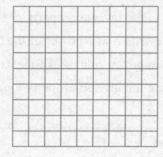

18. $y = \log_{1/2} x$

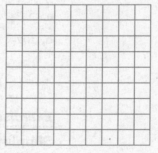

19. $\ln (x + 2)$

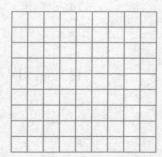

20. $\ln x - 3$

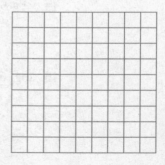

Practice with Examples

For use with pages 493–499

GOAL Use properties of logarithms

VOCABULARY

Properties of Logarithms
Let b, u, and v be positive numbers such that $b \neq 1$.

Product Property $\log_b uv = \log_b u + \log_b v$

Quotient Property $\log_b \dfrac{u}{v} = \log_b u - \log_b v$

Power Property $\log_b u^n = n \log_b u$

Change-of-Base Formula Let u, b, and c be positive numbers with
$b \neq 1$ and $c \neq 1$. Then: $\log_c u = \dfrac{\log_b u}{\log_b c}$.

In particular, $\log_c u = \dfrac{\log u}{\log c}$ and $\log_c u = \dfrac{\ln u}{\ln c}$.

EXAMPLE 1 *Using Properties of Logarithms*

Use $\log_3 2 \approx 0.631$ and $\log_3 5 \approx 1.465$ to approximate the following.

a. $\log_3 \frac{2}{5}$ **b.** $\log_3 10$ **c.** $\log_3 125$

SOLUTION

a. $\log_3 \frac{2}{5} = \log_3 2 - \log_3 5 \approx 0.631 - 1.465 = -0.834$

b. $\log_3 10 = \log_3 (2 \cdot 5) = \log_3 2 + \log_3 5 \approx 0.631 + 1.465 = 2.096$

c. $\log_3 125 = \log_3 5^3 = 3 \log_3 5 \approx 3(1.465) = 4.395$

Exercises for Example 1

Use $\log_6 4 \approx 0.774$ and $\log_6 10 \approx 1.285$ to approximate the value of the expression.

1. $\log_6 40$ **2.** $\log_6 100$

3. $\log_6 \frac{10}{4}$ **4.** $\log_6 64$

NAME _____ DATE _____

Practice with Examples

For use with pages 493–499

EXAMPLE 2 *Expanding a Logarithmic Expression*

Expand $\ln 6x^5$. Assume x is positive.

SOLUTION

$$\ln 6x^5 = \ln 6 + \ln x^5 \qquad \text{Product Property}$$

$$= \ln 6 + 5 \ln x \qquad \text{Power Property}$$

Exercises for Example 2

Expand the expression.

5. $\log 9x$

6. $\log_2 6x^3$

7. $\log_6 \frac{2}{3}$

8. $\log_3 \dfrac{4x}{5}$

9. $\ln 2xy$

10. $\ln \dfrac{2x^2}{y}$

EXAMPLE 3 *Condensing a Logarithmic Expression*

Condense $3 \ln x + \ln 4 - \ln 7x$.

SOLUTION

$$3 \ln x + \ln 4 - \ln 7x = \ln x^3 + \ln 4 - \ln 7x \qquad \text{Power Property}$$

$$= \ln (x^3 \cdot 4) - \ln 7x \qquad \text{Product Property}$$

$$= \ln \frac{4x^3}{7x} \qquad \text{Quotient Property}$$

$$= \ln \frac{4x^2}{7} \qquad \text{Simplify.}$$

NAME _____ DATE _____

Practice with Examples

For use with pages 493–499

Exercises for Example 3

Condense the expression.

11. $\log_4 12 + \log_4 5$ **12.** $\log x - \log y$ **13.** $\ln 3 + \ln 6 - \ln 9$

14. $3 \log_2 3$ **15.** $6 \log_2 x + 3 \log_2 x$ **16.** $\ln 24 - 3 \ln 2$

EXAMPLE 4   *Using the Change-of-Base Formula*

Evaluate the expression $\log_2 9$ using common and natural logarithms.

SOLUTION

Notice that the base of the logarithm is two. Most scientific calculators can only evaluate common logarithms of base ten and natural logarithms of base e. You must use the change-of-base formula.

Using common logarithms: $\log_2 9 = \dfrac{\log 9}{\log 2} \approx \dfrac{0.9542}{0.3010} \approx 3.170$

Using natural logarithms: $\log_2 9 = \dfrac{\ln 9}{\ln 2} \approx \dfrac{2.1972}{0.6931} \approx 3.170$

Notice that you obtain the same result using either common or natural logarithms.

Exercises for Example 4

Use the change-of-base formula to evaluate the expression.

17. $\log_3 30$ **18.** $\log_4 13$

19. $\log_2 17$ **20.** $\log_5 10$

NAME _____ DATE _____

Practice with Examples

For use with pages 501–508

GOAL **Solve exponential equations and logarithmic equations**

VOCABULARY

For $b > 0$ and $b \neq 1$, if $b^x = b^y$, then $x = y$.

For positive numbers b, x, and y where $b \neq 1$, $\log_b x = \log_b y$ if and only if $x = y$.

EXAMPLE 1 *Solving by Equating Exponents*

Solve $9^{x+1} = 27^{x-1}$.

SOLUTION

$9^{x+1} = 27^{x-1}$	Write original equation.
$(3^2)^{x+1} = (3^3)^{x-1}$	Rewrite each power with base 3.
$3^{2x+2} = 3^{3x-3}$	Power of a power property
$2x + 2 = 3x - 3$	Equate exponents
$x = 5$	Solve for x.

The solution is 5.

Exercises for Example 1

Solve the equation.

1. $5^{3x} = 5^{x+8}$　　　　　　　　　　**2.** $10^{2x+3} = 10^{4x-1}$

3. $25^{2x+(1/2)} = 125^x$　　　　　　　　**4.** $16 = 4^{x+1}$

NAME _____   DATE _____

Practice with Examples

EXAMPLE 2 **Taking a Logarithm of Each Side**

Solve $e^{-x} - 6 = 9$.

SOLUTION

Notice that you cannot rewrite each number with the same base. You can solve the equation by taking a logarithm of each side.

$e^{-x} - 6 = 9$	Write original equation.
$e^{-x} = 15$	Add 6 to each side.
$\ln e^{-x} = \ln 15$	Take natural log of each side.
$-x = \ln 15$	$\ln e^x = x$
$x \approx -2.708$	Divide each side by -1 and use a calculator.

The solution is about -2.708.

Exercises for Example 2

Solve the equation.

5. $5^x = 8$

6. $e^{-x} = 5$

7. $2^x + 1 = 5$

8. $10^{2x} - 6 = 146$

9. $9 - 4e^x = 5$

10. $\frac{1}{2}e^{-2x} = 6$

EXAMPLE 3 **Solving a Logarithmic Equation**

Solve $\ln (2x + 3) = \ln (5x - 6)$.

SOLUTION

$\ln (2x + 3) = \ln (5x - 6)$	Write original equation.
$2x + 3 = 5x - 6$	$\log_b x = \log_b y$ implies $x = y$.
$9 = 3x$	Subtract $2x$ and add 6 to each side.
$3 = x$	Divide each side by 3.

The solution is 3.

NAME _____ DATE _____

Practice with Examples

For use with pages 501–508

Exercises for Example 3

Solve the equation.

11. $\log (x + 3) = \log (3x + 1)$

12. $\log_2 (x - 1) = \log_2 (2x + 1)$

13. $\ln (4 - x) = \ln (4x - 11)$

EXAMPLE 4   ## Exponentiating Each Side

Solve $4 \log_3 3x = 20$.

SOLUTION

$4 \log_3 3x = 20$	Write original equation.
$\log_3 3x = 5$	Divide each side by 4.
$3^{\log_3 3x} = 3^5$	Exponentiate each side using base 3.
$3x = 243$	$b^{\log_b x} = x$
$x = 81$	Solve for x.

The solution is 81.

Exercises for Example 4

Solve the equation.

14. $\log_8 (x - 5) = \frac{2}{3}$

15. $3 \log_5 (x + 2) = 6$

16. $4 \ln 2x = 5$

LESSON 8.7

Practice with Examples

For use with pages 509–516

GOAL **Model data with exponential functions and power functions**

EXAMPLE 1 *Writing an Exponential Function*

Write an exponential function $y = ab^x$ whose graph passes through $(2, -36)$ and $(0, -4)$.

SOLUTION

Begin by substituting the coordinates of the two given points to obtain two equations in a and b.

$-36 = ab^2$ Substitute -36 for y and 2 for x.

$-4 = ab^0$ Substitute -4 for y and 0 for x.

Notice that the second equation becomes $-4 = a$ because $b^0 = 1$. Substitute $a = -4$ in the first equation and solve for b:

$-36 = (-4)b^2$ Substitute -4 for a.

$9 = b^2$ Divide each side by -4.

$3 = b$ Take the positive square root.

So, $y = -4 \cdot 3^x$.

Exercises for Example 1

Write an exponential function $y = ab^x$ whose graph passes through the given points.

1. $(0, 7), (1, 14)$

2. $(1, -12), (-1, -3)$

3. $(1, 9), (-1, 1)$

Chapter 8

Practice with Examples

For use with pages 509–516

EXAMPLE 2 *Writing a Power Function*

Write a power function $y = ax^b$ whose graph passes through $(2, 4)$ and $(4, 32)$.

SOLUTION

Begin by substituting the coordinates of the two points to obtain two equations in a and b.

$4 = a \cdot 2^b$ Substitute 4 for y and 2 for x.

$32 = a \cdot 4^b$ Substitute 32 for y and 4 for x.

To solve the system, solve for a in the first equation to get $a = \dfrac{4}{2^b}$, then substitute into the second equation.

$32 = \left(\dfrac{4}{2^b}\right)4^b$

$32 = 4 \cdot 2^b$

$8 = 2^b$

By inspection, $b = 3$, so $a = \dfrac{4}{2^b} = \dfrac{4}{2^3} = \dfrac{4}{8} = 0.5$ and $y = 0.5x^3$.

Practice with Examples

For use with pages 509–516

Exercises for Example 2

Write a power function of the form $y = ax^b$ whose graph passes through the given points.

4. $(2, 1), (6, 9)$

5. $(4, 48), (2, 6)$

6. $(9, 6), (4, 4)$

Chapter 8

Practice with Examples

For use with pages 517–522

GOAL **Evaluate and graph logistic growth functions**

VOCABULARY

Logistic growth functions are written as $y = \dfrac{c}{1 + ae^{-rx}}$, where c, a, and r are positive constants.

The graph of $y = \dfrac{c}{1 + ae^{-rx}}$ has the following characteristics:

- The horizontal lines $y = 0$ and $y = c$ are asymptotes.

- The y-intercept is $\dfrac{c}{1 + a}$.

- The domain is all real numbers, and the range is $0 < y < c$.

- The graph is increasing from left to right. To the left of its point of maximum growth, $\left(\dfrac{\ln a}{r}, \dfrac{c}{2} \right)$, the rate of increase is increasing. To the right of its point of maximum growth, the rate of increase is decreasing.

EXAMPLE 1 *Evaluating a Logistic Growth Function*

Evaluate $f(x) = \dfrac{300}{1 + e^{-2x}}$ for (a) $f(-2)$, (b) $f(0)$, and (c) $f(3)$.

SOLUTION

a. $f(-2) = \dfrac{300}{1 + e^{-2(-2)}} = \dfrac{300}{1 + e^4} \approx 5.4$

b. $f(0) = \dfrac{300}{1 + e^{-2(0)}} = \dfrac{300}{1 + e^0} = \dfrac{300}{1 + 1} = 150$

c. $f(3) = \dfrac{300}{1 + e^{-2(3)}} = \dfrac{300}{1 + e^{-6}} \approx 299.3$

Exercises for Example 1

Evaluate the function $f(x) = \dfrac{5}{1 + e^{-0.3x}}$ for the given value of x.

1. $f(0)$

2. $f(1)$

3. $f(-1)$

NAME _____ DATE _____

Practice with Examples

For use with pages 517–522

4. $f(4)$ **5.** $f(-3)$ **6.** $f(0.6)$

EXAMPLE 2   *Graphing a Logistic Growth Function*

Graph $y = \dfrac{2}{1 + 3e^{-x}}$.

SOLUTION

Begin by sketching the horizontal asymptote, $y = 2$.

Then find the y-intercept at $y = \dfrac{2}{1 + 3} = 0.5$. The point of

maximum growth is $\left(\dfrac{\ln 3}{1}, \dfrac{2}{2}\right) \approx (1.1, 1)$. Plot these points.

Finally, from left to right, draw a curve that starts just above the x-axis, curves up to the point of maximum growth, and then levels off as it approaches the upper horizontal asymptote, $y = 2$.

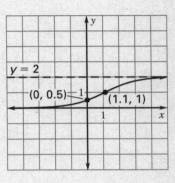

Exercises for Example 2

Graph the function. Identify the asymptotes, *y*-intercept, and point of maximum growth.

7. $y = \dfrac{4}{1 + 3e^{-x}}$ **8.** $y = \dfrac{3}{1 + e^{-0.02x}}$ **9.** $y = \dfrac{2}{1 + 2e^{-3x}}$

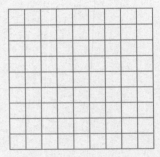 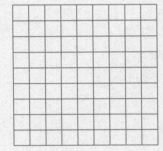 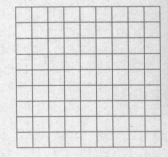

Chapter 8

Practice with Examples

For use with pages 517–522

EXAMPLE 3 *Solving a Logistic Growth Equation*

Solve $\dfrac{12}{1 + 3e^{-2x}} = 10$.

SOLUTION

$\dfrac{12}{1 + 3e^{-2x}} = 10$	Write original equation.
$12 = 10(1 + 3e^{-2x})$	Multiply each side by $1 + 3e^{-2x}$.
$12 = 10 + 30e^{-2x}$	Use distributive property.
$2 = 30e^{-2x}$	Subtract 10 from each side.
$0.067 = e^{-2x}$	Divide each side by 30.
$\ln 0.067 = \ln e^{-2x}$	Take natural log of each side.
$\ln 0.067 = -2x$	$\ln e^x = x$
$-\dfrac{1}{2} \ln 0.067 = x$	Multiply each side by $-\dfrac{1}{2}$.
$1.35 \approx x$	Use a calculator.

The solution is about 1.35.

Exercises for Example 3

Solve the equation.

10. $\dfrac{25}{1 + 2e^{-x}} = 20$

11. $\dfrac{4}{1 + e^{-4x}} = 1$

12. $\dfrac{100}{1 + 5e^{-3x}} = 50$

Practice with Examples

For use with pages 534–539

GOAL **Write and use inverse variation models and joint variation models**

VOCABULARY

Inverse variation is the relationship of two variables x and y if there is a nonzero number k such that $xy = k$, or $y = \dfrac{k}{x}$.

The nonzero constant k is called the **constant of variation.**

Joint variation occurs when a quantity varies directly as the product of two or more other quantities. For instance, if $z = kxy$ where $k \neq 0$, then z varies jointly with x and y.

EXAMPLE 1 *Classifying Direct and Inverse Variation*

Tell whether x and y show *direct variation*, *inverse variation*, or *neither*.

a. $x + y = 12$

b. $\dfrac{5}{y} = x$

c. $x = \dfrac{y}{2}$

SOLUTION

a. Because $x + y = 12$ cannot be rewritten in the form $y = kx$ or $y = \dfrac{k}{x}$, $x + y = 12$ shows neither type of variation.

b. If you cross-multiply in the equation $\dfrac{5}{y} = x$, you obtain $xy = 5$.

When solving for y, the result is $y = \dfrac{5}{x}$, so $\dfrac{5}{y} = x$ shows inverse variation.

c. If you cross-multiply in the equation $x = \dfrac{y}{2}$, you obtain $y = 2x$, so $x = \dfrac{y}{2}$ shows direct variation.

Exercises for Example 1
....

Tell whether *x* and *y* show *direct variation*, *inverse variation*, or *neither*.

1. $xy = 8$

2. $y = x + 5$

3. $y = \dfrac{x}{2}$

4. $x = \dfrac{y}{3}$

Practice with Examples

For use with pages 534–539

EXAMPLE 2 **Writing an Inverse Variation Equation**

The variables x and y vary inversely, and $y = \frac{1}{2}$ when $x = 6$. Write an equation that relates x and y, and find y when $x = -3$.

SOLUTION

Use the general equation for inverse variation to find k, the constant of variation.

$y = \dfrac{k}{x}$ Write general equation for inverse variation.

$\dfrac{1}{2} = \dfrac{k}{6}$ Substitute $\frac{1}{2}$ for y and 6 for x.

$3 = k$ Solve for k.

The inverse variation equation is $y = \dfrac{3}{x}$.

When $x = -3$, the value of y is:

$y = \dfrac{3}{-3} = -1.$

Exercises for Example 2

The variables x and y vary inversely. Use the given values to write an equation relating x and y. Then find y when $x = 4$.

5. $x = 10, y = 2$

6. $x = -3, y = 3$

7. $x = 2, y = 8$

Chapter 9

Practice with Examples

For use with pages 534–539

EXAMPLE 3 *Writing a Joint Variation Model*

The variable z varies jointly with x and the square of y. When $x = 10$ and $y = 9$, $z = 135$. Write an equation relating x, y, and z, then find z when $x = 45$ and $y = 8$.

SOLUTION

$z = kxy^2$	Write an equation for joint variation.
$135 = k(10)(9)^2$	Substitute 135 for z, 10 for x, and 9 for y.
$135 = 810k$	Simplify.
$\frac{1}{6} = k$	Solve for k.

The joint variation equation is $z = \frac{1}{6}xy^2$.

When $x = 45$ and $y = 8$:

$$z = \frac{1}{6}(45)(8)^2 = 480.$$

Exercises for Example 3

The variable z varies jointly with x and y. Use the given values to find an equation that relates the variables. Then find z when $x = 2$ and $y = 8$.

8. $x = 4, y = 3, z = 24$

9. $x = 8, y = -54, z = 144$

10. $x = 1, y = \frac{1}{8}, z = 4$

NAME _____ DATE _____

Practice with Examples

For use with pages 540–545

GOAL Graph simple rational functions and use the graph of a rational function to solve real-life problems

---

VOCABULARY

A **rational function** is a function of the form $f(x) = \dfrac{p(x)}{q(x)}$, where $p(x)$

and $q(x)$ are polynomials and $q(x) \neq 0$.

A **hyperbola** is the graph of a rational function of the form

$f(x) = \dfrac{a}{x - h} + k$, whose center is (h, k), and asymptotes are $x = h$ and

$y = k$. Rational functions of the form $y = \dfrac{ax + b}{cx + d}$ also have graphs that

are hyperbolas. The vertical asymptote occurs at the x-value that makes

the denominator zero, and the horizontal asymptote is the line $y = \dfrac{a}{c}$.

EXAMPLE 1 *Graphing a Rational Function*

Graph $y = \dfrac{3}{x - 4} + 2$. State the domain and range.

SOLUTION

Begin by drawing the asymptotes $x = 4$ and $y = 2$. Then plot two points to the left of the vertical asymptote, such as $(3, -1)$ and $(1, 1)$, and two points to the right, such as $(5, 5)$ and $\left(6, \frac{7}{2}\right)$. Finally, use the asymptotes and plotted points to draw the branches of the hyperbola.

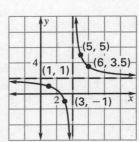

The domain is the set of real numbers except 4, because $x = 4$ will make the denominator zero. The range is the set of real numbers except $y = 2$, because that is where the horizontal asymptote occurs.

NAME _____ DATE _____

Practice with Examples

For use with pages 540–545

Exercises for Example 1

Graph the function. State the domain and range.

1. $y = \dfrac{-2}{x}$

2. $y = \dfrac{3}{x} + 5$

3. $y = \dfrac{2}{x-3} + 1$

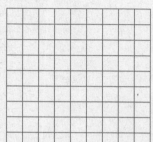

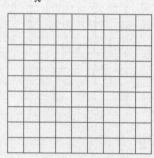

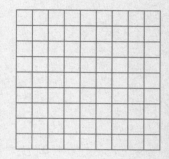

4. $y = \dfrac{1}{x+5} - 2$

5. $y = \dfrac{-3}{x+2} - 1$

6. $y = \dfrac{2}{x-1} - 4$

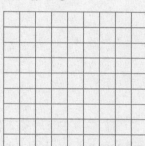

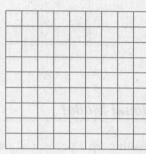

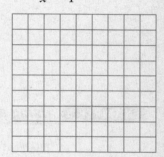

EXAMPLE 2 **Graphing a Rational Function**

Graph $y = \dfrac{x-1}{x-3}$. State the domain and range.

SOLUTION

Begin by drawing the asymptotes. The vertical asymptote occurs at the x-value that makes the denominator zero, $x = 3$. The horizontal asymptote is the line $y = \dfrac{a}{c} = \dfrac{1}{1} = 1$.

Then plot two points to the left of the vertical asymptote, such as $\left(0, \frac{1}{3}\right)$ and $(1, 0)$, and two points to the right, such as $(4, 3)$ and $(5, 2)$. Finally use the asymptotes and plotted points to draw the branches of the hyperbola. The domain is all real numbers except 3, because $x = 3$ makes the denominator zero. The range is all real numbers except 1, because $y = 1$ is a horizontal asymptote.

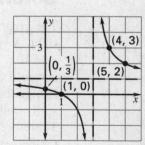

Practice with Examples

For use with pages 540–545

Exercises for Example 2

Graph the function. State the domain and range.

7. $y = \dfrac{x}{x + 2}$

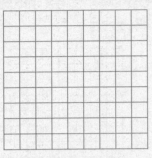

8. $y = \dfrac{2x}{x - 4}$

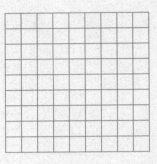

9. $y = \dfrac{x + 2}{x + 3}$

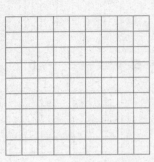

10. $y = \dfrac{x - 1}{2x - 3}$

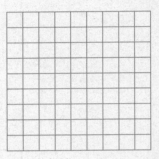

EXAMPLE 3 *Using a Rational Model*

The cost of cleaning up x percent of an oil spill that has washed ashore

can be modeled by $c = \dfrac{20x}{101 - x}$, where c is the cost in thousands of

dollars. Use a graph to approximate the cost to clean up 100% of the oil
spill. Describe what happens to the cost as the percent cleanup increases.

SOLUTION

The graph of the model is shown at the
right. A vertical asymptote occurs at
$x = 101$. To clean up 100% of the oil spill
it would cost approximately \$2,000,000.
Notice that the cleanup of 50% of the oil
spill would cost only about \$20,000.
Therefore, the cost increases drastically as
the percent cleanup approaches 100%.

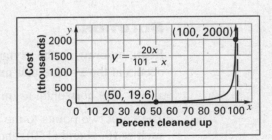

Exercise for Example 3

11. The average cost c of producing x units can be modeled by

$$c = \frac{300,000 + 2x}{x}.$$

Use a graph to approximate the average cost of producing
10,000 units.

NAME _____ DATE _____

Practice with Examples

For use with pages 547–553

GOAL **Graph general rational functions**

EXAMPLE 1 <u>**Graphing a Rational Function (*m* < *n*)**</u>

Graph $y = \dfrac{x}{x^2 - 4}$.

SOLUTION

Begin by finding the x-intercepts of the graph, which are the real zeros of the numerator. The numerator has 0 as its only zero, so the graph has one x-intercept at $(0, 0)$. Then find the vertical asymptotes of the graph, which are the real zeros of the denominator. The denominator contains a difference of two squares that can be factored as $(x - 2)(x + 2)$, so the denominator has zeros 2 and -2, and the graph has vertical asymptotes $x = 2$ and $x = -2$.

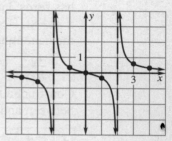

Finally, determine if the graph has a horizontal asymptote. Because the degree of the numerator (1) is less than the degree of the denominator (2), the line $y = 0$ is a horizontal asymptote. Construct a table of values consisting of x-values between and beyond the vertical asymptotes.

x	-4	-3	-1	0	1	3	4
y	$-\frac{1}{3}$	$-\frac{3}{5}$	$\frac{1}{3}$	0	$-\frac{1}{3}$	$\frac{3}{5}$	$\frac{1}{3}$

Plot the points and use the asymptotes to draw the graph.

Exercises for Example 1

Graph the function.

1. $y = \dfrac{2}{x + 1}$

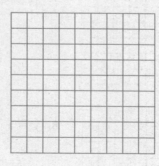

2. $y = \dfrac{x}{x^2 - 1}$

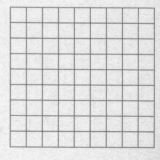

3. $y = \dfrac{-3}{x - 2}$

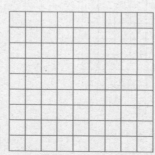

4. $y = \dfrac{2x}{x^2 + 4}$

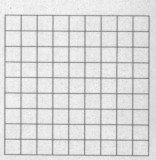

NAME _____ DATE _____

Practice with Examples

For use with pages 547–553

EXAMPLE 2 *Graphing a Rational Function $(m = n)$*

Graph $y = \dfrac{x^2 + 2}{x^2 - x - 6}$.

SOLUTION

The numerator has no zeros, so there are no x-intercepts. The denominator can be factored as $(x - 3)(x + 2)$, so the denominator has zeros 3 and -2 and the graph has vertical asymptotes $x = 3$ and $x = -2$. Because the degree of the numerator (2) equals the degree of the denominator (2), the line

$y = \dfrac{a_m}{b_n} = \dfrac{1}{1} = 1$ is a horizontal asymptote.

Construct a table of values consisting of x-values between and beyond the vertical asymptotes.

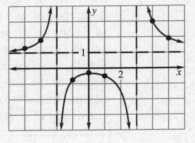

x	-4	-3	-1	0	1	4	5
y	1.3	1.8	-0.75	-0.3	-0.5	3	1.9

Plot the points and use the asymptotes to draw the graph.

Exercises for Example 2

Graph the function.

5. $y = \dfrac{x + 1}{x - 3}$

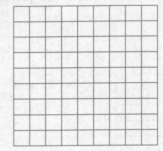

6. $y = \dfrac{2x + 3}{x + 2}$

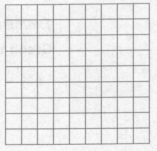

7. $y = \dfrac{3x^2}{x^2 + 9}$

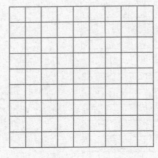

8. $y = \dfrac{2x^2}{x^2 - 1}$

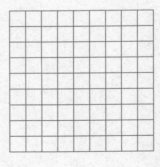

Chapter 9

Practice with Examples

For use with pages 547–553

EXAMPLE 3 *Graphing a Rational Function* $(m > n)$

Graph $y = \dfrac{x^3}{x^2 - 4}$.

SOLUTION

The numerator has 0 as its only zero, so the x-intercept of
the graph is $(0, 0)$. The denominator can be factored as
$(x + 2)(x - 2)$, so the graph has vertical asymptotes
$x = 2$ and $x = -2$. The degree of the numerator (3) is
greater than the degree of the denominator (2), so there is
no horizontal asymptote. But, the end behavior of the
graph is the same as the end behavior of the graph of
$y = x^{3-2} = x$. So, the graph falls to the left and rises
to the right. Construct a table of values consisting of
x-values beyond the vertical asymptote.

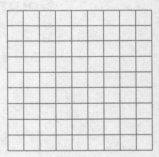

x	-4	-3	-1	1	3	4
y	-5.3	-5.4	0.3	-0.3	5.4	5.3

Plot the points, use the asymptotes, and consider the end behavior to
draw the graph.

Exercises for Example 3

Graph the function.

9. $y = \dfrac{-x^2}{x + 1}$

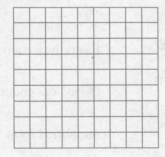

10. $y = \dfrac{x^2 + 1}{x - 2}$

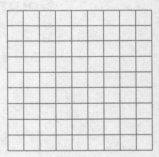

11. $y = \dfrac{x^2 + 3x - 18}{x}$

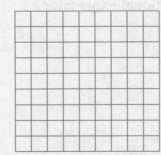

12. $y = \dfrac{x^2 - 9}{2x}$

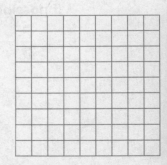

NAME _____ DATE _____

Practice with Examples

For use with pages 554–560

GOAL **Multiply and divide rational expressions**

VOCABULARY

A rational expression is in **simplified form** provided its numerator and denominator have no common factors, other than ± 1.

Simplifying Rational Expressions

Let a, b, and c be nonzero real numbers or variable expressions. Then the following property applies:

$$\frac{a\cancel{c}}{b\cancel{c}} = \frac{a}{b} \qquad \text{Divide out common factor } c.$$

To divide one rational expression by another, multiply the first expression by the reciprocal of the second expression.

$$\frac{a}{b} \div \frac{c}{d} = \frac{a}{b} \cdot \frac{d}{c} = \frac{ad}{bc} \longleftarrow \text{Simplify } \frac{ad}{bc} \text{ if possible.}$$

EXAMPLE 1 *Simplifying a Rational Expression*

Simplify $\dfrac{x^2 + 5x + 6}{x^3 + 3x^2}$.

SOLUTION

$$\frac{x^2 + 5x + 6}{x^3 + 3x^2} = \frac{(x + 2)(x + 3)}{x^2(x + 3)} \qquad \text{Factor numerator and denominator.}$$

$$= \frac{(x + 2)\cancel{(x + 3)}}{x^2\cancel{(x + 3)}} \qquad \text{Divide out common factor.}$$

$$= \frac{x + 2}{x^2} \qquad \text{Simplified form}$$

Exercises for Example 1

If possible, simplify the rational expression.

1. $\dfrac{y^2 - 81}{2y - 18}$

2. $\dfrac{2x - 3}{4x - 6}$

3. $\dfrac{x + 3}{x^2 + 6x + 9}$

4. $\dfrac{y^2 - 7y}{y^2 - 8y + 7}$

NAME _____ DATE _____

Practice with Examples

For use with pages 554–560

EXAMPLE 2 *Multiplying Rational Expressions Involving Polynomials*

Multiply: $\dfrac{x^2 - 2x}{x^2 + 2x + 1} \cdot \dfrac{x^2 + 4x + 3}{x^2 + 3x}$

SOLUTION

$\dfrac{x^2 - 2x}{x^2 + 2x + 1} \cdot \dfrac{x^2 + 4x + 3}{x^2 + 3x} = \dfrac{x(x - 2)}{(x + 1)(x + 1)} \cdot \dfrac{(x + 3)(x + 1)}{x(x + 3)}$ Factor numerators and denominators.

$= \dfrac{\cancel{x}(x - 2)\cancel{(x + 3)}\cancel{(x + 1)}}{\cancel{x}(x + 1)\cancel{(x + 1)}\cancel{(x + 3)}}$ Multiply and divide out common factors.

$= \dfrac{x - 2}{x + 1}$ Simplified form

Exercises for Example 2
....

Multiply the rational expressions. Simplify the result.

5. $\dfrac{x^2 + 2x - 3}{x + 2} \cdot \dfrac{x^2 + 2x}{x^2 - 1}$

6. $\dfrac{5x - 20}{5x + 15} \cdot \dfrac{2x + 6}{x - 4}$

7. $\dfrac{12 - x}{3} \cdot \dfrac{3}{x - 12}$

Algebra 2
Practice Workbook with Examples

185

NAME _____ DATE _____

Practice with Examples

For use with pages 554–560

EXAMPLE 3 *Dividing Rational Expressions*

Divide: $\dfrac{2x^3 - 12x^2}{x^2 - 4x - 12} \div \dfrac{8x^3 + 24x^2}{x^2 + 9x + 18}$

SOLUTION

$$\dfrac{2x^3 - 12x^2}{x^2 - 4x - 12} \div \dfrac{8x^3 + 24x^2}{x^2 + 9x + 18} = \dfrac{2x^3 - 12x^2}{x^2 - 4x - 12} \cdot \dfrac{x^2 + 9x + 18}{8x^3 + 24x^2}$$ Multiply by reciprocal.

$$= \dfrac{2x^2(x - 6)}{(x + 2)(x - 6)} \cdot \dfrac{(x + 6)(x + 3)}{8x^2(x + 3)}$$ Factor.

$$= \dfrac{2x^2(x - 6)(x + 6)(x + 3)}{2 \cdot 4x^2(x + 2)(x - 6)(x + 3)}$$ Multiply and divide out common factors.

$$= \dfrac{x + 6}{4(x + 2)}$$ Simplified form

Exercises for Example 3

Divide the rational expressions. Simplify the result.

8. $\dfrac{48x^2}{y} \div \dfrac{36xy^2}{5}$

9. $\dfrac{x^2}{x^2 - 1} \div \dfrac{3x}{x + 1}$

Practice with Examples

For use with pages 562–567

GOAL **Add and subtract rational expressions and simplify complex fractions**

> **VOCABULARY**
>
> A **complex fraction** is a fraction that contains a fraction in its numerator or denominator.

EXAMPLE 1 *Adding with Unlike Denominators*

Add: $\dfrac{5}{2x} + \dfrac{2}{3x^2}$.

SOLUTION

Begin by finding the least common denominator of $\dfrac{5}{2x}$ and $\dfrac{2}{3x^2}$. Notice that the denominators are already written as factors, and the LCD is $6x^2$.

$$\frac{5}{2x} + \frac{2}{3x^2} = \frac{5(3x)}{2x(3x)} + \frac{2(2)}{3x^2(2)} \qquad \text{Rewrite fractions with LCD.}$$

$$= \frac{15x}{6x^2} + \frac{4}{6x^2} = \frac{15x + 4}{6x^2} \qquad \text{Simplify and add numerators.}$$

Exercises for Example 1

Perform the indicated operation and simplify.

1. $\dfrac{1}{2} + \dfrac{3}{x^2}$

2. $\dfrac{3}{2x} + \dfrac{x}{2x^2 + 6x}$

3. $\dfrac{3}{x + 5} + \dfrac{4}{x + 1}$

4. $\dfrac{x}{x - 1} + \dfrac{3x}{x^2 - 1}$

Chapter 9

Algebra 2
Practice Workbook with Examples

187

NAME _____ DATE _____

Practice with Examples

For use with pages 562–567

EXAMPLE 2 *Subtracting with Unlike Denominators*

Subtract: $\dfrac{3x + 1}{x^2 - x - 12} - \dfrac{5}{3x - 12}$.

SOLUTION

$\dfrac{3x + 1}{x^2 - x - 12} - \dfrac{5}{3x - 12} = \dfrac{3x + 1}{(x - 4)(x + 3)} - \dfrac{5}{3(x - 4)}$ Factor denominators.

$= \dfrac{(3x + 1)(3)}{(x - 4)(x + 3)(3)} - \dfrac{5(x + 3)}{3(x - 4)(x + 3)}$ Rewrite fractions with LCD.

$= \dfrac{9x + 3 - 5(x + 3)}{3(x - 4)(x + 3)}$ Subtract numerators.

$= \dfrac{9x + 3 - 5x - 15}{3(x - 4)(x + 3)}$ Distribute.

$= \dfrac{4x - 12}{3(x - 4)(x + 3)}$ Simplify.

Exercises for Example 2

Perform the indicated operation and simplify.

5. $\dfrac{2x}{x + 2} - \dfrac{8}{x^2 + 2x}$

6. $\dfrac{5x}{x^2 - 4} - \dfrac{7}{x - 2}$

7. $\dfrac{3x + 1}{x^2} - \dfrac{x - 2}{x^3}$

8. $\dfrac{x}{x + 3} - \dfrac{6}{x + 2}$

Practice with Examples

For use with pages 562–567

EXAMPLE 3 *Simplifying a Complex Fraction*

Simplify: $\dfrac{\dfrac{6}{x-1}-3}{\dfrac{3}{x}}$.

SOLUTION

$$\dfrac{\dfrac{6}{x-1}-3}{\dfrac{3}{x}} = \dfrac{\dfrac{6}{x-1}-\dfrac{3(x-1)}{x-1}}{\dfrac{3}{x}} \qquad \text{Rewrite fractions in numerator with LCD.}$$

$$= \dfrac{\dfrac{3(3-x)}{x-1}}{\dfrac{3}{x}} \qquad \text{Subtract fractions in numerator.}$$

$$= \dfrac{3(3-x)}{x-1} \cdot \dfrac{x}{3} \qquad \text{Multiply by reciprocal.}$$

$$= \dfrac{\cancel{3}(3-x)}{x-1} \cdot \dfrac{x}{\cancel{3}} \qquad \text{Divide out common factor.}$$

$$= \dfrac{x(3-x)}{x-1} \qquad \text{Write in simplified form.}$$

Exercises for Example 3

Simplify the complex fraction.

9. $\dfrac{\dfrac{x^2}{x^2-1}}{\dfrac{3x}{x+1}}$

10. $\dfrac{2-\dfrac{1}{x}}{x}$

11. $\dfrac{1+\dfrac{1}{x}}{1-\dfrac{1}{x}}$

Copyright © McDougal Littell Inc.
All rights reserved.

Algebra 2
Practice Workbook with Examples

189

Chapter 9

NAME _____ DATE _____

Practice with Examples

For use with pages 568–574

GOAL Solve rational equations

> ### VOCABULARY
>
> To solve a rational equation, multiply each term on both sides of the equation by the LCD of the terms. Simplify and solve the resulting polynomial equation.
>
> To solve a rational equation for which each side of the equation is a single rational expression, use **cross multiplying.**

EXAMPLE 1 *An Equation with One Solution*

Solve: $\dfrac{7}{x} - \dfrac{1}{3x} = \dfrac{5}{3}$.

SOLUTION

The least common denominator is $3x$.

$$\frac{7}{x} - \frac{1}{3x} = \frac{5}{3} \qquad \text{Write original equation.}$$

$$3x\left(\frac{7}{x} - \frac{1}{3x}\right) = 3x\left(\frac{5}{3}\right) \qquad \text{Multiply each side by the LCD, } 3x.$$

$$21 - 1 = 5x \qquad \text{Simplify.}$$

$$20 = 5x \qquad \text{Subtract.}$$

$$4 = x \qquad \text{Divide each side by 5.}$$

The solution is 4. Check this in the original equation.

Exercises for Example 1

Solve the equation by using the LCD. Check each solution.

1. $\dfrac{3}{x} - \dfrac{2}{x+1} = \dfrac{4}{x}$

2. $\dfrac{2x}{x+3} - 5 = \dfrac{1}{x+3}$

3. $\dfrac{4}{x} - \dfrac{1}{x+2} = \dfrac{2}{x}$

Practice with Examples

For use with pages 568–574

EXAMPLE 2 *An Equation with Two Solutions*

Solve: $\dfrac{5x}{x-1} - 2 = \dfrac{14}{x^2 - 1}$.

SOLUTION

Begin by writing each denominator in factored form.
The LCD is $(x + 1)(x - 1)$.

$$\frac{5x}{x-1} - 2 = \frac{14}{(x+1)(x-1)}$$

$$(x+1)(x-1) \cdot \frac{5x}{x-1} - (x+1)(x-1) \cdot 2$$

$$= (x+1)(x-1) \cdot \frac{14}{(x+1)(x-1)} \qquad \text{Multiply each term by LCD.}$$

$$5x(x+1) - 2(x+1)(x-1) = 14 \qquad \text{Simplify.}$$

$$5x^2 + 5x - 2x^2 + 2 = 14 \qquad \text{Distribute and use FOIL.}$$

$$3x^2 + 5x + 2 = 14 \qquad \text{Combine like terms.}$$

$$3x^2 + 5x - 12 = 0 \qquad \text{Write in standard form.}$$

$$(3x - 4)(x + 3) = 0 \qquad \text{Factor.}$$

$$3x - 4 = 0 \text{ or } x + 3 = 0 \qquad \text{Use zero product property.}$$

$$x = \frac{4}{3} \qquad x = -3$$

The solutions are $\frac{4}{3}$ and -3. Check these in the original equation.

Practice with Examples

For use with pages 568–574

Exercises for Example 2

Solve the equation by using the LCD. Check each solution.

4. $\dfrac{5x}{x-1} - 3 = \dfrac{2x+5}{x^2-1}$

5. $\dfrac{2x}{x-2} - \dfrac{4x-1}{3x+2} = \dfrac{17x+4}{3x^2-4x-4}$

6. $x - \dfrac{24}{x} = 5$

NAME _____ DATE _____

Practice with Examples

For use with pages 589–594

GOAL Find the distance between two points and find the midpoint of the line segment joining two points

---

VOCABULARY

The Distance Formula

The distance d between the points (x_1, y_1) and (x_2, y_2) is as follows:

$$d = \sqrt{(x_2 - x_1)^2 + (y_2 - y_1)^2}$$

The Midpoint Formula

The midpoint of the line segment joining $A(x_1, y_1)$ and $B(x_2, y_2)$ is as follows:

$$M\left(\frac{x_1 + x_2}{2}, \frac{y_1 + y_2}{2}\right)$$

Each coordinate of M is the mean of the corresponding coordinates of A and B.

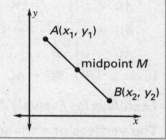

EXAMPLE 1 *Finding the Distance Between Two Points*

Find the distance between $(4, -3)$ and $(6, 2)$.

SOLUTION

Let $(x_1, y_1) = (4, -3)$ and $(x_2, y_2) = (6, 2)$.

$$
\begin{aligned}
d &= \sqrt{(x_2 - x_1)^2 + (y_2 - y_1)^2} && \text{Use distance formula.}\\
&= \sqrt{(6 - 4)^2 + (2 - (-3))^2} && \text{Substitute.}\\
&= \sqrt{2^2 + 5^2} && \text{Simplify.}\\
&= \sqrt{4 + 25} && \text{Simplify.}\\
&= \sqrt{29} \approx 5.39 && \text{Use a calculator.}
\end{aligned}
$$

Exercises for Example 1
....

Find the distance between the two points.

1. $(1, 7), (5, 4)$ **2.** $(-5, 0), (-2, 2)$

3. $(-4, 7), (0, -1)$ **4.** $(-2, -5), (4, 6)$

NAME _____ DATE _____

Practice with Examples

For use with pages 589–594

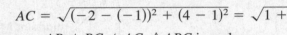

EXAMPLE 2 *Classifying a Triangle Using the Distance Formula*

Classify $\triangle ABC$ as *scalene*, *isosceles*, or *equilateral*.

SOLUTION

Begin by finding the lengths of the three sides using the
distance formula. Recall from geometry that a scalene triangle
has no equal sides, an isosceles triangle has two equal sides,
and an equilateral triangle has three equal sides.

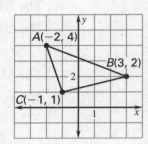

$$AB = \sqrt{(3 - (-2))^2 + (2 - 4)^2} = \sqrt{25 + 4} = \sqrt{29}$$

$$BC = \sqrt{(-1 - 3)^2 + (1 - 2)^2} = \sqrt{16 + 1} = \sqrt{17}$$

$$AC = \sqrt{(-2 - (-1))^2 + (4 - 1)^2} = \sqrt{1 + 9} = \sqrt{10}$$

Because $AB \neq BC \neq AC$, $\triangle ABC$ is scalene.

Exercises for Example 2

**The vertices of a triangle are given. Classify the triangle as
scalene, isosceles, or equilateral.**

5. $(4, 2), (0, 5), (7, -2)$

6. $(1, 2), (3, 3), (4, 0)$

7. $(1, 2), (4, 2), (1, 5)$

Algebra 2
Practice Workbook with Examples

Practice with Examples

For use with pages 589–594

EXAMPLE 3 *Finding the Midpoint of a Segment*

Find the midpoint of the line segment joining $(-2, 3)$ and $(4, 1)$.

SOLUTION

Let $(x_1, y_1) = (-2, 3)$ and $(x_2, y_2) = (4, 1)$.

$$\text{midpoint} = \left(\frac{x_1 + x_2}{2}, \frac{y_1 + y_2}{2} \right) \qquad \text{Use midpoint formula.}$$

$$= \left(\frac{-2 + 4}{2}, \frac{3 + 1}{2} \right) \qquad \text{Substitute.}$$

$$= (1, 2) \qquad \text{Simplify.}$$

Exercises for Example 3

Find the midpoint of the line segment joining the two points.

8. $(1, 7), (5, 5)$ **9.** $(-5, 0), (-1, 2)$

10. $(-4, 7), (0, -1)$ **11.** $(-2, -5), (4, 6)$

NAME _____   DATE _____

Practice with Examples

For use with pages 595–600

GOAL **Graph and write equations of parabolas and use parabolas to solve real-life problems**

VOCABULARY

Every parabola has the property that any point on it is equidistant from a point called the **focus** (which lies on the axis of symmetry) and a line called the **directrix** (which is perpendicular to the axis of symmetry).

Standard Equation of a Parabola (Vertex at Origin)

The standard form of the equation of a parabola with vertex at $(0, 0)$ is as follows.

Equation	Focus	Directrix	Axis of Symmetry
$x^2 = 4py$	$(0, p)$	$y = -p$	Vertical $(x = 0)$
$y^2 = 4px$	$(p, 0)$	$x = -p$	Horizontal $(y = 0)$

EXAMPLE 1 *Graphing an Equation of a Parabola*

Identify the focus and directrix of the parabola given by $x^2 = 12y$.
Graph the parabola.

SOLUTION

Because the variable x is squared, the axis of symmetry is the vertical line $x = 0$. Since the equation is written in standard form, $4p = 12$ and $p = 3$. The focus is $(0, p) = (0, 3)$ and the directrix is $y = -p = -3$. Because $p > 0$, the parabola opens up. To draw the parabola, construct a table of values and plot the points.

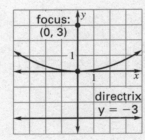

x	-2	-1	0	1	2
y	0.33	0.08	0	0.08	0.33

NAME _____ DATE _____

Practice with Examples

For use with pages 595–600

Exercises for Example 1

Graph the equation. Identify the focus and directrix of the parabola.

1. $x^2 = 2y$

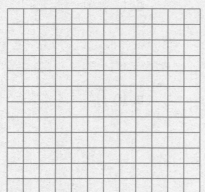

2. $y^2 = 16x$

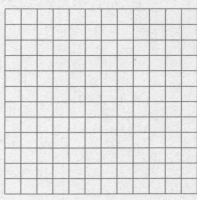

3. $x^2 = -\dfrac{1}{4}y$

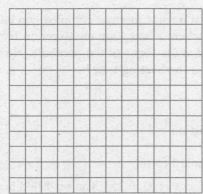

4. $y^2 = -4x$

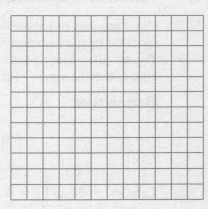

EXAMPLE 2 *Writing an Equation of a Parabola*

Write an equation of the parabola with vertex $(0, 0)$ and focus $(4, 0)$.

SOLUTION

Because the focus is $(4, 0)$ you know that $p = 4$ and the parabola has a horizontal axis of symmetry.

$y^2 = 4px$ Standard form, horizontal axis of symmetry

$y^2 = 4(4)x$ Substitute 4 for p.

$y^2 = 16x$ Simplify.

Algebra 2
Practice Workbook with Examples

NAME _____ DATE _____

Practice with Examples

For use with pages 595–600

Exercises for Example 2

Write the standard form of the equation of the parabola with the given focus and vertex at (0, 0).

5. $(0, 1)$

6. $\left(-\frac{1}{2}, 0\right)$

7. $(-2, 0)$

8. $\left(0, \frac{1}{4}\right)$

EXAMPLE 3 *Modeling a Parabolic Reflector*

Cross sections of parabolic mirrors at a solar-thermal complex can be modeled by the equation $\frac{1}{25}x^2 = y$, where x and y are measured in feet. The oil-filled heating tube is located at the focus of the parabola. How high above the vertex of the mirror is the heating tube?

SOLUTION

$$\frac{1}{25}x^2 = y \qquad \text{Original equation}$$

$$x^2 = 25y \qquad \text{Write in standard form.}$$

Thus, $4p = 25$ and $p = 6.25$. The focus is $(0, 6.25)$. The oil-filled heating tube is located 6.25 feet above the vertex of the mirror.

Exercises for Example 3

9. A searchlight reflector is designed so that a cross section through its axis is a parabola and the light source is at the focus. Find the focus if the reflector is 3 feet across at the opening and 1 foot deep.

10. One of the largest radio telescopes has a diameter of 250 feet and a focal length of 50 feet. If the cross section of the radio telescope is a parabola, find the depth.

NAME _____ DATE _____

Practice with Examples

For use with pages 601–607

GOAL **Graph and write equations of circles**

> ### VOCABULARY
>
> A **circle** is the set of all points (x, y) that are equidistant from a fixed point, called the **center** of the circle.
>
> The distance r between the center and any point (x, y) on the circle is the **radius.**
>
> The **standard form of the equation of a circle** with center at $(0, 0)$ and radius r is as follows:
>
> $$x^2 + y^2 = r^2$$

EXAMPLE 1 *Graphing an Equation of a Circle*

Draw the circle given by $x^2 + y^2 = 5$.

SOLUTION

The equation is already written in standard form. In this form, you can see that the graph is a circle whose center is the origin and whose radius is $r = \sqrt{5} \approx 2.2$.

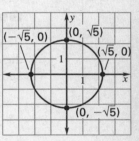

Plot several points that are $\sqrt{5}$ units from the origin, such as $(0, \sqrt{5})$, $(\sqrt{5}, 0)$, $(0, -\sqrt{5})$, and $(-\sqrt{5}, 0)$.

Draw a circle that passes through the four points.

Exercises for Example 1

Graph the equation. Give the radius of the circle.

1. $x^2 + y^2 = 4$

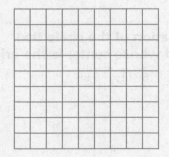

2. $x^2 + y^2 = 100$

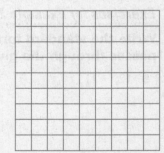

NAME _____ DATE _____

Practice with Examples

For use with pages 601–607

3. $x^2 + y^2 = 36$

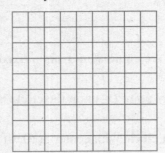

4. $x^2 + y^2 = 12$

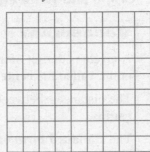

EXAMPLE 2 *Writing an Equation of a Circle*

Write the standard form of the equation of the circle that passes through
the point $(-3, 4)$ and whose center is the origin.

SOLUTION

Begin by finding the radius of the circle. Because the point $(-3, 4)$ is on
the circle, the radius of the circle must be the distance between the center
and the point $(-3, 4)$.

$r = \sqrt{(-3 - 0)^2 + (4 - 0)^2}$ Use the distance formula.

$ = \sqrt{9 + 16}$ Simplify.

$ = \sqrt{25} = 5$

Then use the radius and the standard form to find an equation of the circle.

$x^2 + y^2 = r^2$ Standard form

$x^2 + y^2 = 5^2$ Substitute 5 for r.

$x^2 + y^2 = 25$ Simplify.

Exercises for Example 2

**Write the standard form of the equation of the circle that
passes through the given point and whose center is the origin.**

5. $(2, -1)$

6. $(1, -9)$

7. $(2, 3)$

8. $(-1, -4)$

Practice with Examples

For use with pages 601–607

EXAMPLE 3 *Finding a Tangent Line*

Write an equation of the line that is tangent to the circle $x^2 + y^2 = 10$ at $(-1, 3)$.

SOLUTION

Recall the theorem in geometry that states that a line tangent to a circle is perpendicular to the circle's radius at the point of tangency. To find the equation of this tangent line, you must begin by finding the slope of the radius through the point $(-1, 3)$.

$$m = \frac{y_2 - y_1}{x_2 - x_1} = \frac{3 - 0}{-1 - 0} = -3$$

Because the tangent line at $(-1, 3)$ is perpendicular to the radius, its

slope must be the negative reciprocal of -3, or $\frac{1}{3}$.

$$y - y_1 = m(x - x_1) \qquad \text{Point-slope form}$$

$$y - 3 = \frac{1}{3}(x + 1) \qquad \text{Substitute.}$$

$$y = \frac{1}{3}x + \frac{10}{3} \qquad \text{Simplify.}$$

The equation of the tangent line is $y = \frac{1}{3}x + \frac{10}{3}$.

Exercises for Example 3

Write an equation of the line that is tangent to the given circle at the given point.

9. $x^2 + y^2 = 25$; $(3, -4)$

10. $x^2 + y^2 = 2$; $(1, -1)$

11. $x^2 + y^2 = 8$; $(-2, -2)$

12. $x^2 + y^2 = 20$; $(4, 2)$

NAME _____ DATE _____

Practice with Examples

For use with pages 609–614

GOAL   **Graph and write equations of ellipses**

VOCABULARY

An **ellipse** is the set of all points P such that the sum of the distances between P and two distinct fixed points, called the **foci**, is a constant.

The line through the foci intersects the ellipse at two points, the **vertices.**

The line segment joining the vertices is the **major axis,** and its midpoint is the **center** of the ellipse.

The line perpendicular to the major axis at the center intersects the ellipse at two points called the **co-vertices.**

The line segment joining the co-vertices is the **minor axis.**

The **standard form of the equation of the ellipse** with center at $(0, 0)$ and major and minor axes of lengths $2a$ and $2b$, where $a > b > 0$, is as follows.

Equation	Major Axis	Vertices	Co-Vertices
$\dfrac{x^2}{a^2} + \dfrac{y^2}{b^2} = 1$	Horizontal	$(\pm a, 0)$	$(0, \pm b)$
$\dfrac{x^2}{b^2} + \dfrac{y^2}{a^2} = 1$	Vertical	$(0, \pm a)$	$(\pm b, 0)$

The foci of the ellipse lie on the major axis, c units from the center where $c^2 = a^2 - b^2$.

EXAMPLE 1   *Graphing an Equation of an Ellipse*

Draw the ellipse given by $\dfrac{x^2}{4} + \dfrac{y^2}{25} = 1$. Identify the foci.

SOLUTION

Because the denominator of the y^2-term is greater than that of the x^2-term, the major axis is vertical. So, $a = 5$ and $b = 2$. Plot the vertices $(0, 5)$ and $(0, -5)$, and the co-vertices $(2, 0)$ and $(-2, 0)$. Then draw the ellipse that passes through these four points. The foci are at $(0, c)$ and $(0, -c)$. To find c, use the equation $c^2 = a^2 - b^2$.

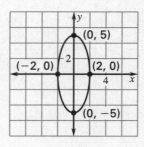

$$c^2 = 5^2 - 2^2 = 25 - 4 = 21$$

$$c = \sqrt{21}$$

The foci are at $\left(0, \sqrt{21}\right)$ and $\left(0, -\sqrt{21}\right)$.

Algebra 2
Practice Workbook with Examples

NAME _____ DATE _____

Practice with Examples

For use with pages 609–614

Exercises for Example 1

Graph the equation. Then identify the vertices, co-vertices, and foci of the ellipse.

1. $\dfrac{x^2}{4} + \dfrac{y^2}{9} = 1$

2. $\dfrac{x^2}{9} + \dfrac{y^2}{1} = 1$

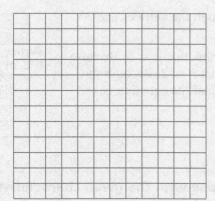

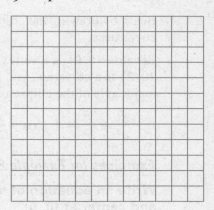

3. $\dfrac{x^2}{9} + \dfrac{y^2}{36} = 1$

4. $\dfrac{x^2}{49} + \dfrac{y^2}{16} = 1$

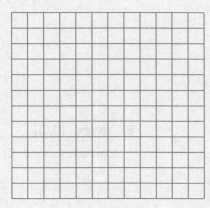

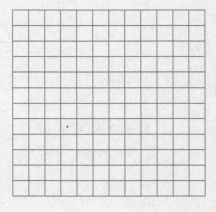

NAME _____ DATE _____

Practice with Examples

EXAMPLE 2 *Writing an Equation of an Ellipse*

Write an equation of the ellipse whose center is at the origin and that has a vertex at $(5, 0)$ and a co-vertex at $(0, 2)$.

SOLUTION

Begin by drawing the ellipse through the vertices and co-vertices.

Because $(5, 0)$ is a vertex, you know that $a = 5$. Because $(0, 2)$ is a co-vertex, you know that $b = 2$. Because the major axis of the ellipse is horizontal, its equation is:

$$\frac{x^2}{a^2} + \frac{y^2}{b^2} = 1 \quad \text{or} \quad \frac{x^2}{25} + \frac{y^2}{4} = 1$$

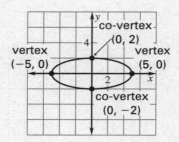

Exercises for Example 2

Write an equation of the ellipse with the given characteristics and center at (0, 0).

5. Vertex: $(3, 0)$

    Co-vertex: $(0, 1)$

6. Vertex: $(0, -4)$

    Co-vertex: $(3, 0)$

7. Vertex: $(-4, 0)$

    Co-vertex: $(0, 2)$

8. Vertex: $(0, 5)$

    Co-vertex: $(-2, 0)$

Algebra 2
Practice Workbook with Examples

LESSON 10.5

Practice with Examples

For use with pages 615–621

GOAL   **Graph and write equations of hyperbolas**

VOCABULARY

A **hyperbola** is the set of all points P such that the difference of the distances from P to two fixed points, called the **foci,** is constant. The line through the foci intersects the hyperbola at two points, the **vertices.** The line segment joining the vertices is the **transverse axis,** and its midpoint is the **center** of the hyperbola.

The **standard form of the equation of a hyperbola** with center at $(0, 0)$ is as follows.

Equation	Transverse Axis	Asymptotes	Vertices
$\dfrac{x^2}{a^2} - \dfrac{y^2}{b^2} = 1$	Horizontal	$y = \pm\dfrac{b}{a}x$	$(\pm a, 0)$
$\dfrac{y^2}{a^2} - \dfrac{x^2}{b^2} = 1$	Vertical	$y = \pm\dfrac{a}{b}x$	$(0, \pm a)$

The foci of the hyperbola lie on the transverse axis, c units from the center where $c^2 = a^2 + b^2$.

EXAMPLE 1   *Graphing an Equation of a Hyperbola*

Draw the hyperbola given by $\dfrac{y^2}{4} - \dfrac{x^2}{9} = 1$.

SOLUTION

Note from the equation that $a^2 = 4$ and $b^2 = 9$, so $a = 2$ and $b = 3$. Because the y^2-term is positive, the transverse axis is vertical and the vertices are $(0, 2)$ and $(0, -2)$. Sketch a rectangle that is centered at the origin, $2a = 4$ units high and $2b = 6$ units wide. To draw the asymptotes, draw lines passing through opposite corners of the rectangle. Finally, draw the hyperbola above and below the rectangle.

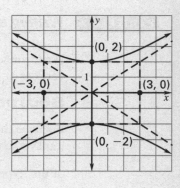

NAME _____ DATE _____

Practice with Examples

For use with pages 615–621

Exercises for Example 1

Graph the equation.

1. $\dfrac{x^2}{1} - \dfrac{y^2}{4} = 1$

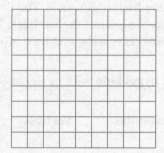

2. $\dfrac{y^2}{9} - \dfrac{x^2}{16} = 1$

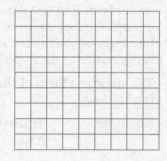

3. $\dfrac{x^2}{4} - \dfrac{y^2}{9} = 1$

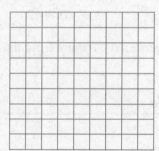

4. $\dfrac{y^2}{25} - \dfrac{x^2}{9} = 1$

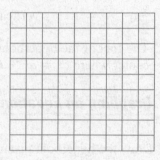

EXAMPLE 2 *Writing an Equation of a Hyperbola*

Write an equation of the hyperbola with foci at $(4, 0)$ and $(-4, 0)$ and vertices at $(3, 0)$ and $(-3, 0)$.

SOLUTION

Because the foci and vertices lie on the x-axis, the transverse axis is horizontal. Thus, the standard form of the hyperbola is $\dfrac{x^2}{a^2} - \dfrac{y^2}{b^2} = 1$.

The distance between each vertex and the origin is 3 units, so $a = 3$. The distance between each focus and the origin is 4 units, so $c = 4$. To find b, use the equation $c^2 = a^2 + b^2$.

$$b^2 = c^2 - a^2$$
$$= 4^2 - 3^2 = 16 - 9 = 7$$
$$b = \sqrt{7}$$

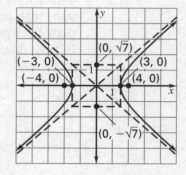

continued

Practice with Examples

For use with pages 615–621

Substitute 3 for a and $\sqrt{7}$ for b in the standard form of the equation of a hyperbola with center at $(0, 0)$ and a horizontal transverse axis.

$$\frac{x^2}{3^2} - \frac{y^2}{(\sqrt{7})^2} = 1 \qquad \text{Substitute 3 for } a \text{ and } \sqrt{7} \text{ for } b.$$

$$\frac{x^2}{9} - \frac{y^2}{7} = 1 \qquad \text{Simplify.}$$

Exercises for Example 2

Write an equation of the hyperbola with the given foci and vertices.

5. Foci: $(-5, 0), (5, 0)$

Vertices: $(-2, 0), (2, 0)$

6. Foci: $(-3, 0), (3, 0)$

Vertices: $(-2, 0), (2, 0)$

7. Foci: $(0, -7), (0, 7)$

Vertices: $(0, -1), (0, 1)$

8. Foci: $(-5, 0), (5, 0)$

Vertices: $(-4, 0), (4, 0)$

NAME _____ DATE _____

Practice with Examples

For use with pages 623–631

GOAL Write and graph an equation of a parabola with its vertex at (*h*, *k*) and an equation of a circle, ellipse, or hyperbola with its center at (*h*, *k*), and classify a conic using its equation

---

VOCABULARY

Parabolas, circles, ellipses, and hyperbolas are all curves that are formed by the intersection of a plane and a double-napped cone and are all called **conic sections** or **conics.**

EXAMPLE 1 *Writing an Equation of a Translated Parabola*

Write an equation of the parabola whose vertex is at $(-4, -1)$ and whose focus is at $(-4, 2)$.

SOLUTION

Begin by choosing the correct form of the parabola. It is helpful to plot the vertex and focus to see that they are vertically aligned. Therefore the parabola has a vertical axis, opens upward, and has the form $(x - h)^2 = 4p(y - k)$. Then find h and k by using the fact that the vertex $(h, k) = (-4, -1)$. So, $h = -4$ and $k = -1$.

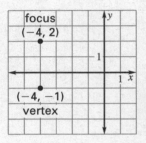

Finally, find p by calculating the distance between the vertex $(-4, -1)$ and the focus $(-4, 2)$.

$$|p| = \sqrt{(x_2 - x_1)^2 + (y_2 - y_1)^2} = \sqrt{(-4 - (-4))^2 + (2 - (-1))^2} = \sqrt{9} = 3$$

Since the parabola opens up, $p > 0$ and thus $p = 3$. The standard form of the equation is $(x + 4)^2 = 12(y + 1)$.

Exercises for Example 1

Write an equation for the parabola.

1. Vertex: $(3, 2)$
   Focus: $(3, 4)$

2. Vertex: $(1, 2)$
   Focus: $(5, 2)$

3. Vertex: $(-2, -3)$
   Focus: $(-2, -5)$

NAME _____ DATE _____

Practice with Examples

For use with pages 623–631

EXAMPLE 2 *Graphing the Equation of a Translated Ellipse*

Graph $\dfrac{(x + 4)^2}{25} + \dfrac{(y - 2)^2}{9} = 1$.

SOLUTION

Because the denominator of the x^2-term is greater than that of the y^2-term, the major axis is horizontal. Since $a^2 = 25$ and $b^2 = 9$, $a = 5$ and $b = 3$. Plot the center $(h, k) = (-4, 2)$. Plot the vertices 5 units to the left and right of the center, and the co-vertices 3 units above and below the center. Draw an ellipse through the vertices and co-vertices.

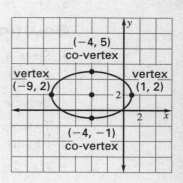

Exercises for Example 2

Graph the equation.

4. $(x + 3)^2 + (y - 1)^2 = 9$

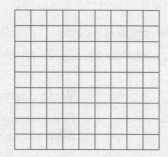

5. $\dfrac{(y - 2)^2}{4} + \dfrac{(x - 4)^2}{1} = 1$

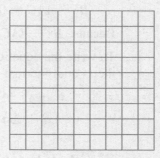

6. $(x + 2)^2 = 4(y + 3)$

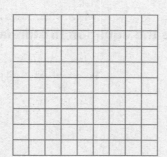

7. $\dfrac{(x - 2)^2}{9} - \dfrac{(y + 5)^2}{16} = 1$

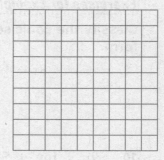

Practice with Examples

For use with pages 623–631

EXAMPLE 3 *Classifying Conics*

Classify the given conic and write the equation in standard form.

a. $y^2 - 2y - 4x - 7 = 0$ **b.** $x^2 + y^2 + 2x + 6y + 6 = 0$

SOLUTION

a. Since $A = 0$, $B = 0$, and $C = 1$, the value of the discriminant is as follows:

$$B^2 - 4AC = 0^2 - 4(0)(1) = 0$$

Because $B^2 - 4AC = 0$, the graph is a parabola.

To write the equation in standard form, complete the square for the y-terms:

$y^2 - 2y - 4x - 7 = 0$	Write original equation.
$(y^2 - 2y) = 4x + 7$	Group the terms containing y.
$(y^2 - 2y + 1) = 4x + 7 + 1$	Complete the square.
$(y - 1)^2 = 4(x + 2)$	Simplify.

b. Since $A = 1$, $B = 0$, and $C = 1$, the value of the discriminant is as follows:

$$B^2 - 4AC = 0^2 - 4(1)(1) = -4$$

Because $B^2 - 4AC < 0$ and $A = C$, the graph is a circle.

To write the equation in standard form, complete the square for both the x- and y-terms:

$x^2 + y^2 + 2x + 6y + 6 = 0$	Write original equation.
$(x^2 + 2x) + (y^2 + 6y) = -6$	Group terms and subtract 6 from each side.
$(x^2 + 2x + 1) + (y^2 + 6y + 9) = -6 + 1 + 9$	Complete the square.
$(x + 1)^2 + (y + 3)^2 = 4$	Simplify.

Exercises for Example 3

Classify the conic section and write the equation in standard form.

8. $x^2 + y^2 + 8x - 4y + 11 = 0$ **9.** $x^2 - 6x + 4y + 13 = 0$

10. $-9x^2 + 16y^2 + 54x + 64y - 161 = 0$ **11.** $4x^2 + y^2 - 8x - 4y + 4 = 0$

Practice with Examples

For use with pages 632–638

GOAL **Solve systems of quadratic equations**

EXAMPLE 1 *Finding Points of Intersection*

Find the points of intersection of the graphs of
$4x^2 + 4xy + 6y^2 - 2x + 3y = 0$ and $y = 2x - 1$.

SOLUTION

The graph of $4x^2 + 4xy + 6y^2 - 2x + 3y = 0$ is an ellipse because
$B^2 - 4AC = 4^2 - 4(4)(6) = -80 < 0$ and $A \neq C$. The graph of
$y = 2x - 1$ is a straight line.

To find the points of intersection, substitute $2x - 1$ for y in the equation
of the ellipse.

$$4x^2 + 4xy + 6y^2 - 2x + 3y = 0 \quad \text{Equation of ellipse}$$
$$4x^2 + 4x(2x - 1) + 6(2x - 1)^2 - 2x + 3(2x - 1) = 0 \quad \text{Substitute } 2x - 1 \text{ for } y.$$
$$4x^2 + 4x(2x - 1) + 6(4x^2 - 4x + 1) - 2x + 3(2x - 1) = 0 \quad \text{Expand power.}$$
$$4x^2 + 8x^2 - 4x + 24x^2 - 24x + 6 - 2x + 6x - 3 = 0 \quad \text{Use distributive property.}$$
$$36x^2 - 24x + 3 = 0 \quad \text{Combine like terms.}$$
$$3(12x^2 - 8x + 1) = 0 \quad \text{Factor out a 3.}$$
$$3(6x - 1)(2x - 1) = 0 \quad \text{Factor trinomial.}$$
$$x = \tfrac{1}{6} \quad \text{or} \quad x = \tfrac{1}{2} \quad \text{Zero-product property}$$

To find the y-coordinates of the points of intersection, substitute $x = \tfrac{1}{6}$
and $x = \tfrac{1}{2}$ into the linear equation and solve for y.

$$y = 2x - 1 = \tfrac{2}{6} - 1 = -\tfrac{2}{3}$$
$$y = 2x - 1 = 1 - 1 = 0$$

The points of intersection are $\left(\tfrac{1}{6}, -\tfrac{2}{3}\right)$ and $\left(\tfrac{1}{2}, 0\right)$.

Exercises for Example 1

Find the points of intersection of the graphs in the system.

1. $x^2 + y^2 = 8$

$y = x$

2. $x^2 - 2x + 3y - 11 = 0$

$y = x + 3$

Practice with Examples

For use with pages 632–638

3. $2x^2 + 4y^2 = 54$

$y = -x$

4. $x^2 - y^2 = 24$

$y = x - 2$

EXAMPLE 2 *Solving a System by Substitution*

Find the points of intersection of the graphs in the system.

$x^2 + y^2 - 8y + 7 = 0$ Equation 1

$-x^2 + y - 1 = 0$ Equation 2

SOLUTION

Because Equation 2 has no y^2-term, solve that equation for y and substitute into Equation 1.

$$x^2 + y^2 - 8y + 7 = 0 \qquad \text{Equation 1}$$

$$x^2 + (x^2 + 1)^2 - 8(x^2 + 1) + 7 = 0 \qquad \text{Substitute } x^2 + 1 \text{ for } y.$$

$$x^2 + x^4 + 2x^2 + 1 - 8x^2 - 8 + 7 = 0 \qquad \text{Expand power and distribute.}$$

$$x^4 - 5x^2 = 0 \qquad \text{Combine like terms.}$$

$$x^2(x^2 - 5) = 0 \qquad \text{Factor out an } x^2.$$

$$x^2(x + \sqrt{5})(x - \sqrt{5}) = 0 \qquad \text{Factor difference of two squares.}$$

$$x = 0 \quad \text{or} \quad x = -\sqrt{5} \quad \text{or} \quad x = \sqrt{5} \qquad \text{Zero product property}$$

To find the corresponding y-values, substitute $x = 0$, $x = -\sqrt{5}$, and $x = \sqrt{5}$ into Equation 2.

$$y = x^2 + 1 = 0^2 + 1 = 1$$

$$y = x^2 + 1 = \left(-\sqrt{5}\right)^2 + 1 = 6$$

$$y = x^2 + 1 = \left(\sqrt{5}\right)^2 + 1 = 6$$

The graphs intersect at $(0, 1)$, $\left(-\sqrt{5}, 6\right)$, and $\left(\sqrt{5}, 6\right)$.

Practice with Examples

For use with pages 632–638

Exercises for Example 2

Find points of intersection, if any, of the graphs in the system.

5. $x^2 - y - 2 = 0$

$2x^2 + y - 6x - 7 = 0$

6. $x^2 + y^2 - 3 = 0$

$2x^2 - y = 0$

7. $x^2 + y^2 - 1 = 0$

$x^2 - y - 2 = 0$

NAME _____   DATE _____

Practice with Examples

For use with pages 651–657

GOAL Use and write sequences, and use summation notation to write series and find sums of series

---

VOCABULARY

A **sequence** could be considered a function whose domain is a set of consecutive integers. If the domain is not specified, it begins at 1.

Finite sequences contain a last term, whereas **infinite sequences** continue without stopping.

When the terms of a sequence are added, the resulting expression is a **series**.

Summation notation, also called **sigma notation,** is used to write series. For example, in $\sum_{i=1}^{4} 2i$, i is the *index of summation,* 1 is the *lower limit of summation,* and 4 is the *upper limit of summation.*

EXAMPLE 1   *Writing Terms of Sequences*

Write the first five terms of the sequence.

a. $a_n = -4n + 3$

b. $a_n = (-1)^{n+1}$

SOLUTION

Because no domain was specified, begin with $n = 1$.

a. $a_1 = -4(1) + 3 = -1$

$a_2 = -4(2) + 3 = -5$

$a_3 = -4(3) + 3 = -9$

$a_4 = -4(4) + 3 = -13$

$a_5 = -4(5) + 3 = -17$

Notice that the terms decrease by 4 each time.

b. $a_1 = (-1)^{1+1} = 1$

$a_2 = (-1)^{2+1} = -1$

$a_3 = (-1)^{3+1} = 1$

$a_4 = (-1)^{4+1} = -1$

$a_5 = (-1)^{5+1} = 1$

Notice that the terms in the series alternate from positive to negative.

Exercises for Example 1

Write the first five terms of the sequence.

1. $a_n = 5n - 3$

2. $a_n = n - 2$

3. $a_n = 2^n$

4. $a_n = \dfrac{(-1)^n}{n}$

Practice with Examples

For use with pages 651–657

EXAMPLE 2 *Writing Rules for Sequences*

Write the next term in the given sequence. Then write a rule for the *n*th term.

$$1, \frac{4}{3}, \frac{6}{4}, \frac{8}{5}, \ldots$$

SOLUTION

Notice that beyond the first term, in each term the numerator is a multiple of 2 and the denominator increases by 1.

You can rewrite the terms as $\frac{2}{2}, \frac{4}{3}, \frac{6}{4}, \frac{8}{5}, \ldots$.

The next term is $a_5 = \frac{2 \cdot 5}{5 + 1} = \frac{10}{6}$. A rule for the *n*th term is $a_n = \frac{2n}{n + 1}$.

Exercises for Example 2

Write the next term in the sequence. Then write a rule for the *n*th term.

5. 3, 6, 9, 12, . . .

6. $\frac{1}{1}, \frac{1}{3}, \frac{1}{5}, \frac{1}{7}, \ldots$

7. $-4, -3, -2, -1, \ldots$

8. $\frac{2}{3}, \frac{3}{4}, \frac{4}{5}, \frac{5}{6}, \ldots$

Practice with Examples

For use with pages 651–657

EXAMPLE 3 *Writing Series with Summation Notation*

Write the series with summation notation.

a. $1 + 4 + 9 + 16 + \cdots$ **b.** $-2 + 4 - 6 + \cdots + 20$

SOLUTION

a. Notice that the first term is 1^2, the second is 2^2, the third is 3^2, and the fourth is 4^2. So, the terms of the series can be written as:

$$a_i = i^2 \text{ where } i = 1, 2, 3, 4, \cdots$$

The summation notation for the series is $\displaystyle\sum_{i=1}^{\infty} i^2$.

b. Notice that for each terms the signs are alternating negative and positive and the values are multiples of 2. So, the terms of the series can be written as:

$$a_i = (-1)^i 2i \text{ where } i = 1, 2, 3, \ldots, 10.$$

The summation notation for the series is $\displaystyle\sum_{i=1}^{10} (-1)^i 2i$.

Exercises for Example 3

Write the series with summation notation.

9. $5 + 6 + 7 + \cdots + 12$

10. $-3 - 6 - 9 - \ldots$

11. $\frac{1}{3} + \frac{2}{4} + \frac{3}{5} + \cdots + \frac{12}{14}$

12. $3 + 5 + 7 + \ldots$

Practice with Examples

For use with pages 659–665

GOAL **Write rules for arithmetic sequences and find sums of arithmetic series**

VOCABULARY

In an **arithmetic sequence,** the difference between consecutive terms is constant, and this constant difference is called the **common difference,** denoted by d. The nth term of an arithmetic sequence with first term a_1 and common difference d is given by:

$$a_n = a_1 + (n - 1)d.$$

The expression formed by adding the terms of an arithmetic sequence is called an **arithmetic series.**

The sum of the first n terms of an arithmetic series is:

$$S_n = n\left(\frac{a_1 + a_n}{2}\right).$$

In words, S_n is the mean of the first and nth terms, multiplied by the number of terms.

EXAMPLE 1 *Identifying Arithmetic Sequences*

Decide whether each sequence is arithmetic.

a. 2, 11, 20, 29, 38, . . .   **b.** 2, 4, 7, 11, 16, . . .

SOLUTION

To decide whether a sequence is arithmetic, find the difference of consecutive terms. If the differences are constant, then the sequence is arithmetic.

a. $a_2 - a_1 = 11 - 2 = 9$ **b.** $a_2 - a_1 = 4 - 2 = 2$

$a_3 - a_2 = 20 - 11 = 9$ $a_3 - a_2 = 7 - 4 = 3$

$a_4 - a_3 = 29 - 20 = 9$ $a_4 - a_3 = 11 - 7 = 4$

$a_5 - a_4 = 38 - 29 = 9$ $a_5 - a_4 = 16 - 11 = 5$

Because each difference is 9, the sequence is arithmetic.

Because the differences are not constant, the sequence is not arithmetic.

Exercises for Example 1

Decide whether the sequence is arithmetic.

1. 12, 7, 2, -3, -8, . . .   **2.** 4, 8, 16, 22, 32, . . .

3. 1, 2, 4, 6, 8, . . .   **4.** 19, 23, 27, 31, 35, . . .

Practice with Examples

For use with pages 659–665

Chapter 11

EXAMPLE 2 *Writing a Rule for the nth Term*

Write a rule for the *n*th term of the sequence 2, 11, 20, 29, 38, ...
Then find a_{15}.

SOLUTION

The sequence is arithmetic because each difference is 9. So, you can use
the rule for the *n*th term:

$$a_n = a_1 + (n - 1)d \qquad \text{Write general rule.}$$
$$= 2 + (n - 1)9 \qquad \text{Substitute 2 for } a_1 \text{ and 9 for } d.$$
$$= 2 + 9n - 9 \qquad \text{Use distributive property.}$$
$$= 9n - 7 \qquad \text{Simplify.}$$

The 15th term is $a_{15} = 9(15) - 7 = 135 - 7 = 128$.

Exercises for Example 2

Write a rule for the *n*th term of the sequence and find a_{15}.

5. 12, 7, 2, −3, −8, . . .

6. 19, 23, 27, 31, 35, . . .

7. 5, 7, 9, 11, 13, . . .

8. 4, 3, 2, 1, 0, . . .

9. 12, 6, 0, −6, −12, . . .

10. 5, 8, 11, 14, 17, . . .

NAME _____ DATE _____

Practice with Examples

For use with pages 659–665

EXAMPLE 3 *Finding a Sum*

Find the sum of the first 50 terms of the arithmetic series
$3 + 6 + 9 + 12 + 15 + \cdots$.

SOLUTION

Begin by finding the common difference, $d = 6 - 3 = 3$. Then, find a
formula for the nth term.

$a_n = a_1 + (n - 1)d$	Write rule for the nth term.
$\quad = 3 + (n - 1)(3)$	Substitute 3 for a_1 and 3 for d.
$\quad = 3n$	Simplify.

The 50th term is $a_{50} = 3(50) = 150$. So, the sum of the first 50 terms is:

$S_{50} = 50\left(\dfrac{a_1 + a_{50}}{2}\right)$	Write rule for S_{50}.
$\quad = 50\left(\dfrac{3 + 150}{2}\right)$	Substitute 3 for a_1 and 150 for a_{50}.
$\quad = 3825$	Simplify. The sum of the first 50 terms is 3825.

Exercises for Example 3

Find the sum of the first n terms of the arithmetic series.

11. $2 + 3 + 4 + 5 + \cdots ; n = 19$

12. $25 + 35 + 45 + 55 + \cdots ; n = 50$

NAME _____ DATE _____

Practice with Examples

For use with pages 666–673

GOAL Write rules for geometric sequences and find sums of geometric series

---

VOCABULARY

In a **geometric sequence,** the ratio of any term to the previous term is constant, and this constant ratio is called the **common ratio,** denoted by r. The nth term of a geometric sequence with first term a_1 and common ratio r is given by:

$$a_n = a_1 r^{n-1}.$$

The expression formed by adding the terms of a geometric sequence is called a **geometric series.** The sum S_n of the first n terms of a geometric series with common ratio $r \neq 1$ is:

$$S_n = a_1 \left(\frac{1 - r^n}{1 - r} \right).$$

EXAMPLE 1 *Writing a Rule for the nth Term*

Write a rule for the nth term of the sequence $6, 24, 96, 384, \ldots$. Then find a_7.

SOLUTION

The sequence is geometric because the common ratio $r = \frac{24}{6} = 4$. So, a rule for the nth term is:

$$a_n = a_1 r^{n-1}$$
$$= 6(4)^{n-1}$$

The 7th term is $a_7 = 6(4)^{7-1} = 6(4)^6 = 24{,}576$.

Exercises for Example 1
Write a rule for the *n*th term of the geometric sequence.

   1. $4, 12, 36, 108, 324, \ldots$ **2.** $1, 6, 36, 216, 1296, \ldots$

   3. $2, -6, 18, -54, 162, \ldots$ **4.** $7, 14, 28, 56, 128, \ldots$

Practice with Examples

For use with pages 666–673

EXAMPLE 2 ***Finding the nth Term Given a Term and the Common Ratio***

One term of a geometric sequence is $a_4 = 64$. The common ratio is $r = 4$. Write a rule for the *n*th term.

SOLUTION

Begin by finding the first term as follows.

$a_n = a_1 r^{n-1}$	Write general rule.
$a_4 = a_1 r^{4-1}$	Substitute 4 for *n*.
$64 = a_1(4)^3$	Substitute 64 for a_4 and 4 for *r*.
$1 = a_1$	Solve for a_1.

So, the rule for the *n*th term is:

$a_n = a_1 r^{n-1}$	Write general rule.
$\quad = 1(4)^{n-1}$	Substitute 1 for a_1 and 4 for *r*.

Exercises for Example 2

Write a rule for the *n*th term of the geometric sequence.

5. $a_1 = 2, r = -\frac{1}{3}$

6. $a_5 = 3, r = -1$

7. $a_3 = -12, r = -2$

NAME _____ DATE _____

Practice with Examples

For use with pages 666–673

EXAMPLE 3 *Finding a Sum*

Find the sum of the first ten terms of the geometric series
$-3 + 6 - 12 + 24 - \ldots$.

SOLUTION

Begin by finding the common ratio, $r = \dfrac{6}{-3} = -2$. So, the sum of the first 10 terms is:

$$S_{10} = a_1\left(\frac{1 - r^{10}}{1 - r}\right) \qquad \text{Write rule for } S_{10}.$$

$$= -3\left(\frac{1 - (-2)^{10}}{1 - (-2)}\right) \qquad \text{Substitute } -3 \text{ for } a_1 \text{ and } -2 \text{ for } r.$$

$$= -3\left(-\frac{1023}{3}\right) \qquad \text{Simplify.}$$

$$= 1023 \qquad\qquad \text{Simplify.}$$

The sum of the first 10 terms is 1028.

Exercises for Example 3

Find the sum of the first *n* terms of the geometric series.

8. $2 + 8 + 32 + 128 + \cdots ; n = 12$

9. $1 + (-6) + 36 + (-216) + \cdots ; n = 9$

NAME _____ DATE _____

Practice with Examples

For use with pages 675–680

GOAL **Find sums of infinite geometric series**

> ### VOCABULARY
>
> The **sum of an infinite geometric series** with first term a_1 and common ratio r is given by
>
> $$S = \frac{a_1}{1 - r}$$
>
> provided $|r| < 1$. If $|r| \geq 1$, the series has no sum.

EXAMPLE 1 *Finding Sums of Infinite Geometric Series*

Find the sum of the infinite geometric series, if it has one.

a. $\displaystyle\sum_{n=1}^{\infty} 4\left(-\frac{1}{3}\right)^{n-1}$
    b. $\displaystyle\sum_{n=0}^{\infty} 2\left(\frac{5}{4}\right)^{n}$

SOLUTION

a. Begin by checking to see if the infinite geometric series has a sum. Because $|r| = \left|-\frac{1}{3}\right| = \frac{1}{3} < 1$, the series has a sum. For this series, $a_1 = 4\left(-\frac{1}{3}\right)^{1-1} = 4\left(-\frac{1}{3}\right)^{0} = 4(1) = 4$ and $r = -\frac{1}{3}$. The sum is as follows:

$$S = \frac{a_1}{1 - r} = \frac{4}{1 - \left(-\frac{1}{3}\right)} = \frac{4}{1 + \frac{1}{3}} = \frac{4}{\frac{4}{3}} = 4 \cdot \frac{3}{4} = 3.$$

b. Because $|r| = \left|\frac{5}{4}\right| = \frac{5}{4} > 1$, you can conclude that the series has no sum.

Exercises for Example 1

Find the sum of the infinite geometric series, if it has one.

1. $\displaystyle\sum_{n=0}^{\infty} 3\left(\frac{1}{2}\right)^{n}$
    2. $\displaystyle\sum_{n=0}^{\infty} 2\left(-\frac{1}{2}\right)^{n}$

3. $\displaystyle\sum_{n=1}^{\infty} (0.9)^{n-1}$
    4. $\displaystyle\sum_{n=0}^{\infty} 3\left(\frac{4}{3}\right)^{n}$

Algebra 2   **223**
Practice Workbook with Examples

Chapter 11

Practice with Examples

For use with pages 675–680

EXAMPLE 2 *Finding the Common Ratio*

An infinite geometric series with first term $a_1 = 7$ has a sum of 4.
What is the common ratio of the series?

SOLUTION

$$S = \frac{a_1}{1 - r}$$ Write rule for sum.

$$4 = \frac{7}{1 - r}$$ Substitute 4 for S and 7 for a_1.

$4(1 - r) = 7$ Multiply each side by $1 - r$.

$1 - r = \frac{7}{4}$ Divide each side by 4.

$-r = \frac{3}{4}$ Subtract 1 from each side.

$r = -\frac{3}{4}$ Solve for r.

Exercises for Example 2

Find the common ratio of the infinite geometric series with the given sum and first term.

5. $S = 30, a_1 = 9$

6. $S = 3, a_1 = 4$

7. $S = 2, a_1 = 1$

8. $S = 100, a_1 = 20$

Practice with Examples

For use with pages 675–680

EXAMPLE 3 *Writing a Repeating Decimal as a Fraction*

Write 0.888 . . . as a fraction.

SOLUTION

Notice that only one digit, 8, is repeated in the pattern. So, $r = 0.1$.

$$0.888 \ldots = 8(0.1) + 8(0.1)^2 + 8(0.1)^3 + \cdots$$

$$S = \frac{a_1}{1 - r}$$ Write rule for sum.

$$= \frac{8(0.1)}{1 - 0.1}$$ Substitute for a_1 and r.

$$= \frac{0.8}{0.9}$$ Simplify.

$$= \frac{8}{9}$$ Write as a quotient of integers.

The repeating decimal 0.888 . . . is $\frac{8}{9}$ as a fraction.

Exercises for Example 3

Write the repeating decimal as a fraction.

9. 0.111 . . .

10. 0.333 . . .

11. 0.7171 . . .

12. 0.2727 . . .

NAME _____ DATE _____

Practice with Examples

For use with pages 681–687

GOAL **Evaluate and write recursive rules for sequences**

VOCABULARY

A **recursive rule** gives the beginning term or terms of a sequence and then a recursive equation that tells how a_n is related to one or more preceding terms. The expression $n!$ is read "**n factorial**" and represents the product of all integers from 1 to n. For example, $4! = 4 \cdot 3 \cdot 2 \cdot 1 = 24$.

EXAMPLE 1 *Evaluating Recursive Rules*

Write the first five terms of the sequence.

a. $a_1 = 1, a_n = a_{n-1} + 3$

b. $a_0 = 1, a_n = a_{n-1} + 2n$

SOLUTION

a.
$a_1 = 1$
$a_2 = a_{2-1} + 3 = a_1 + 3 = 1 + 3 = 4$
$a_3 = a_{3-1} + 3 = a_2 + 3 = 4 + 3 = 7$
$a_4 = a_{4-1} + 3 = a_3 + 3 = 7 + 3 = 10$
$a_5 = a_{5-1} + 3 = a_4 + 3 = 10 + 3 = 13$

b.
$a_0 = 1$
$a_1 = a_{1-1} + 2 \cdot 1 = a_0 + 2 = 1 + 2 = 3$
$a_2 = a_{2-1} + 2 \cdot 2 = a_1 + 4 = 3 + 4 = 7$
$a_3 = a_{3-1} + 2 \cdot 3 = a_2 + 6 = 7 + 6 = 13$
$a_4 = a_{4-1} + 2 \cdot 4 = a_3 + 8 = 13 + 8 = 21$

Exercises for Example 1

Find the first five terms of the sequence.

1. $a_1 = 10, a_n = a_{n-1} - 2$

2. $a_1 = 2, a_n = a_{n-1} + n - 1$

3. $a_1 = 3, a_n = a_{n-1} + 2$

4. $a_1 = 1, a_n = 2a_{n-1}$

Practice with Examples

For use with pages 681–687

EXAMPLE 2 ***Writing a Recursive Rule for an Arithmetic Sequence***

Write a recursive rule for the arithmetic sequence with $a_1 = 5$ and $d = -3$.

SOLUTION

Use the fact that you can obtain a_n in an arithmetic sequence by adding the common difference to the previous term.

$$a_n = a_{n-1} + d \qquad \text{General recursive rule for } a_n.$$
$$\quad = a_{n-1} - 3 \qquad \text{Substitute } -3 \text{ for } d.$$

A recursive rule for the sequence is $a_1 = 5$, $a_n = a_{n-1} - 3$.

Exercises for Example 2

Write a recursive rule for the arithmetic sequence.

5. $a_1 = 2$
  $d = 4$

6. $a_1 = 0$
  $d = -2$

7. $a_1 = -3$
  $d = 1$

8. $a_1 = 12$
  $d = -4$

EXAMPLE 3 ***Writing a Recursive Rule for a Geometric Sequence***

Write a recursive rule for a geometric sequence with $a_1 = 2$ and $r = -3$.

SOLUTION

Use the fact that you can obtain a_n in a geometric sequence by multiplying the previous term by the constant ratio, r.

$$a_n = r \cdot a_{n-1}$$
$$\quad = -3a_{n-1}$$

A recursive rule for the sequence is $a_1 = 2$, $a_n = -3a_{n-1}$.

NAME _____ DATE _____

Practice with Examples

For use with pages 681–687

Exercises for Example 3

Write a recursive rule for the geometric sequence.

9. $a_1 = 3$
$r = 8$

10. $a_1 = 10$
$r = \frac{1}{2}$

11. $a_1 = -2$
$r = 0.3$

12. $a_1 = -1$
$r = -2$

EXAMPLE 4 *Writing a Recursive Rule*

Write a recursive rule for the sequence 2, 6, 10, 14, 18, ...

SOLUTION

Notice that the common difference of the terms is 4. This tells you the sequence is arithmetic. Therefore, each term is obtained by adding 4 to the previous term.

A recursive rule is given by:

$a_1 = 2, a_n = a_{n-1} + 4.$

Exercises for Example 4

Write a recursive rule for the sequence.

13. 1, 2, 4, 8, 16, . . .

14. 11, 23, 35, 47, 59, . . .

15. $-12, -8, -4, 0, 4, . . .$

16. $1, -3, 9, -27, . . .$

Practice with Examples

For use with pages 701–707

GOAL Use the fundamental counting principle and permutations to count the number of ways an event can happen

---

VOCABULARY

Fundamental Counting Principle

If one event can occur in m ways and another event can occur in n ways, then the number of ways that *both* events can occur is $m \cdot n$. This principle can be extended to three or more events.

An ordering of n objects is a **permutation** of the objects. There are six permutations of the letters A, B, and C: ABC, ACB, BAC, BCA, CAB, and CBA.

Permutations of n Objects Taken r at a Time

The number of permutations of r objects taken from a group of n distinct objects is denoted by $_nP_r$ and is given by: $_nP_r = \dfrac{n!}{(n-r)!}$

Permutations with Repetition

The number of distinguishable permutations of n objects where one object is repeated q_1 times, another is repeated q_2 times, and so on is:

$$\frac{n!}{q_1! \cdot q_2! \cdot \cdots \cdot q_k!}$$

EXAMPLE 1 *Using the Fundamental Counting Principle*

Radio station call letters consist of four letters beginning with either a K or a W.

a. How many different radio station call letters are possible if letters can be repeated?

b. How many different radio station call letters are possible if letters *cannot* be repeated?

SOLUTION

a. There are 2 choices for the first letter and 26 choices for the remaining three letters. Use the fundamental counting principle to find the number of different possibilities.

Number of call letters $= 2 \cdot 26 \cdot 26 \cdot 26 = 35{,}152$

b. If you cannot repeat letters, there are still 2 choices for the first letter, but then there are only 25 remaining choices for the second letter, 24 choices for the third letter, and 23 for the fourth letter. Use the fundamental counting principle to find the number of different possibilities.

Number of call letters without repetition $= 2 \cdot 25 \cdot 24 \cdot 23 = 27{,}600$

Chapter 12

NAME _____ DATE _____

Practice with Examples

For use with pages 701–707

Exercises for Example 1

1. A baseball coach is determining the batting order for the team. The team has 9 players, but the coach does not want the pitcher to be one of the first four to bat. How many batting orders are possible?

2. How many different 4-digit numbers can be formed from the digits 1, 2, 3, and 4 if digits can be repeated? If digits cannot be repeated?

3. How many different 5-digit zip codes can be formed if digits can be repeated? If digits cannot be repeated?

EXAMPLE 2 *Finding the Number of Permutations*

a. In how many different ways can 2 students out of a twenty-five-member class be elected president and vice president?

b. Find the number of distinguishable permutations of the letters in MATHEMATICS.

SOLUTION

a. Any of the 25 students can be elected president, then any of the remaining 24 can be elected vice president. So the number of ways the students can be elected is $25 \cdot 24 = 600$.

b. MATHEMATICS has 11 letters of which M is repeated 2 times, A is repeated 2 times, and T is repeated 2 times. Therefore, the number of distinguishable permutations is given by

$$\frac{n!}{q_1! \cdot q_2! \cdot \ldots \cdot q_n!} = \frac{11!}{2! \cdot 2! \cdot 2!} = \frac{39,916,800}{8} = 4,989,600.$$

NAME _____ DATE _____

Practice with Examples

For use with pages 701–707

Exercises for Example 2

4. If eight basketball teams are in a tournament, find the number of different ways that first, second, and third place can be decided. (Assume there are no ties.)

5. There are 15 members in a committee. In how many different ways can a president, vice president, secretary, and treasurer be chosen?

6. Find the number of distinguishable permutations of the letters in CAT.

7. Find the number of distinguishable permutations of the letters in CINCINNATI.

Practice with Examples

For use with pages 708–715

GOAL **Use combinations to count the number of ways an event can happen, and use the binomial theorem to expand a binomial that is raised to a power**

VOCABULARY

A **combination** is a selection of r objects from a group of n objects where the order is not important.

Combinations of n Objects Taken r at a Time

The number of combinations of r objects taken from a group of n distinct objects is denoted by $_nC_r$ and is given by:

$$_nC_r = \frac{n!}{(n - r)! \cdot r!}$$

If you arrange the values of $_nC_r$ in a triangular pattern in which each row corresponds to a value of n, you get **Pascal's triangle.**

The following theorem uses combinations to find the coefficients in the expansion of the binomial $a + b$ raised to the nth power.

The Binomial Theorem

The binomial expansion of $(a + b)^n$ for any positive integer n is:

$$(a + b)^n = {}_nC_0 a^n b^0 + {}_nC_1 a^{n-1}b^1 + {}_nC_2 a^{n-2}b^2 + \cdots + {}_nC_n a^0 b^n$$

$$= \sum_{r=0}^{n} {}_nC_r a^{n-r}b^r$$

EXAMPLE 1 *Finding Combinations*

A committee of five people is to be chosen from a group of 20 people, 12 of which are men and 8 are women.

a. If the order in which the people are chosen is not important, how many different five-people committees are possible?

b. How many different ways can 3 men and 2 women be chosen for the committee?

SOLUTION

a. The number of ways to chose 5 people from a group of 20 is:

$$_{20}C_5 = \frac{20!}{15! \cdot 5!} = \frac{20 \cdot 19 \cdot 18 \cdot 17 \cdot 16 \cdot 15!}{15! \cdot 5!} = 15{,}504$$

b. Because you need to choose 3 of the 12 men and 2 of the 8 women, the number of possible committees is:

$$_{12}C_3 \cdot {}_8C_2 = \frac{12!}{9! \cdot 3!} \cdot \frac{8!}{6! \cdot 2!} = \frac{12 \cdot 11 \cdot 10 \cdot 9!}{9! \cdot 3!} \cdot \frac{8 \cdot 7 \cdot 6!}{6! \cdot 2!} = 6160$$

Chapter 12

Practice with Examples

For use with pages 708–715

Exercises for Example 1

1. An ice cream shop has a choice of 10 toppings. In how many ways can you choose 3 different toppings for your ice cream?

2. Out of a group of 30 people, 20 of which are women, how many different committees of 6 people can be chosen?

3. In Exercise 2, determine the possible number of committees of 6 in which 4 are women and 2 are men.

EXAMPLE 2 ### Using the Binomial Theorem

a. Expand $(x + 3)^5$.

b. Find the coefficient of x^6 in the expansion of $(x + 2)^{10}$.

SOLUTION

a. $(x + 3)^5 = {}_5C_0x^53^0 + {}_5C_1x^43^1 + {}_5C_2x^33^2 + {}_5C_3x^23^3 + {}_5C_4x^13^4 + {}_5C_5x^03^5$

$\quad = (1)(x^5)(1) + (5)(x^4)(3) + (10)(x^3)(9) + (10)(x^2)(27) +$

$\qquad (5)(x)(81) + (1)(1)(243)$

$\quad = x^5 + 15x^4 + 90x^3 + 270x^2 + 405x + 243$

b. From the binomial theorem, you know that

$$(x + 2)^{10} = \sum_{r=0}^{10} {}_{10}C_r(x)^{10-r}(2)^r.$$

The term that has x^6 is ${}_{10}C_4(x)^6(2)^4 = (210)(x^6)(16) = 3360x^6$.
The coefficient is 3360.

NAME _____ DATE _____

Practice with Examples

For use with pages 708–715

Exercises for Example 2

Use the binomial theorem to write the binomial expansion.

4. $(x + 1)^4$

5. $(x - 2)^5$

6. $(x - y)^4$

7. $(x + y)^5$

8. Find the coefficient of x^5 in the expansion of $(x + 4)^7$.

NAME _____ DATE _____

Practice with Examples

For use with pages 716–722

GOAL **Find theoretical and experimental probabilities**

VOCABULARY

The **probability** of an event is a number between 0 and 1 that indicates the likelihood the event will occur.

Theoretical probability is a type of probability that is based on all outcomes of an event *A* being equally likely and is given by:

$$P(A) = \frac{\text{number of outcomes in A}}{\text{total number of outcomes}}.$$

Experimental probability is a type of probability that is based on the results of an experiment, a survey, or the history of an event.

EXAMPLE 1 ## Finding Probabilities of Events

You draw a card from a standard deck of 52 cards. Find the probability of drawing a face card.

SOLUTION

Twelve outcomes correspond to drawing a face card: J, Q and K from the four suits.

$$P(\text{drawing a face card}) = \frac{\text{number of ways to draw a face card}}{\text{number of ways to draw a card}} = \frac{12}{52} = \frac{3}{13}$$

Exercises for Example 1

Simplify the expression.

1. Find the probability of choosing an E when selecting a letter from those in the word COLLEGE.

2. A card is drawn from a standard deck of 52 cards. Find the probability the card is either a club or a spade.

Practice with Examples

For use with pages 716–722

EXAMPLE 2 **Probabilities Involving Permutations and Combinations**

For next year's schedule of classes, mathematics, English, history, and science are each scheduled during the first four periods of the day. Your schedule is randomly selected by a computer.

a. What is the probability that English, math, science, and history will be scheduled in that order?

b. Your favorite subjects are math and science. What is the probability that your favorite subjects will be scheduled the first two periods, in any order?

SOLUTION

a. Because there are four subjects, you have four choices for first period, three choices for second period, two choices for third period, and one choice for fourth period. So, there are 4! different permutations of subjects. Because there is only one way to schedule your classes with English first, math second, science third, and history fourth,

$$P(E, M, S, H) = \frac{1}{4!} = \frac{1}{24} \approx 0.042.$$

b. There are $_4C_2$ different combinations of 2 subjects. Of these $_2C_2$ contain 2 of your favorite subjects. So, the probability is:

$$P(\text{scheduling 2 favorites first}) = \frac{_2C_2}{_4C_2} = \frac{1}{6} \approx 0.167.$$

Exercises for Example 2

Seven letters are chosen, one at a time, at random from those in the word ENGLISH.

3. Find the probability that they will be chosen in alphabetical order.

4. Find the probability that the first letter will be a vowel.

Practice with Examples

For use with pages 716–722

EXAMPLE 3 *Finding Experimental Probabilities*

In order to choose a mascot for a new school, 1847 students were surveyed: 529 chose a falcon, 762 chose a ram, and 501 chose a panther. The remaining students did not vote. If a student is selected at random, what is the probability that the student's choice was a panther?

SOLUTION

Of the 1847 students surveyed, 501 chose a panther. So, the probability is:

$$P(\text{panther}) = \frac{501}{1847} \approx 0.271$$

Exercises for Example 3

Thirty students in an Algebra 2 class took a test: 8 received A's, 13 received B's, and 9 received C's. If a student from the class is randomly chosen,

5. What is the probability the student received a C on the test?

6. What is the probability the student received an A or B on the test?

Chapter 12

NAME _____ DATE _____

Practice with Examples

For use with pages 724–729

GOAL Find probabilities of unions and intersections of two events, and use complements to find the probability of an event

---

VOCABULARY

A union or intersection of two events is called a **compound event.** If no outcomes are in the intersection of two events, then the events are **mutually exclusive.**

The event A' called the **complement** of event A, consists of all outcomes that are not in A.

Probability of Compound Events

If A and B are two events, then the probability of A or B is

$$P(A \text{ or } B) = P(A) + P(B) - P(A \text{ and } B)$$

If A and B are mutually exclusive, then the probability of A or B is:

$$P(A \text{ or } B) = P(A) + P(B)$$

Probability of the Complement of an Event

The probability of the complement of A is $P(A') = 1 - P(A)$.

EXAMPLE 1 *Probability of Events*

A standard six-sided number cube is rolled.

a. What is the probability that it is a 4 *or* a prime number?

b. What is the probability that it is an even number *or* a prime number?

SOLUTION

a. Let event A be rolling a 4, and let event B be rolling a prime number. Event A has 1 outcome. Recall that a prime number is a number greater than 1 that has only factors of 1 and itself. So, event B has 3 outcomes. Because A and B are mutually exclusive, the probability is:

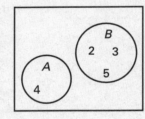

$$P(A \text{ or } B) = P(A) + P(B) = \frac{1}{6} + \frac{3}{6} = \frac{4}{6} = \frac{2}{3} \approx 0.667$$

NAME _____ DATE _____

Practice with Examples

For use with pages 724–729

b. Let event *A* be rolling an even number, and let event B be rolling a prime number. Event *A* has 3 outcomes and event B has 3 outcomes. Of these, one outcome is common to A and *B*. So, the probability of rolling an even or prime number is:

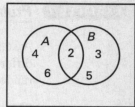

$$P(A \text{ or } B) = P(A) + P(B) - P(A \text{ and } B)$$ 　　　Write general formula.

$$= \frac{3}{6} + \frac{3}{6} - \frac{1}{6}$$ 　　　Substitute known probabilities.

$$= \frac{5}{6}$$ 　　　Combine like terms.

$$\approx 0.833$$ 　　　Convert to a decimal.

Exercises for Example 1

A standard six-sided number cube is rolled. Find the probability of the given event.

1. an even number or a one

2. a six or a number less than 3

3. an even number or number greater than 5

4. an odd number or number divisible by 3

5. A weather forecaster says that the probability it will rain on Monday or Tuesday is 40%, the probability it will rain on Monday is 30%, and the probability it will rain on Tuesday is 60%. What is the probability that it will rain on both Monday and Tuesday?

Chapter 12

NAME _____ DATE _____

Practice with Examples

For use with pages 724–729

EXAMPLE 2 *Probabilities of Complements*

A standard deck of 52 playing cards has 4 suits with 13 different cards in each suit as shown. A card is drawn at random. Find the probability that the card is *not* a King.

Standard 52-card deck

K♠	K♣	K♦	K♥
Q♠	Q♣	Q♦	Q♥
J♠	J♣	J♦	J♥
10♠	10♣	10♦	10♥
9♠	9♣	9♦	9♥
8♠	8♣	8♦	8♥
7♠	7♣	7♦	7♥
6♠	6♣	6♦	6♥
5♠	5♣	5♦	5♥
4♠	4♣	4♦	4♥
3♠	3♣	3♦	3♥
2♠	2♣	2♦	2♥
A♠	A♣	A♦	A♥

SOLUTION

$P(\text{card is not a King}) = 1 - P(\text{card is a King})$

$$= 1 - \frac{4}{52}$$

$$= \frac{48}{52} = \frac{12}{13}$$

$$\approx 0.923$$

Exercises for Example 2

Find the probability of the given event.

6. the card is not a face card (face cards are Jacks, Queens, and Kings)

7. the card is not less than or equal to 4 (an ace is one)

Chapter 12

NAME _____ DATE _____

Practice with Examples

For use with pages 730–737

GOAL **Find the probability of independent and dependent events**

VOCABULARY

Two events are **independent** if the occurrence of one has no effect on the occurrence of the other.

Probability of Independent Events

If A and B are independent events, then the probability that both A and B occur is $P(A \text{ and } B) = P(A) \cdot P(B)$.

Two events are **dependent** if the occurrence of one affects the occurrence of the other. The probability that B will occur given that A has occurred is called the **conditional probability** of B given A and is written $P(B|A)$.

Probability of Dependent Events

If A and B are dependent events, then the probability that both A and B occur is $P(A \text{ and } B) = P(A) \cdot P(B|A)$.

EXAMPLE 1 **Probability of Independent Events**

You are playing a game. On your first turn you roll two number cubes and roll doubles. On your second roll, you roll a ten. What is the probability of this occurring?

SOLUTION

Let event A be rolling doubles on your first roll, and let event B be rolling a sum of 10 on the second roll. Events A and B are independent of each other. So, the probability is:

$$P(A \text{ and } B) = P(A) \cdot P(B) = \frac{6}{36} \cdot \frac{3}{36} = \frac{1}{6} \cdot \frac{1}{12} = \frac{1}{72} \approx 0.014$$

Exercises for Example 1

Find the probability of rolling the given events.

  1. sum of 8, then doubles

  2. an even sum, then a sum greater than 8

Algebra 2
Practice Workbook with Examples

Chapter 12

Practice with Examples

For use with pages 730–737

EXAMPLE 2 *Using a Complement to Find a Probability*

The probability of selecting a rotten apple from a basket of apples is 12%. What is the probability of selecting three good apples when selecting one from each of three different baskets?

SOLUTION

Let event A represent selecting a rotten apple. Then A' represents selecting a good apple. Because $P(A) = 0.12$, it follows that $P(A') = 0.88$. So, the probability of selecting three good apples is:

$$P(A' \text{ and } A' \text{ and } A') = P(A') \cdot P(A') \cdot P(A')$$
$$= (0.88)(0.88)(0.88)$$
$$\approx 0.681$$

Exercises for Example 2

Use the information from Example 2 to find the probability of the given event.

3. selecting 2 good apples and 1 rotten apple

4. selecting 3 rotten apples

Practice with Examples
For use with pages 730–737

EXAMPLE 3 *Probability of Dependent Events*

A gumball machine contains 100 gumballs, twenty of each of the colors red, blue, green, white, and yellow. What is the probability of you and your friend both getting red gumballs?

SOLUTION

Because the gumballs are not replaced in the machine, A and B are dependent events. Notice that for $P(B|A)$ there will be one less red gumball and one less gumball in the total. So, the probability is:

$$P(A \text{ and } B) = P(A) \cdot P(B|A) = \frac{20}{100} \cdot \frac{19}{99} = \frac{1}{5} \cdot \frac{19}{99} = \frac{19}{495} \approx 0.0384$$

Exercises for Example 3

Use the information from Example 3 to find the probability of the dependent events.

5. blue, then white

6. green, then red, then blue

7. blue, then blue, then blue

8. yellow, then yellow

NAME _____ DATE _____

Practice with Examples

For use with pages 739–744

GOAL **Find binomial probabilities and analyze binomial distributions**

VOCABULARY

In a **binomial experiment** there are n independent trials with each trial having only two possible outcomes: success and failure. The probability of success is the same for each trial.

Finding a Binomial Probability

For a binomial experiment consisting of n trials, the probability of exactly k successes is

$$P(k \text{ successes}) = {}_nC_k p^k (1 - p)^{n-k},$$

where the probability of success on each trial is p.

A **binomial distribution** shows the probabilities of all possible number of successes in a binomial experiment.
A distribution is **symmetric** if the left half of the histogram is a mirror image of the right half, otherwise the distribution is **skewed.**

EXAMPLE 1 *Finding a Binomial Probability*

A scientist claims that 40% of the mice used in an experiment will become very aggressive after having been administered an experimental drug. Suppose you randomly select 8 mice. What is the probability that exactly 5 of them exhibit aggressive behavior?

SOLUTION

Because the mice are either aggressive or not aggressive, this is a binomial distribution. Let $p = 0.4$ be the probability that a randomly selected mouse is aggressive. By selecting 8 mice, you are conducting $n = 8$ independent trials. The probability of getting exactly $K = 5$ successes (aggressiveness) is:

$$P(K = 5) = {}_8C_5 (0.4)^5 (1 - 0.4)^{8-5}$$

$$= (56)(0.4)^5 (0.6)^3$$

$$\approx 0.124$$

The probability that exactly 5 of the 8 mice surveyed exhibited aggressive behavior is about 12%.

NAME _____ DATE _____

Practice with Examples

For use with pages 739–744

Exercises for Example 1

1. An automobile safety engineer claims that 10% of automobile accidents are due to driver fatigue. Suppose you randomly surveyed 6 people who had been in an accident. What is the probability that exactly 3 of them were due to driver fatigue?

2. The probability that a stolen car will be recovered is 63%. Find the probability that exactly 4 of 5 stolen cars will be recovered.

EXAMPLE 2 *Constructing a Binomial Distribution*

Draw a histogram of the binomial distribution for the experiment in Example 1. Then find the probability that at least 5 of the mice will exhibit aggressive behavior.

SOLUTION

$P(K = 0) = {}_8C_0(0.4)^0(0.6)^8 \approx 0.017$

$P(K = 1) = {}_8C_1(0.4)^1(0.6)^7 \approx 0.090$

$P(K = 2) = {}_8C_2(0.4)^2(0.6)^6 \approx 0.209$

$P(K = 3) = {}_8C_3(0.4)^3(0.6)^5 \approx 0.279$

$P(K = 4) = {}_8C_4(0.4)^4(0.6)^4 \approx 0.232$

$P(K = 5) = {}_8C_5(0.4)^5(0.6)^3 \approx 0.124$

$P(K = 6) = {}_8C_6(0.4)^6(0.6)^2 \approx 0.041$

$P(K = 7) = {}_8C_7(0.4)^7(0.6)^1 \approx 0.008$

$P(K = 8) = {}_8C_8(0.4)^8(0.6)^0 \approx 0.001$

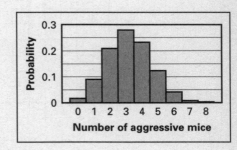

The probability of getting at least $K = 5$ successes is:

$P(K \geq 5) = P(5) + P(6) + P(7) + P(8) \approx 0.124 + 0.041 + 0.008 + 0.001 = 0.174$

The probability that at least 5 of the mice selected will exhibit aggressive behavior is about 17%.

NAME _____ DATE _____

Practice with Examples

For use with pages 739–744

Exercises for Example 2

3. Draw a histogram of the binomial distribution in Exercise 1. Find the probability that at most 3 of the accidents were due to driver fatigue.

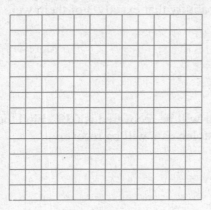

4. Draw a histogram of the binomial distribution in Exercise 2. Find the probability that at least 2 of the stolen cars will be recovered.

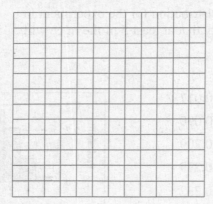

Practice with Examples

For use with pages 746–752

GOAL **Calculate probabilities using normal distributions, and use normal distributions to approximate binomial distributions**

VOCABULARY

A smooth, symmetrical, bell-shaped curve which approximates a binomial distribution is called a **normal curve.** Areas under this curve represent probabilities from **normal distributions.**

Area Under a Normal Curve

The mean $\bar{x}$ and standard deviation σ of a normal distribution determine the following areas.

• The total area under the curve is 1.

• 68% of the area lies within 1 standard deviation of the mean.

• 95% of the area lies within 2 standard deviations of the mean.

• 99.7% of the area lies within 3 standard deviations of the mean.

Normal Approximation of a Binomial Distribution

Consider the binomial distribution consisting of n trials with probability p of success on each trial. If $np \geq 5$ and $n(1 - p) \geq 5$, then binomial distribution can be approximated by a normal distribution with a mean of

$$\bar{x} = np$$

and a standard deviation of

$$\sigma = \sqrt{np(1 - p)}.$$

EXAMPLE 1 *Using a Normal Distribution*

A normal distribution of IQ scores has a mean of 100 and a standard deviation of 16. Find the probability that a randomly selected person's IQ will be between 84 and 116.

SOLUTION

The score of 84 is one standard deviation to the left of the mean and the score of 116 is one standard deviation to the right of the mean. The diagram shows the partial areas based on the properties of a normal curve. So, the probability that a randomly selected person will have an IQ between 84 and 116 is found by adding the two probabilities $0.34 + 0.34 = 0.68.$

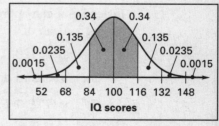

Chapter 12

Practice with Examples

For use with pages 746–752

Exercises for Example 1

A normal distribution has a mean of 80 and a standard deviation of 7. Find the probability that a randomly selected x-value is in the given interval.

1. between 66 and 87

2. at most 94

3. The waiting time for drive-through customers at a certain bank during the busiest hours is normally distributed with a mean of 8 minutes and a standard deviation of 2 minutes. What is the probability that the next two customers will wait longer than 8 minutes?

EXAMPLE 2 *Finding a Binomial Probability*

A scientist claims that 23% of all patients with high blood pressure have negative side effects from a certain kind of medicine. There are 120 patients in a random study. What is the probability that you will find more than 33 patients with negative side effects?

SOLUTION

This is a binomial distribution because the patient either has negative side effects (success) or does not (failure). To answer the question using the binomial probability formula, you would have to calculate the following:

$$P(x \geq 33) = P(33) + P(34) + P(35) + \cdots + P(120)$$

Instead you can approximate the answer with a normal distribution having a mean of

$$\bar{x} = np = 120(0.23) \approx 28$$

and a standard deviation of

$$\sigma = \sqrt{np(1 - p)} = \sqrt{(120)(0.23)(0.77)} \approx 5$$

Because 33 is one standard deviation to the right of the mean, the probability of finding more than 33 patients with negative side effects is:

$$p(x \geq 33) \approx 0.135 + 0.0235 + 0.0015$$

$$= 0.16$$

NAME _____ DATE _____

Practice with Examples

For use with pages 746–752

Exercises for Example 2
....
Look at Example 2. Suppose advances in medicine reduced the
percentage of patients having negative side effects to 18%.

4. What is the probability that you will find at most 30 patients with
negative side effects?

5. What is the probability that you will find at least 18 patients with
negative side effects?

Practice with Examples

For use with pages 769–775

GOAL **Use trigonometric relationships to evaluate trigonometric functions of acute angles**

VOCABULARY

Right Triangle Definition of Trigonometric Functions

Let θ be an acute angle of a right triangle. The six trigonometric functions of θ are defined as follows.

$$\sin\theta = \frac{opp}{hyp} \qquad \cos\theta = \frac{adj}{hyp} \qquad \tan\theta = \frac{opp}{adj}$$

$$\csc\theta = \frac{hyp}{opp} \qquad \sec\theta = \frac{hyp}{adj} \qquad \cot\theta = \frac{adj}{opp}$$

The abbreviations *opp, adj,* and *hyp* represent the lengths of the three sides of the right triangle. Note that the ratios in the second row are the reciprocals of the ratios in the first row. That is:

$$\csc\theta = \frac{1}{\sin\theta} \qquad \sec\theta = \frac{1}{\cos\theta} \qquad \cot\theta = \frac{1}{\tan\theta}$$

The table below gives values of the six trigonometric functions for the common angles 30°, 45°, and 60°.

θ	$\sin\theta$	$\cos\theta$	$\tan\theta$	$\csc\theta$	$\sec\theta$	$\cot\theta$
30°	$\dfrac{1}{2}$	$\dfrac{\sqrt{3}}{2}$	$\dfrac{\sqrt{3}}{3}$	2	$\dfrac{2\sqrt{3}}{3}$	$\sqrt{3}$
45°	$\dfrac{\sqrt{2}}{2}$	$\dfrac{\sqrt{2}}{2}$	1	$\sqrt{2}$	$\sqrt{2}$	1
60°	$\dfrac{\sqrt{3}}{2}$	$\dfrac{1}{2}$	$\sqrt{3}$	$\dfrac{2\sqrt{3}}{3}$	2	$\dfrac{\sqrt{3}}{3}$

Finding all missing side lengths and angle measures is called **solving a right triangle**.

NAME _____ DATE _____

Practice with Examples

For use with pages 769–775

EXAMPLE 1 *Evaluating Trigonometric Functions*

Evaluate the six trigonometric functions of the angle θ
shown in the right triangle.

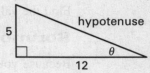

SOLUTION

The sides opposite and adjacent to the angle θ are given.
To find the length of the hypotenuse, use the Pythagorean Theorem.

$$\sqrt{5^2 + 12^2} = \sqrt{25 + 144} = \sqrt{169} = 13$$

Using adj = 12, opp = 5, and hyp = 13, you can evaluate the trigonometric functions.

$$\sin \theta = \frac{\text{opp}}{\text{hyp}} = \frac{5}{13} \qquad \cos \theta = \frac{\text{adj}}{\text{hyp}} = \frac{12}{13} \qquad \tan \theta = \frac{\text{opp}}{\text{adj}} = \frac{5}{12}$$

$$\csc \theta = \frac{\text{hyp}}{\text{opp}} = \frac{13}{5} \qquad \sec \theta = \frac{\text{hyp}}{\text{adj}} = \frac{13}{12} \qquad \cot \theta = \frac{\text{adj}}{\text{opp}} = \frac{12}{5}$$

Exercises for Example 1

Evaluate the six trigonometric functions of the given angle θ.

1.

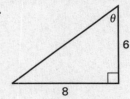

2.

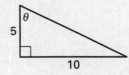

3.

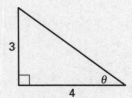

NAME _____ DATE _____

Practice with Examples

For use with pages 769–775

EXAMPLE 2 ***Finding a Missing Side Length of a Right Triangle***

Find the value of x for the right triangle shown.

SOLUTION

Because you are given the hypotenuse and the side adjacent to $\theta = 45°$, write the equation of the trigonometric function involving the ratio of these sides, then solve the equation for x.

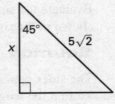

$\cos 45° = \dfrac{\text{adj}}{\text{hyp}}$ Write trigonometric equation.

$\dfrac{1}{\sqrt{2}} = \dfrac{x}{5\sqrt{2}}$ Substitute $\dfrac{1}{\sqrt{2}}$ for $\cos 45°$ and $5\sqrt{2}$ for hypotenuse.

$5 = x$ Multiply each side by $5\sqrt{2}$.

The length of the side is $x = 5$.

Exercises for Example 2

Find the missing side lengths x and y.

4.

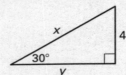

5.

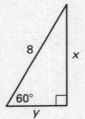

6.

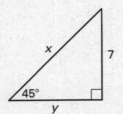

NAME _____ DATE _____

Practice with Examples

For use with pages 776–783

GOAL Measure angles in standard position using degree measure and radian measure, and calculate arc lengths and areas of sectors

---

VOCABULARY

An angle is formed by two rays, the fixed ray called the **initial side** and the rotating ray called the **terminal side**. An angle is in **standard position** if its vertex is at the origin and its initial side is the positive x-axis.

One **radian** is the measure of an angle in standard position whose terminal side intercepts an arc of length r.

A **sector** is a region of a circle that is bounded by two radii and an arc of the circle with a **central angle** θ formed by the two radii.

The **arc length** s of a sector with radius r and central angle θ is given by the formula $s = r\theta$.

The **area** A of a sector with radius r and central angle θ is given by the formula $A = \frac{1}{2}r^2\theta$.

EXAMPLE 1 *Drawing Angles in Standard Position*

Draw an angle with the given measure in standard position. Then tell in which quadrant the terminal side lies.

a. $120°$ **b.** $-210°$ **c.** $570°$

SOLUTION

a. Use the fact that $120° = 180° - 120° = 60°$. So, the terminal side is $60°$ counterclockwise before the negative x-axis.

b. Because $-210°$ is negative, and $210° = 180° + 30°$, the terminal side is $30°$ clockwise past the negative x-axis.

c. Use the fact that $570° = 360° + 210°$. So, the terminal side makes one complete revolution counterclockwise and continues another $210°$.

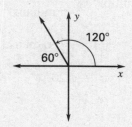

Quadrant II

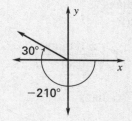

Quadrant II

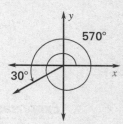

Quadrant III

Chapter 13

NAME _____ DATE _____

Practice with Examples

For use with pages 776–783

Exercises for Example 1

Draw an angle with the given measure in standard position. Then tell in which quadrant the terminal side lies.

1. $-60°$
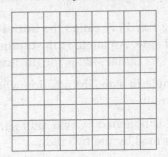

2. $225°$
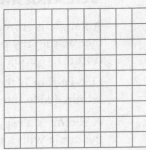

3. $420°$
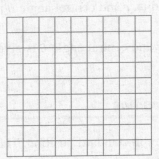

4. $-200°$
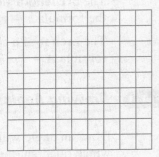

EXAMPLE 2 ## Converting Between Degrees and Radians

a. Convert $-20°$ to radians.

b. Convert $\frac{2\pi}{3}$ radians to degrees.

SOLUTION

a. To rewrite a degree measure in radians, multiply by $\frac{\pi \text{ radians}}{180°}$.

$$-20° = (-20°)\left(\frac{\pi \text{ radians}}{180°}\right)$$

$$= -\frac{\pi}{9} \text{ radians}$$

b. To rewrite a radian measure in degrees, multiply by $\frac{180°}{\pi \text{ radians}}$.

$$\frac{2\pi}{3} = \frac{2\pi}{3} \text{ radians} \left(\frac{180°}{\pi \text{ radians}}\right)$$

$$= 120°$$

Exercises for Example 2

Rewrite each degree measure in radians and each radian measure in degrees.

5. $315°$

6. $-150°$

Algebra 2
Practice Workbook with Examples

Practice with Examples

For use with pages 776–783

7. $\dfrac{5\pi}{6}$

8. $-\dfrac{3\pi}{4}$

EXAMPLE 3 **Finding Arc Length and Area**

Find the arc length and area of a sector with a radius of 3 km and a central angle of 20°.

SOLUTION

Begin by converting the angle measure to radians.

$$\theta = 20°\left(\frac{\pi \text{ radians}}{180°}\right) = \frac{\pi}{9} \text{ radians}$$

Then use the formulas for arc length and area.

Arc length: $s = r\theta = 3\left(\dfrac{\pi}{9}\right) = \dfrac{\pi}{3}$ kilometers

Area: $A = \dfrac{1}{2}r^2\theta = \dfrac{1}{2}(3^2)\left(\dfrac{\pi}{9}\right) = \dfrac{\pi}{2}$ square kilometers

Exercises for Example 3

Find the arc length and area of a sector with the given radius *r* and central angle *θ*.

9. $r = 9$ in., $\theta = 50°$

10. $r = 5$ cm, $\theta = 240°$

11. $r = 6$ ft, $\theta = 180°$

NAME _____ DATE _____

Practice with Examples

For use with pages 784–790

GOAL **Evaluate trigonometric functions of any angle**

VOCABULARY

General Definition of Trigonometric Functions

Let θ be an angle in standard position and (x, y) be any point (except the origin) on the terminal side of θ. The six trigonometric functions of θ are defined as follows.

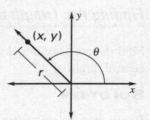

$$\sin \theta = \frac{y}{r} \qquad\qquad \csc \theta = \frac{r}{y}, y \neq 0$$

$$\cos \theta = \frac{x}{r} \qquad\qquad \sec \theta = \frac{r}{x}, x \neq 0$$

Pythagorean theorem gives $r = \sqrt{x^2 + y^2}$.

$$\tan \theta = \frac{y}{x}, x \neq 0 \qquad \cot \theta = \frac{x}{y}, y \neq 0$$

For acute angles, these definitions give the same values as those given by the definitions in Lesson 13.1.

EXAMPLE 1 *Evaluating Trigonometric Functions Given a Point*

Let $(-1, 1)$ be a point on the terminal aide of an angle θ in standard position. Evaluate the six trigonometric functions of θ.

SOLUTION

Begin by sketching the angle in the second quadrant as shown. Then use the Pythagorean theorem to find r.

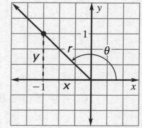

$$r = \sqrt{x^2 + y^2}$$
$$= \sqrt{(-1)^2 + 1^2}$$
$$= \sqrt{2}$$

Then using $x = -1$, $y = 1$, and $r = \sqrt{2}$, you can write the following:

$$\sin \theta = \frac{y}{r} = \frac{1}{\sqrt{2}} = \frac{\sqrt{2}}{2} \qquad \cos \theta = \frac{x}{r} = -\frac{1}{\sqrt{2}} = -\frac{\sqrt{2}}{2} \qquad \tan \theta = \frac{y}{x} = \frac{1}{-1} = -1$$

$$\csc \theta = \frac{r}{y} = \frac{\sqrt{2}}{1} = \sqrt{2} \qquad \sec \theta = \frac{r}{x} = \frac{\sqrt{2}}{-1} = -\sqrt{2} \qquad \cot \theta = \frac{x}{y} = \frac{-1}{1} = -1$$

Practice with Examples

For use with pages 784–790

Exercises for Example 1

Use the given point on the terminal side of an angle θ in standard position. Then evaluate the six trigonometric functions.

1. $(-15, -8)$ **2.** $(1, -1)$

3. $\left(1, \sqrt{3}\right)$ **4.** $(-3, 4)$

EXAMPLE 2 *Finding Reference Angles*

Find the reference angle θ' for each angle θ.

a. $\theta = 120°$ **b.** $\theta = \dfrac{5\pi}{3}$

SOLUTION

a. Because $90° < \theta < 180°$, the reference angle is $\theta' = 180° - \theta = 180° - 120° = 60°$.

b. Because $\dfrac{3\pi}{2} < \theta < 2\pi$, the reference angle is $\theta' = 2\pi - \theta = $

$2\pi - \dfrac{5\pi}{3} = \dfrac{6\pi}{3} - \dfrac{5\pi}{3} = \dfrac{\pi}{3}.$

Exercises for Example 2

Find the reference angle θ' for each angle θ.

5. $\theta = 210°$ **6.** $\theta = -300°$

7. $\theta = -\dfrac{4\pi}{3}$ **8.** $\theta = \dfrac{5\pi}{4}$

Chapter 13

Practice with Examples

For use with pages 784–790

EXAMPLE 3 **Using Reference Angles to Evaluate Trigonometric Functions**

Evaluate (a) $\sec\left(\dfrac{5\pi}{4}\right)$ and (b) $\cot(-240°)$.

SOLUTION

a. Because $\pi < \theta < \dfrac{3\pi}{2}$, the reference angle is $\theta' = \theta - \pi =$

$\dfrac{5\pi}{4} - \pi = \dfrac{5\pi}{4} - \dfrac{4\pi}{4} = \dfrac{\pi}{4}$. The secant function is negative in

Quadrant III, so $\sec\left(\dfrac{5\pi}{4}\right) = -\sec\left(\dfrac{\pi}{4}\right) = -\dfrac{\sqrt{2}}{1} = -\sqrt{2}$.

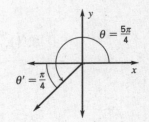

b. The angle $-240°$ is coterminal with $120°$. The reference
angle is $\theta' = 180° - 120° = 60°$. The cotangent function
is negative in Quadrant II, so

$$\cot(-240°) = -\cot(60°) = -\dfrac{1}{\sqrt{3}} = -\dfrac{\sqrt{3}}{3}.$$

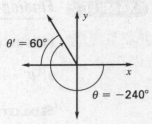

Exercises for Example 3

Evaluate the function without using a calculator.

9. $\cos(-225°)$

10. $\tan(330°)$

11. $\cot\left(\dfrac{4\pi}{3}\right)$

12. $\sin\left(-\dfrac{5\pi}{3}\right)$

Practice with Examples

For use with pages 792–798

GOAL Evaluate inverse trigonometric functions

VOCABULARY

If $-1 \leq a \leq 1$, then the **inverse sine** of a is $\sin^{-1} a = \theta$ where $\sin \theta = a$ and $-\dfrac{\pi}{2} \leq \theta \leq \dfrac{\pi}{2}$ (or $-90° \leq \theta \leq 90°$).

If $-1 \leq a \leq 1$, then the **inverse cosine** of a is $\cos^{-1} a = \theta$ where $\cos \theta = a$ and $0 \leq \theta \leq \pi$ (or $0° \leq \theta \leq 180°$.)

If a is any real number, then the **inverse tangent** of a is $\tan^{-1} a = \theta$ where $\tan \theta = a$ and $-\dfrac{\pi}{2} < \theta < \dfrac{\pi}{2}$ (or $-90° < \theta < 90°$).

EXAMPLE 1 *Evaluating Inverse Trigonometric Functions*

Evaluate the expression in both radians and degrees.

a. $\sin^{-1}(-3)$ **b.** $\tan^{-1}\sqrt{3}$ **c.** $\cos^{-1}\left(-\dfrac{\sqrt{3}}{2}\right)$

SOLUTION

a. Because $-1 \leq \sin \theta \leq 1$, there is no angle whose sine is -3. So $\sin^{-1}(-3)$ is undefined.

b. When $-\dfrac{\pi}{2} < \theta < \dfrac{\pi}{2}$ or $-90° < \theta < 90°$, the angle whose tangent is $\sqrt{3}$ is:

$$\theta = \tan^{-1}\sqrt{3} = \frac{\pi}{3} \quad \text{or} \quad \theta = \tan^{-1}\sqrt{3} = 60°.$$

c. When $0 \leq \theta \leq \pi$ or $0 \leq \theta \leq 180°$, the angle whose cosine is $-\dfrac{\sqrt{3}}{2}$ is:

$$\theta = \cos^{-1}\left(-\frac{\sqrt{3}}{2}\right) = \frac{5\pi}{6} \quad \text{or} \quad \theta = \cos^{-1}\left(-\frac{\sqrt{3}}{2}\right) = 150°.$$

Exercises for Example 1
....

Evaluate the expression in both radians and degrees.

1. $\sin^{-1}\left(-\dfrac{1}{2}\right)$ **2.** $\tan^{-1}(1)$

Chapter 13

NAME _____ DATE _____

Practice with Examples

For use with pages 792–798

3. $\tan^{-1}\left(-\dfrac{\sqrt{3}}{3}\right)$

4. $\cos^{-1}\left(-\dfrac{\sqrt{2}}{2}\right)$

EXAMPLE 2 *Finding an Angle Measure*

Find the measure of the angle θ for the triangle shown.

SOLUTION

In the right triangle, you are given the adjacent side and the opposite side. So, you want to use the tangent function.

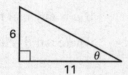

$$\tan \theta = \frac{\text{opp}}{\text{adj}} = \frac{6}{11}$$

You are being asked to find the angle whose tangent is $\frac{6}{11}$. Use a calculator and the inverse tangent key to find the measure of θ.

In radian mode, $\quad \theta = \tan^{-1}\dfrac{6}{11} \approx 0.499$ radians or

in degree mode, $\quad \theta = \tan^{-1}\dfrac{6}{11} \approx 28.6°.$

Exercises for Example 2

Find the measure of the angle θ in both radians and degrees. Round to three significant digits.

5.
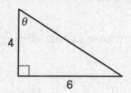

6.

7.

Algebra 2
Practice Workbook with Examples

Practice with Examples

For use with pages 792–798

EXAMPLE 3 *Solving a Trigonometric Equation*

Solve the equation $\cos \theta = -0.84$ where $90° < \theta < 180°$.

SOLUTION

You want to find the angle whose cosine is -0.84. The cosine is negative in Quadrant II and Quadrant III. In Quadrant II (where $90° < \theta < 180°$), the angle that has this cosine value is:

$$\theta = \cos^{-1}(-0.84) \approx 147°.$$

Exercises for Example 3

Solve the equation for θ. Round to three significant digits.

8. $\sin \theta = -0.72; 270° < \theta < 360°$

9. $\tan \theta = -2.4; 90° < \theta < 180°$

10. $\cos \theta = -0.13; 180° < \theta < 270°$

11. $\sin \theta = 0.54; 90° < \theta < 180°$

Chapter 13

NAME _____ DATE _____

Practice with Examples

For use with pages 799–806

GOAL Use the law of sines to find the sides and angles of a triangle

---

VOCABULARY

If ABC is a triangle with sides a, b, and c, then according to the **law of sines,**

$$\frac{a}{\sin A} = \frac{b}{\sin B} = \frac{c}{\sin C} \quad \text{or} \quad \frac{\sin A}{a} = \frac{\sin B}{b} = \frac{\sin C}{c}.$$

EXAMPLE 1 *The AAS or ASA Case*

Solve $\triangle ABC$ with $A = 23°$, $B = 57°$, and $c = 12$ meters.

SOLUTION

To solve a triangle, you must find all unknown angles and sides. Because the sum of the three angles of any triangle is 180°, you can find angle C:

$\quad C = 180° - 23° - 57° = 100°$.

Using the law of sines, you can find the unknown sides a and b.

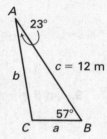

$$\frac{a}{\sin 23°} = \frac{b}{\sin 57°} = \frac{12}{\sin 100°}$$

$\dfrac{a}{\sin 23°} = \dfrac{12}{\sin 100°}$	Write two equations, each with one variable.	$\dfrac{b}{\sin 57°} = \dfrac{12}{\sin 100°}$
$a = \dfrac{12 \sin 23°}{\sin 100°}$	Cross-multiply to solve for variable.	$b = \dfrac{12 \sin 57°}{\sin 100°}$
$a \approx 4.76$ meters	Use a calculator.	$b \approx 10.22$ meters

---

Exercises for Example 1

Solve $\triangle ABC$.

1. $A = 23°$, $B = 57°$, $a = 12$ in.

2. $B = 34°$, $C = 108°$, $b = 20$ mi

NAME _____   DATE _____

Practice with Examples

For use with pages 799–806

Solve △*ABC*.

3. $A = 41°$, $C = 77°$, $a = 10.5$ ft

4. $B = 20°$, $C = 31°$, $b = 210$ mm

Two angles and one side (AAS or ASA) determine exactly one triangle.
Two sides and an angle opposite one of the sides (SSA) may determine
no triangle, one triangle, or two triangles. The one-triangle case is dis-
cussed in Example 2.

EXAMPLE 2   *The SSA Case—One Triangle*

Solve △*ABC* with $B = 40°$, $a = 5$ in., and $b = 7$ in.

SOLUTION

First make a sketch. Because *B* is acute and the side
opposite *B* is longer than the adjacent side, you know
that only one triangle can be formed. Use the law of
sines to find *A*.

$$\frac{5}{\sin A} = \frac{7}{\sin 40°} \qquad \text{Law of sines}$$

$$\sin A = \frac{5 \sin 40°}{7} \qquad \text{Solve for } \sin A.$$

$$\sin A \approx 0.4591 \qquad \text{Use a calculator.}$$

$$A \approx 27.3° \qquad \text{Use inverse sine function.}$$

You then know that $C \approx 180° - 40° - 27.3° = 112.7°$. Use the law of
sines to find length *c*.

$$\frac{c}{\sin 112.7°} = \frac{7}{\sin 40°}$$

$$c = \frac{7 \sin 112.7°}{\sin 40°} \approx 10.0 \text{ inches}$$

Chapter 13

Practice with Examples

For use with pages 799–806

Exercises for Example 2

Solve △ABC.

5. $A = 75°$, $a = 4$ in., $c = 2$ in.

6. $C = 100°$, $b = 7$ in., $c = 9$ in.

7. $B = 25°$, $a = 4$ m, $b = 6$ m

Chapter 13

NAME _____ DATE _____

Practice with Examples

For use with pages 807–812

GOAL Use the law of cosines to find the sides and angles of a triangle

---

VOCABULARY

If △ABC has sides of length a, b, and c as shown, then:

$$a^2 = b^2 + c^2 - 2bc \cos A$$

$$b^2 = a^2 + c^2 - 2ac \cos B$$

$$c^2 = a^2 + b^2 - 2ab \cos C$$

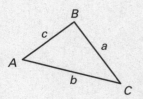

EXAMPLE 1 **The SAS Case**

Solve △ABC with $a = 18$, $b = 11$, and $C = 58°$.

SOLUTION

Because you were not given a side opposite an angle, you cannot use the law of sines. To find the length c of the side, use the law of cosines.

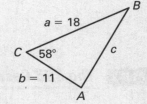

$c^2 = a^2 + b^2 - 2ab \cos C$	Write law of cosines.
$c^2 = 18^2 + 11^2 - 2(18)(11) \cos 58°$	Substitute for a, b, and C.
$c^2 \approx 235.2$	Simplify.
$c \approx \sqrt{235.2} \approx 15.3$	Take square root.

Now that you have an angle and a side opposite it, you can use the law of sines to find a second angle.

$\dfrac{a}{\sin A} = \dfrac{c}{\sin C}$	Write law of sines.
$\dfrac{18}{\sin A} = \dfrac{15.3}{\sin 58°}$	Substitute for a, c, and C.
$\sin A \approx 0.9977$	Solve for $\sin A$.
$A \approx \sin^{-1} 0.9977 \approx 86.1°$	Use inverse sine.

You can find the third angle as follows.

$$B = 180° - 58° - 86.1° = 35.9°$$

Practice with Examples

For use with pages 807–812

Exercises for Example 1

Solve △*ABC*.

1. $A = 62°$, $b = 56$, $c = 40$ **2.** $B = 100°$, $a = 12$, $c = 13$

3. $C = 42°$, $a = 22$, $b = 35$ **4.** $A = 56°$, $b = 15$, $c = 17$

EXAMPLE 2   *The SSS Case*

Solve △*ABC* with $a = 22$ meters, $b = 19$ meters, and $c = 14$ meters.

SOLUTION

Begin by sketching the triangle. Then find the angle
opposite the longest side, $\overline{CB}$, using the law of cosines.

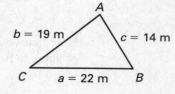

$$\cos A = \frac{b^2 + c^2 - a^2}{2bc} = \frac{19^2 + 14^2 - 22^2}{2(19)(14)} \approx 0.1372$$

$$A = \cos^{-1} 0.1372 \approx 82.1°$$

Now use the law of sines to find B.

$\dfrac{a}{\sin A} = \dfrac{b}{\sin B}$	Write law of sines.
$\dfrac{22}{\sin 82.1°} = \dfrac{19}{\sin B}$	Substitute for a, A, and b.
$\sin B = \dfrac{19 \sin 82.1°}{22}$	Solve for $\sin B$.
$\sin B \approx 0.8554$	Simplify.
$B \approx \sin^{-1} 0.8554 \approx 58.8°$	Use inverse sine.

Finally, you can find the measure of angle C.

$$C = 180° - 82.1° - 58.8° = 39.1°$$

NAME _____ DATE _____

Practice with Examples

For use with pages 807–812

Exercises for Example 2

Solve △ABC.

5. $a = 39, b = 14, c = 27$

6. $a = 7, b = 7, c = 10$

7. $a = 19, b = 21, c = 13$

Chapter 13

Practice with Examples

For use with pages 813–819

GOAL **Use parametric equations to represent motion in a plane**

> ### VOCABULARY
>
> A pair of equations that expresses x and y in terms of a third variable t, written as $x = f(t)$ and $y = g(t)$, are called **parametric equations,** and t is called the **parameter.**

EXAMPLE 1 *Graphing a Set of Parametric Equations*

Graph $x = t - 3$ and $y = -2t + 1$ for $1 \leq t \leq 5$.

SOLUTION

Begin by making a table of values.

t	1	2	3	4	5
x	-2	-1	0	1	2
y	-1	-3	-5	-7	-9

Then plot the points (x, y) given in the table:

$(-2, -1), (-1, -3), (0, -5), (1, -7), (2, -9)$

Now connect the points with a line segment as shown.

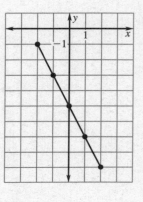

Exercises for Example 1

Graph the parametric equations.

1. $x = 2t + 1$ and $y = -t + 2$
for $0 \leq t \leq 4$

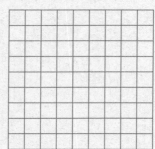

2. $x = t$ and $y = -t$
for $2 \leq t \leq 6$

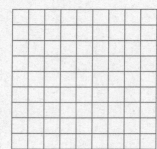

NAME _____ DATE _____

Practice with Examples

For use with pages 813–819

3. $x = -3t + 4$ and $y = t + 1$
for $1 \leq t \leq 4$

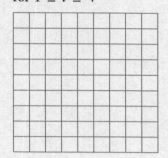

4. $x = -2t + 2$ and $y = t - 1$
for $0 \leq t \leq 4$

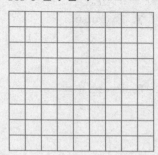

EXAMPLE 2 *Eliminating the Parameter*

Write an *xy*-equation for the parametric equations in Example 1:
$x = t - 3$ and $y = -2t + 1$ for $1 \leq t \leq 5$. State the domain for the
equation.

SOLUTION

First solve one of the parametric equations for *t*. It is more convenient to
solve the *x*-equation because the coefficient of *t* is one.

$x = t - 3$ Write original equation.

$x + 3 = t$ Add 3 to each side.

Then substitute this value for *t* in the other parametric equation.

$y = -2t + 1$ Write original equation.

$y = -2(x + 3) + 1$ Substitute for *t*.

$y = -2x - 6 + 1$ Use distributive property.

$y = -2x - 5$ Simplify.

To find the domain of the *xy*-equation, determine the values of *x* when
$t = 1$ and $t = 5$. When $t = 1$, $x = t - 3 = 1 - 3 = -2$, and when
$t = 5$, $x = t - 3 = 5 - 3 = 2$. So, the domain is $-2 \leq x \leq 2$.

Exercises for Example 2

**Write an *xy*-equation for the parametric equations. State the
domain.**

  5. Exercise 1

  6. Exercise 2

Chapter 13

Practice with Examples

For use with pages 813–819

Write an *xy*-equation for the parametric equations. State the domain.

7. Exercise 3

8. Exercise 4

EXAMPLE 3 *Modeling Linear Motion*

An object is at $(0, 12)$ at time $t = 0$ and then at $(50, 0)$ at time 4. Write parametric equations describing the linear motion.

SOLUTION

The angle of elevation is $\theta = \tan^{-1} \frac{12}{50} \approx 13.5°$. To find the constant speed V, divide the distance by the change in time, $t = 4$ seconds.

The distance traveled is the hypotenuse of the right triangle, so

$$d = \sqrt{12^2 + 50^2} = \sqrt{2644} \approx 51.4 \text{ ft and}$$

$$v \approx \frac{51.4 \text{ ft}}{4 \text{ sec}} \approx 12.9 \text{ ft/sec}$$

Using $v = 12.9$, $\theta = 13.5°$, and $(x_0, y_0) = (0, 12)$, you can write:

$$x = (v \cos \theta)t + x_0 \quad \text{and} \quad y = (v \sin \theta)t + y_0$$
$$\approx (12.9 \cos 13.5°)t + 0 \qquad \approx (12.9 \sin 13.5°)t + 12$$
$$\approx 12.5t \qquad\qquad\qquad \approx 3.01t + 12$$

Exercises for Example 3

Use the given information to write parametric equations describing the linear motion.

9. An object is at $(0, 0)$ at time $t = 0$ and then at $(15, 80)$ at time $t = 5$.

10. An object is at $(0, 20)$ at time $t = 0$ and then at $(100, 0)$ at time $t = 10$.

Algebra 2
Practice Workbook with Examples

NAME _____ DATE _____

Practice with Examples

For use with pages 831–837

GOAL **Graph sine, cosine, and tangent functions**

> ## VOCABULARY
>
> The **amplitude** of the graphs for the sine and cosine functions is the average between the maximum and minimum values.
>
> The **frequency** gives the number of cycles per unit of time, and is the reciprocal of the period.
>
> The graphs of $y = a \sin bx$ and $y = a \cos bx$, where a and b are nonzero real numbers, have an amplitude of $|a|$ and a period of $\dfrac{2\pi}{|b|}$.
>
> If a and b are nonzero real numbers, the graph of $y = a \tan bx$ has a period of $\dfrac{\pi}{|b|}$ and vertical asymptotes at odd multiples of $\dfrac{\pi}{2|b|}$.

EXAMPLE 1 *Graphing a Sine Function*

Graph $y = 3 \sin \frac{1}{2}x$.

SOLUTION

The amplitude is $a = 3$ and the period is $\dfrac{2\pi}{b} = \dfrac{2\pi}{\frac{1}{2}} = 4\pi$. The five key points are:

Intercepts: $(0, 0)$; $\left(\dfrac{1}{2} \cdot \dfrac{2\pi}{b}, 0\right) = \left(\dfrac{1}{2} \cdot \dfrac{2\pi}{\frac{1}{2}}, 0\right) = (2\pi, 0)$;

$\left(\dfrac{2\pi}{b}, 0\right) = \left(\dfrac{2\pi}{\frac{1}{2}}, 0\right) = (4\pi, 0)$

Maximum: $\left(\dfrac{1}{4} \cdot \dfrac{2\pi}{b}, a\right) = \left(\dfrac{1}{4} \cdot \dfrac{2\pi}{\frac{1}{2}}, 3\right) = (\pi, 3)$

Minimum: $\left(\dfrac{3}{4} \cdot \dfrac{2\pi}{b}, -a\right) = \left(\dfrac{3}{4} \cdot \dfrac{2\pi}{\frac{1}{2}}, -3\right) = (3\pi, -3)$

Chapter 14

NAME _____ DATE _____

Practice with Examples

For use with pages 831–837

Exercises for Example 1

Draw one cycle of the function's graph.

1. $y = \sin 2x$

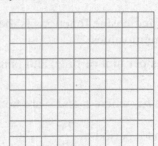

2. $y = 4 \sin x$

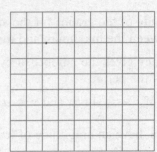

3. $y = 3 \sin 4x$

EXAMPLE 2 *Graphing a Cosine Function*

Graph $y = \frac{1}{2} \cos 2x$.

SOLUTION

The amplitude is $a = \frac{1}{2}$ and the period is $\frac{2\pi}{b} = \frac{2\pi}{2} = \pi$. The five key points are:

Intercepts: $\left(\frac{1}{4} \cdot \frac{2\pi}{b}, 0\right) = \left(\frac{1}{4} \cdot \pi, 0\right) = \left(\frac{\pi}{4}, 0\right)$

$\left(\frac{3}{4} \cdot \frac{2\pi}{b}, 0\right) = \left(\frac{3}{4} \cdot \pi, 0\right) = \left(\frac{3\pi}{4}, 0\right)$

Maximum: $(0, a) = \left(0, \frac{1}{2}\right); \left(\frac{2\pi}{b}, a\right) = \left(\pi, \frac{1}{2}\right)$

Minimum: $\left(\frac{1}{2} \cdot \frac{2\pi}{b}, -a\right) = \left(\frac{1}{2} \cdot \pi, -\frac{1}{2}\right) = \left(\frac{\pi}{2}, -\frac{1}{2}\right)$

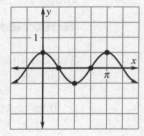

Exercises for Example 2

Draw one cycle of the function's graph.

4. $y = \cos 3x$

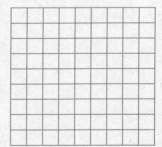

5. $y = 2 \cos 2\pi x$

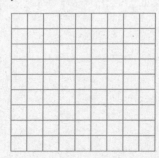

6. $y = 3 \cos 2x$

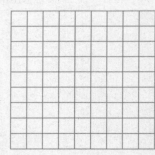

Chapter 14

NAME _____ DATE _____

Practice with Examples

For use with pages 831–837

EXAMPLE 3 *Graphing a Tangent Function*

Graph $y = 2 \tan 2\pi x$.

SOLUTION

The period is $\dfrac{\pi}{b} = \dfrac{\pi}{2\pi} = \dfrac{1}{2}$.

Intercept: $(0, 0)$

Asymptotes: $x = \dfrac{1}{2} \cdot \dfrac{\pi}{b} = \dfrac{1}{2} \cdot \dfrac{1}{2} = \dfrac{1}{4}$

$$x = -\dfrac{1}{2} \cdot \dfrac{\pi}{b} = -\dfrac{1}{2} \cdot \dfrac{1}{2} = -\dfrac{1}{4}$$

Halfway points: $\left(\dfrac{1}{4} \cdot \dfrac{\pi}{b}, a\right) = \left(\dfrac{1}{4} \cdot \dfrac{1}{2}, 2\right) = \left(\dfrac{1}{8}, 2\right)$

$$\left(-\dfrac{1}{4} \cdot \dfrac{\pi}{b}, -a\right) = \left(-\dfrac{1}{4} \cdot \dfrac{1}{2}, -2\right) = \left(-\dfrac{1}{8}, -2\right)$$

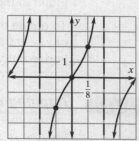

Exercises for Example 3

Draw one cycle of the function's graph.

7. $y = 4 \tan x$

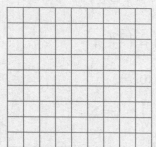

8. $y = \tan \frac{1}{3}x$

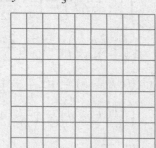

9. $y = 2 \tan \pi x$

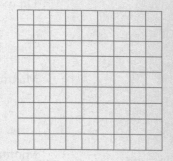

NAME _____ DATE _____

Practice with Examples

For use with pages 840–847

GOAL **Graph translations and reflections of sine, cosine, and tangent graphs**

VOCABULARY

To obtain the graph of $y = a \sin b(x - h) + k$ or $y = a \cos b(x - h) + k$, transform the graph of $y = |a| \sin bx$ or $y = |a| \cos bx$ by shifting the graph k units vertically and h units horizontally. Then, if $a < 0$, reflect the graph in the line $y = k$.

To obtain the graph of $y = a \tan b(x - h) + k$, transform the graph of $y = |a| \tan bx$ by shifting the graph k units vertically and h units horizontally. Then, if $a < 0$, reflect the graph in the line $y = k$.

EXAMPLE 1 *Graphing a Vertical Translation*

Graph $y = 4 + \cos 2x$.

SOLUTION

Because the graph is a transformation of the graph if $y = \cos 2x$, the amplitude is 1 and the period is $\dfrac{2\pi}{2} = \pi$. Because $k = 4$, translate the graph of $y = \cos 2x$ up 4 units. The five key points are:

On $y = k$: $\left(\dfrac{1}{4} \cdot \dfrac{2\pi}{b}, k\right) = \left(\dfrac{1}{4} \cdot \dfrac{2\pi}{2}, 4\right) = \left(\dfrac{\pi}{4}, 4\right)$

$\left(\dfrac{3}{4} \cdot \dfrac{2\pi}{b}, a\right) = \left(\dfrac{3}{4} \cdot \dfrac{2\pi}{2}, 4\right) = \left(\dfrac{3\pi}{4}, 4\right)$

Maximum: $(0, k + a) = (0, 4 + 1) = (0, 5)$

$\left(\dfrac{2\pi}{b}, k + a\right) = \left(\dfrac{2\pi}{2}, 4 + 1\right) = (\pi, 5)$

Minimum: $\left(\dfrac{1}{2} \cdot \dfrac{2\pi}{b}, k - a\right) = \left(\dfrac{1}{2} \cdot \dfrac{2\pi}{2}, 4 - 1\right) = \left(\dfrac{\pi}{2}, 3\right)$

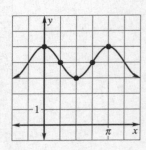

Exercises for Example 1

Graph the function.

1. $y = -2 + \cos x$ **2.** $y = 3 + \sin x$ **3.** $y = -3 + \tan x$

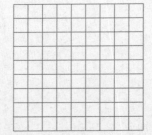 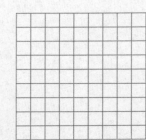 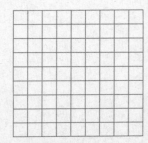

Chapter 14

NAME _____ DATE _____

Practice with Examples

For use with pages 840–847

EXAMPLE 2 *Graphing a Horizontal Translation*

Graph $y = 3 \sin \frac{1}{2}\left(x + \frac{\pi}{2}\right)$.

SOLUTION

The amplitude is 3 and the period is $\frac{2\pi}{\frac{1}{2}} = 4\pi$. Because $h = -\frac{\pi}{2}$,

translate the graph of $y = 3 \sin \frac{1}{2}x$ left $\frac{\pi}{2}$ units. The five key points are:

On $y = k$: $(h, 0) = \left(-\frac{\pi}{2}, 0\right)$; $\left(\frac{2\pi}{b} + h, 0\right) = \left(4\pi - \frac{\pi}{2}, 0\right) = \left(\frac{7\pi}{2}, 0\right)$;

$\left(\frac{1}{2} \cdot \frac{2\pi}{b} + h, 0\right) = \left(\frac{3\pi}{2}, 0\right)$

Maximum: $\left(\frac{1}{4} \cdot \frac{2\pi}{b} + h, a\right) = \left(\frac{\pi}{2}, 3\right)$

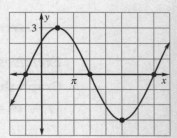

Minimum: $\left(\frac{3}{4} \cdot \frac{2\pi}{b} + h, -a\right) = \left(\frac{5\pi}{2}, -3\right)$

Exercises for Example 2

Graph the function.

4. $y = \sin(x - \pi)$ **5.** $y = \cos(x + \pi)$ **6.** $y = 3 \cos\left(x - \frac{\pi}{2}\right)$

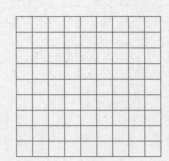 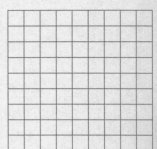

NAME _____ DATE _____

Practice with Examples

For use with pages 840–847

EXAMPLE 3 *Graphing a Reflection*

Graph $y = -2 \tan x$.

SOLUTION

Because the graph is a reflection of the graph of $y = 2 \tan x$, the period is π. The intercepts and asymptotes are the same as they are for the graph of $y = 2 \tan x$. However, the halfway points are reflected in the x-axis.

Asymptotes: $x = \dfrac{1}{2} \cdot \dfrac{\pi}{b} = \dfrac{1}{2} \cdot \pi = \dfrac{\pi}{2}$

$x = -\dfrac{1}{2} \cdot \dfrac{\pi}{b} = -\dfrac{1}{2} \cdot \pi = -\dfrac{\pi}{2}$

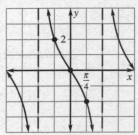

Halfway points: $\left(\dfrac{1}{4} \cdot \dfrac{\pi}{b}, -a \right) = \left(\dfrac{1}{4} \cdot \pi, -2 \right) = \left(\dfrac{\pi}{4}, -2 \right)$

$\left(-\dfrac{1}{4} \cdot \dfrac{\pi}{b}, a \right) = \left(-\dfrac{1}{4} \cdot \pi, 2 \right) = \left(-\dfrac{\pi}{4}, 2 \right)$

Exercises for Example 3

Graph the function.

7. $y = -\cos x$

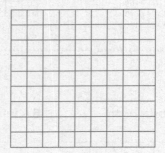

8. $y = -\dfrac{1}{2} \sin x$

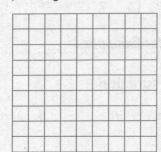

9. $y = -3 \tan \dfrac{1}{2}x$

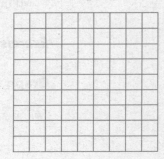

Chapter 14

NAME _____ DATE _____

Practice with Examples

For use with pages 848–854

GOAL Use trigonometric identities to simplify trigonometric expressions.

EXAMPLE 1 *Finding Trigonometric Values*

Given that $\tan \theta = -\dfrac{2}{3}$ and $\dfrac{3\pi}{2} < \theta < 2\pi$, find the values of the other five trigonometric functions of θ.

SOLUTION

Begin by finding $\sec \theta$.

$$1 + \tan^2 \theta = \sec^2 \theta \qquad \text{Write Pythagorean identity.}$$

$$1 + \left(-\frac{2}{3}\right)^2 = \sec^2 \theta \qquad \text{Substitute } -\frac{2}{3} \text{ for } \tan \theta.$$

$$\frac{13}{9} = \sec^2 \theta \qquad \text{Simplify.}$$

$$\pm \frac{\sqrt{13}}{3} = \sec \theta \qquad \text{Take square roots of each side.}$$

$$\frac{\sqrt{13}}{3} = \sec \theta \qquad \text{Because } \theta \text{ is in Quadrant IV, } \sec \theta \text{ is positive.}$$

Now, knowing $\tan \theta$ and $\sec \theta$, you can find the values of the other four trigonometric functions.

$$\sec \theta = \frac{1}{\cos \theta} \qquad\qquad\qquad \cot \theta = \frac{1}{\tan \theta}$$

$$\frac{\sqrt{13}}{3} = \frac{1}{\cos \theta} \qquad\qquad\qquad = \frac{1}{-\frac{2}{3}}$$

$$\cos \theta = \frac{3}{\sqrt{13}} = \frac{3\sqrt{13}}{13} \qquad\qquad = -\frac{3}{2}$$

$$\tan \theta = \frac{\sin \theta}{\cos \theta} \qquad\qquad\qquad \csc \theta = \frac{1}{\sin \theta}$$

$$-\frac{2}{3} = \frac{\sin \theta}{\frac{3}{\sqrt{13}}} \qquad\qquad\qquad = \frac{1}{\frac{-2}{\sqrt{13}}}$$

$$\sin \theta = -\frac{6}{\sqrt{13}} \cdot \frac{1}{3} = -\frac{2\sqrt{13}}{13} \qquad\qquad = -\frac{\sqrt{13}}{2}$$

Algebra 2
Practice Workbook with Examples

Chapter 14

Practice with Examples

For use with pages 848–854

Exercises for Example 1

Find the values of the other five trigonometric functions of θ.

1. $\sin \theta = \dfrac{1}{2}, \dfrac{\pi}{2} < \theta < \pi$

2. $\cos \theta = -\dfrac{2}{3}, \pi < \theta < \dfrac{3\pi}{2}$

3. $\tan \theta = \dfrac{3}{4}, 0 < \theta < \dfrac{\pi}{2}$

4. $\sec \theta = -\dfrac{6}{5}, \dfrac{\pi}{2} < 0 < \pi$

5. $\csc \theta = -\dfrac{5}{3}, \dfrac{3\pi}{2} < \theta < 2\pi$

6. $\cot \theta = \dfrac{1}{2}, \pi < \theta < \dfrac{3\pi}{2}$

EXAMPLE 2 *Simplifying a Trigonometric Expression*

Simplify the expression $\csc(-x) - \csc(-x)\cos^2 x$.

SOLUTION

$$\csc(-x) - \csc(-x)\cos^2 x = \csc(-x)(1 - \cos^2 x) \qquad \text{Factor out } \csc(-x).$$

$$= \csc(-x)(\sin^2 x) \qquad \text{Pythagorean identity}$$

$$= \frac{1}{\sin(-x)} \cdot \sin^2 x \qquad \text{Reciprocal identity}$$

$$= -\frac{1}{\sin x} \cdot \sin^2 x \qquad \text{Negative angle identity}$$

$$= -\sin x \qquad \text{Simplify.}$$

Chapter 14

NAME _____ DATE _____

Practice with Examples

For use with pages 848–854

Exercises for Example 2

Simplify the expression.

7. $\dfrac{\csc^2 \theta}{1 + \tan^2 \theta}$

8. $\cos\left(\dfrac{\pi}{2} - \theta\right) \cot \theta$

9. $\dfrac{\csc \theta}{\sec \theta}$

10. $(1 + \cos \theta)(1 - \cos \theta)$

11. $\tan\left(\dfrac{\pi}{2} - \theta\right) \sin \theta$

12. $\dfrac{\tan^2 \theta}{\sec \theta}$

13. $\dfrac{\cot \theta \, \sin \theta}{1 - \sin^2 \theta}$

14. $\cos^2 \theta \, (1 + \tan^2 \theta)$

Practice with Examples

For use with pages 855–861

GOAL Solve a trigonometric equation

EXAMPLE 1 *Solving a Trigonometric Equation*

Solve $\tan^2 x - 1 = 2$.

SOLUTION

$\tan^2 x - 1 = 2$ Write original equation.

$\tan^2 x = 3$ Isolate $\tan^2 x$ on one side by adding 1 to each side.

$\tan x = \pm\sqrt{3}$ Take square roots of each side.

Two solutions in the interval $0 \le x < 2\pi$ are $x = \dfrac{\pi}{3}$ and $x = \dfrac{2\pi}{3}$. Because $\tan x$ is a periodic function, there are infinitely many other solutions. Since the period of the tangent function is π, you can write the general solution as: $x = \dfrac{\pi}{3} + n\pi$ or $x = \dfrac{2\pi}{3} + n\pi$ where n is any integer.

Exercises for Example 1

Find the general solution of the equation.

1. $2\cos^2 x = 1$

2. $7\tan x + 9 = 2$

3. $\cot^2 x - 1 = 2$

4. $2\cos x = \sqrt{3}$

5. $\cot x + 1 = 0$

6. $4\sin^2 x - 3 = 0$

NAME _____ DATE _____

Practice with Examples

For use with pages 855–861

EXAMPLE 2 *Factoring to Solve a Trigonometric Equation*

Solve $\sqrt{2} \cos x \tan x = \tan x$.

SOLUTION

$\sqrt{2} \cos x \tan x = \tan x$	Write original equation.
$\sqrt{2} \cos x \tan x - \tan x = 0$	Subtract $\tan x$ from each side.
$\tan x(\sqrt{2} \cos x - 1) = 0$	Factor out $\tan x$.

Set each factor equal to 0 and solve for x, if possible.

$\tan x = 0$ $\qquad\qquad$ $\sqrt{2} \cos x - 1 = 0$

$x = 0 \text{ or } x = \pi$ $\qquad\qquad$ $\cos x = \dfrac{1}{\sqrt{2}}$

$\qquad\qquad\qquad\qquad\qquad\qquad x = \dfrac{\pi}{4} \text{ or } x = \dfrac{7\pi}{4}$

The general solution is $x = n\pi$, $x = \dfrac{\pi}{4} + 2n\pi$, or $x = \dfrac{7\pi}{4} + 2n\pi$ where n is any integer.

Exercises for Example 2

Solve the equation in the interval $0 \le x < 2\pi$.

7. $\sin^3 x - \sin x = 0$ $\qquad\qquad\qquad$ **8.** $\sqrt{3} \sin x = 2 \sin x \cos x$

9. $(\cos x - 1)(\sin x - 1) = 0$ $\qquad\qquad$ **10.** $\tan x \sec x = \sqrt{2} \tan x$

11. $\sin x \tan x = \sin x$ $\qquad\qquad\qquad$ **12.** $\tan x + \tan^2 x = 0$

Chapter 14

Practice with Examples

For use with pages 855–861

EXAMPLE 3 *Using the Quadratic Formula*

Solve $2 \sin^2 x + \sin x = 1$ in the interval $0 \le x \le \pi$.

SOLUTION

Because the right side of the equation does not equal 0, you cannot factor out $\sin x$. So, rewrite the equation in standard form and use the quadratic formula.

$2 \sin^2 x + \sin x - 1 = 0$ Write original equation in standard form.

$$\sin x = \frac{-1 \pm \sqrt{1^2 - 4(2)(-1)}}{2(2)}$$ Quadratic formula

$$= \frac{-1 \pm \sqrt{9}}{4}$$ Simplify.

$$= \frac{1}{2} \text{ or } -1$$ Simplify.

$x = \sin^{-1}\frac{1}{2}$ or $x = \sin^{-1}(-1)$ Use inverse sine.

$x = \frac{\pi}{6}$ or $\frac{5\pi}{6}$ $x = \frac{3\pi}{2}$

In the interval $0 \le x \le \pi$, the solutions are $x = \frac{\pi}{6}$ or $x = \frac{5\pi}{6}$.

Exercises for Example 3

Solve the equation in the interval $0 \le x \le \pi$.

13. $2 \sin^2 x + \sin x - 3 = 0$ **14.** $2 \tan^2 x - 3 \tan x - 1 = 0$

15. $5 \cos^2 x + 3 \cos x = 2$ **16.** $\cos^2 x - 4 \cos x = -2$

Chapter 14

Practice with Examples

For use with pages 862–867

GOAL **Model data with a sine or a cosine function**

EXAMPLE 1 **Writing Trigonometric Functions**

Write a function for the sinusoid whose graph is shown.

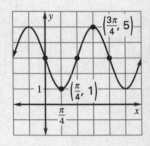

SOLUTION

Since the maximum and minimum values of the function do not occur at points equidistant from the *x*-axis, the curve has a vertical shift. To find the value of *k,* add the maximum and minimum *y*-values and divide by 2:

$$k = \frac{M + m}{2} = \frac{5 + 1}{2} = \frac{6}{2} = 3$$

Because the graph crosses the *y*-axis at $y = k$, the graph is a sine curve

with no horizontal shift. So, the function has the form $y = a \sin bx + 3$.

To find the value of *b,* use the fact that the period is $\frac{2\pi}{b} = \pi$. So, $b = 2$.

The amplitude is $|a| = \frac{M - m}{2} = \frac{5 - 1}{2} = \frac{4}{2} = 2$. Since the graph is a

reflection, $a = -2 < 0$.

The function is $y = -2 \sin 2x + 3$.

Exercises for Example 1

Write a function for the sinusoid.

1.

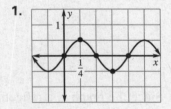

2.

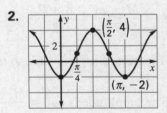

Chapter 14

NAME _____ DATE _____

Practice with Examples

For use with pages 862–867

3.

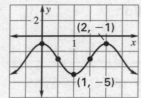

4.

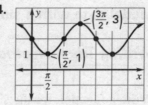

EXAMPLE 2 | *Modeling a Sinusoid*

The depth of the Atlantic Ocean at a channel buoy off the coast of Maine varies sinusoidally over time. On a certain day, a high tide of 8 feet occurs at 6:00 A.M. and a low tide of 2 feet occurs at 12:00 midnight. Write a model for the depth d (in feet) of the water as a function of time t (in hours since midnight).

SOLUTION

The high tide is the maximum value of the curve and occurs at $(6, 8)$. The low tide is the minimum value of the curve and it occurs at $(0, 2)$. Because the minimum point is on the d-axis, you can model the depth curve with a cosine function with a reflection and no horizontal shift of the form $d = a \cos bt + k$. To find the value of k, calculate the mean of the minimum and maximum y-values:

$$k = \frac{M + m}{2} = \frac{8 + 2}{2} = 5$$

The period is $\frac{2\pi}{b} = 12$, so $b = \frac{\pi}{6}$.

The amplitude is $|a| = \frac{M - m}{2} = \frac{8 - 2}{2} = 3$. Since the graph is a reflection, $a = -3 < 0$.

The model is $d = -3 \cos \frac{\pi}{6} t + 5$, where t is time in hours since midnight.

Practice with Examples

Exercises for Example 2

5. One complete breathing cycle for a human, consisting of inhaling and exhaling, takes place every 5 seconds on average. If the maximum air flow rate is 0.6 liter per second and varies sinusoidally over time, write a model for the air flow rate *r* (in liters per second) as a sine function of time *t* (in seconds).

6. A beating heart consists of two phases. In the systolic phase blood rushes through the heart, and in the diastolic phase the heart relaxes. Write a model of the form $r = a \sin bt$ for a person whose systolic phase lasts 0.25 second and whose maximum blood flow rate is 0.13 liter per second.

NAME _____ DATE _____

Practice with Examples

For use with pages 869–874

GOAL Evaluate trigonometric functions of the sum and difference of two angles

> ### VOCABULARY
>
> **Sum Formulas**
>
> $\sin(u + v) = \sin u \cos v + \cos u \sin v$
>
> $\cos(u + v) = \cos u \cos v - \sin u \sin v$
>
> $\tan(u + v) = \dfrac{\tan u + \tan v}{1 - \tan u \tan v}$
>
> **Difference Formulas**
>
> $\sin(u - v) = \sin u \cos v - \cos u \sin v$
>
> $\cos(u - v) = \cos u \cos v + \sin u \sin v$
>
> $\tan(u - v) = \dfrac{\tan u - \tan v}{1 + \tan u \tan v}$

EXAMPLE 1 *Evaluating a Trigonometric Expression*

Find the exact value of sin 15°.

SOLUTION

Begin by rewriting the sine as the sum or difference of angles that you know the sine of.

$\sin 15° = \sin(45° - 30°)$ Substitute 45° − 30° for 15°.

$\quad\quad\;\; = \sin 45° \cos 30° - \cos 45° \sin 30°$ Difference formula for sine

$\quad\quad\;\; = \dfrac{\sqrt{2}}{2}\left(\dfrac{\sqrt{3}}{2}\right) - \dfrac{\sqrt{2}}{2}\left(\dfrac{1}{2}\right)$ Evaluate.

$\quad\quad\;\; = \dfrac{\sqrt{6} - \sqrt{2}}{4}$ Simplify.

Using a calculator in degree mode, notice that sin 15° ≈ 0.2588 and $\left(\sqrt{6} - \sqrt{2}\right) \div 4 \approx 0.2588$. So, the result is correct.

Exercises for Example 1

Find the exact value of the expression.

1. cos 15°   **2.** tan 15°   **3.** sin 75°   **4.** cos 105°

5. $\sin \dfrac{\pi}{12}$ **6.** $\cos \dfrac{5\pi}{12}$ **7.** $\tan \dfrac{13\pi}{12}$ **8.** $\sin \dfrac{7\pi}{12}$

Practice with Examples

For use with pages 869–874

EXAMPLE 2 *Using a Difference Formula*

Find $\cos(u - v)$ given that $\sin u = \frac{4}{5}$ with $0 < u < \frac{\pi}{2}$ and $\cos v = -\frac{12}{13}$ with $\pi < v < \frac{3\pi}{2}$.

SOLUTION

Begin by finding $\cos u$ for the angle in Quadrant I that has a sine of $\frac{4}{5}$.
Using the Pythagorean theorem,

$$x = \sqrt{5^2 - 4^2} = \sqrt{25 - 16} = \sqrt{9} = 3.$$

Since the angle u is in Quadrant I, $\cos u = \frac{3}{5}$.

Then find $\sin v$ for the angle in Quadrant II that has a cosine of $-\frac{12}{13}$.

Using the Pythagorean theorem,

$$v = \sqrt{13^2 - (-12)^2} = \sqrt{169 - 144} = \sqrt{25} = 5.$$

Since the angle v is in Quadrant III, $\sin v = -\frac{5}{13}$.

$\cos(u - v) = \cos u \cos v + \sin u \sin v$	Difference formula for cosine
$= \frac{3}{5}\left(-\frac{12}{13}\right) + \frac{4}{5}\left(-\frac{5}{13}\right)$	Substitute.
$= -\frac{36}{65} + \left(-\frac{20}{65}\right)$	Multiply.
$= -\frac{56}{65}$	Add.

Exercises for Example 2

Evaluate the expression given $\cos u = -\frac{1}{3}$ with $\frac{\pi}{2} < u < \pi$, and $\sin v = \frac{2}{3}$ with $0 < v < \frac{\pi}{2}$.

9. $\sin(u + v)$ **10.** $\cos(u - v)$ **11.** $\tan(u + v)$

12. $\sin(u - v)$ **13.** $\cos(u + v)$ **14.** $\tan(u - v)$

Practice with Examples

For use with pages 869–874

EXAMPLE 3 *Simplifying an Expression*

Simplify the expression $\sin\left(x + \dfrac{\pi}{2}\right)$.

SOLUTION

$$\sin\left(x + \frac{\pi}{2}\right) = \sin x \cos \frac{\pi}{2} + \cos x \sin \frac{\pi}{2} \qquad \text{Sum formula for sine}$$

$$= \sin x(0) + \cos x(1) \qquad\qquad \text{Evaluate.}$$

$$= \cos x \qquad\qquad\qquad\qquad \text{Simplify.}$$

Exercises for Example 3

Simplify the expression.

15. $\cos\left(x - \dfrac{\pi}{2}\right)$

16. $\sin(x - \pi)$

17. $\tan(x + 2\pi)$

Practice with Examples

For use with pages 875–882

GOAL **Evaluate expressions using double- and half-angle formulas**

The half-angle formulas are as follows:

$$\sin\frac{u}{2} = \pm\sqrt{\frac{1-\cos u}{2}} \qquad \cos\frac{u}{2} = \pm\sqrt{\frac{1+\cos u}{2}}$$

$$\tan\frac{u}{2} = \frac{1-\cos u}{\sin u} = \frac{\sin u}{1+\cos u}$$

EXAMPLE 1 *Evaluating Trigonometric Expressions*

Find the exact value of $\tan\dfrac{\pi}{12}$.

SOLUTION

Use the fact that $\dfrac{\pi}{12}$ is half of $\dfrac{\pi}{6}$.

$$\tan\frac{\pi}{12} = \tan\frac{1}{2}\left(\frac{\pi}{6}\right) = \frac{1-\cos\frac{\pi}{6}}{\sin\frac{\pi}{6}} = \frac{1-\frac{\sqrt{3}}{2}}{\frac{1}{2}} = 2-\sqrt{3}$$

To simplify, multiply the numerator and denominator by 2.

Exercises for Example 1 ....

1. $\sin 15°$

2. $\cos 22.5°$

3. $\tan(-15°)$

4. $\sin\left(-\dfrac{\pi}{12}\right)$

5. $\cos\dfrac{5\pi}{8}$

6. $\tan\dfrac{\pi}{8}$

Chapter 14

NAME _____ DATE _____

Practice with Examples

For use with pages 875–882

EXAMPLE 2 *Evaluating Trigonometric Expressions*

Given $\sin u = \dfrac{1}{3}$ with $0 \le u < \dfrac{\pi}{2}$, find (a) $\cos \dfrac{u}{2}$ and (b) $\cos 2u$.

SOLUTION

Begin by finding $\cos u$ for the angle in Quadrant I that has a sine of $\frac{1}{3}$.
Using the Pythagorean theorem,

$$x = \sqrt{3^2 - 1^2} = \sqrt{9-1} = \sqrt{8} = 2\sqrt{2}. \text{ So, } \cos u = \frac{2\sqrt{2}}{3}.$$

a. $\cos \dfrac{u}{2} = +\sqrt{\dfrac{1 + \cos u}{2}} = \sqrt{\dfrac{1 + (2\sqrt{2}/3)}{2}} = \sqrt{\dfrac{3 + 2\sqrt{2}}{6}}$

b. $\cos 2u = \cos^2 u - \sin^2 u = \left(\dfrac{2\sqrt{2}}{3}\right)^2 - \left(\dfrac{1}{3}\right)^2 = \dfrac{8}{9} - \dfrac{1}{9} = \dfrac{7}{9}$

Note that $\sin 2u = 2 \sin u \cos u$ and $\tan 2u = \dfrac{2 \tan u}{1 - \tan^2 u}$.

Exercises for Example 2

Find the exact value of the function.

7. $\cos \dfrac{u}{2}$ if $\cos u = \dfrac{4}{5}, 0 \le u < \dfrac{\pi}{2}$ **8.** $\tan 2u$ if $\sin u = \dfrac{4}{5}, \dfrac{\pi}{2} \le u < \pi$

EXAMPLE 3 *Verifying a Trigonometric Identity*

Verify the identity $4 \sin x \cos x(1 - 2 \sin^2 x) = \sin 4x$.

SOLUTION

$$4 \sin x \cos x(1 - 2 \sin^2 x) = 4 \sin x \cos x(\cos 2x) \quad \text{Use double-angle formula.}$$
$$= 2(2 \sin x \cos x) \cos 2x \quad \text{Regroup factors.}$$
$$= 2(\sin 2x) \cos 2x \quad \text{Use double-angle formula.}$$
$$= \sin 4x \quad \text{Use double-angle formula.}$$

Practice with Examples

For use with pages 875–882

Exercises for Example 3

Verify the identity.

9. $2 \sin^2 2x + \cos 4x = 1$

10. $(\sin x + \cos x)^2 = 1 + \sin 2x$

EXAMPLE 4 *Solving a Trigonometric Equation*

Solve $2 \cos 2x + 4 \sin x - 3 = 0$ for $0 \le x < 2\pi$.

SOLUTION

$2 \cos 2x + 4 \sin x - 3 = 0$	Write original equation.
$2(1 - 2 \sin^2 x) + 4 \sin x - 3 = 0$	Use double-angle formula.
$2 - 4 \sin^2 x + 4 \sin x - 3 = 0$	Use distributive property.
$-4 \sin^2 x + 4 \sin x - 1 = 0$	Combine like terms.
$\sin x = \dfrac{-4 \pm \sqrt{4^2 - 4(-4)(-1)}}{2(-4)} = \dfrac{-4 \pm \sqrt{0}}{-8} = \dfrac{1}{2}$	Use quadratic formula.
$x = \dfrac{\pi}{6}, \dfrac{5\pi}{6}$	Solve for x.

Exercises for Example 4

Solve the equation for $0 \le x < 2\pi$.

11. $\sin x = \cos 2x$

12. $\cos 2x - \cos x - 2 = 0$